SHATTERED JUSTICE

The Oklahoma Girl Scout Murders

J. D. MORRISON

Copyright © 2022 by J. D. Morrison

Shattered Justice
by J.D. Morrison

All rights reserved solely by the author. The author guarantees all contents are original and do not infringe upon the legal rights of any other person or work. No part of this book may be reproduced in any form without the permission of the author.

Paul,
I miss your mug

Dedicated to the friend of David Sack:
If you had not mailed his letter, this book would have never come to be. You are now my friend, as well, and I love you. Thank you for your prayers and inspiration.

For
Lori, Denise and Michelle

WW2 Soldier Paul Smith

Mayes County Sheriff Paul Smith

98-year-old Paul

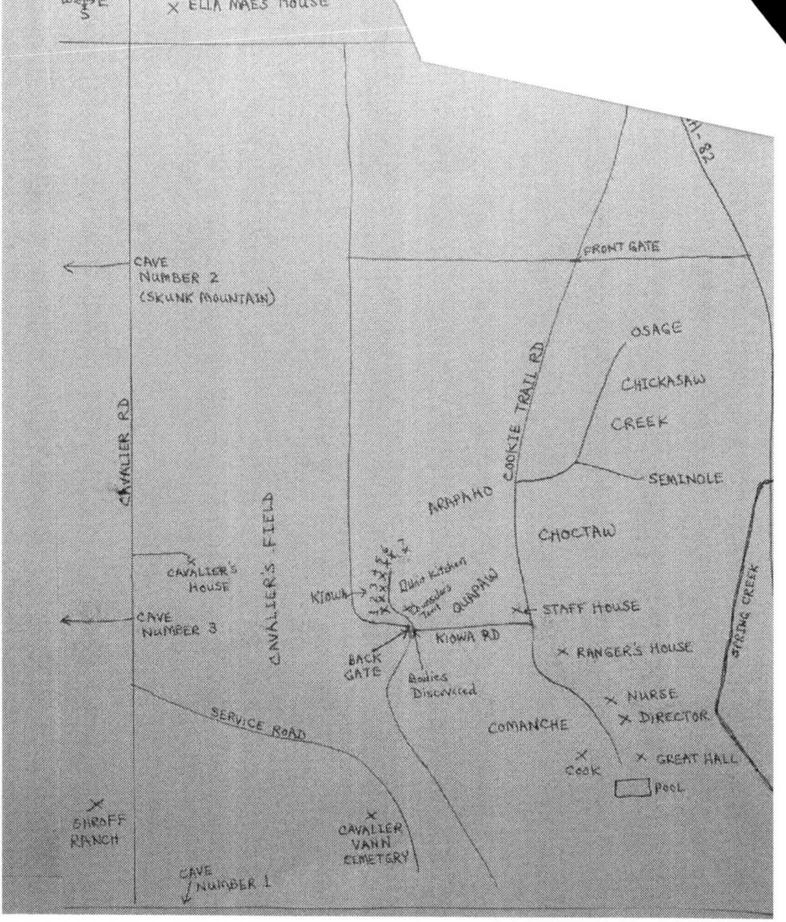

ELLA MAES HOUSE
HI-82
FRONT GATE
CAVE
NUMBER 2
(SKUNK MOUNTAIN)
OSAGE
CHICKASAW
CREEK
COOKIE TRAIL RD
SEMINOLE
CAVALIER RD
ARAPAHO
CAVALIER'S FIELD
CHOCTAW
CAVALIER'S
HOUSE
Kiowa
QUAPAW
STAFF HOUSE
STRING CREEK
CAVE
NUMBER 3
KIOWA RD
RANGER'S HOUSE
BACK
GATE
Bodies
Discovered
NURSE
DIRECTOR
SERVICE ROAD
COMANCHE
GREAT HALL
COOK
POOL
SHROFF
RANCH
CAVALIER
VANN
CEMETERY
CAVE
NUMBER 1

Information contained in this book relies on the following sources:

The private files and notes of Paul Smith (Sheriff of Mayes County, OK 1981-1985)

Files obtained from Herb Weaver, son of Glen "Pete" Weaver (Sheriff of Mayes County, OK 1969-1971, 1973-1981)

The transcripts of the preliminary hearings of Gene Leroy Hart (1966 and 1978)

Personal interviews

OSBI sources, including *Someone Cry For the Children,* by authors Michael and Dick Wilkerson (New York: The Dial Press, 1981)

Tent Number Eight, by Gloyd McCoy (Oklahoma: Tate Publishing, 2011)

Various press accounts, as noted within text

Opinions formed by Jennifer Morrison

NOTE: NO ONE NAMED IN THIS BOOK IS CURRENTLY CHARGED WITH A CRIME RELATING TO THE GIRL SCOUT MURDERS

CONTENTS

Acknowledgments .... *xxiii*

Chapter 1 – Best Day Ever 1
Chapter 2 – Worst Day Ever 13
Chapter 3 – Three Little Angels 29
Chapter 4 – Case Solved? 35
Chapter 5 – Sonny 51
Chapter 6 – Catch Me If You Can 85
Chapter 7 – Trials and Tribulations 99
Chapter 8 – Son of a Preacher Man 115
Chapter 9 – I Fought the Law 131
Chapter 10 – . . . And the Law Won 139
Chapter 11 – Justice for Truth 151
Chapter 12 – You Gotta Have Faith 165
Chapter 13 – Better Together 175
Chapter 14 – If Tomorrow Never Comes 191
Chapter 15 – Into the Lion's Den 199
Chapter 16 – Ready or Not, Here I Come! 215
Chapter 17 – Nooks and Crannies 229
Chapter 18 – DNA = Do Not Ask 251
Chapter 19 – Over and Out 261

Epitaph *263*
Author's Notes *265*
Prayer For Salvation *269*
Author Contact Information *271*

ACKNOWLEDGMENTS

To Larry Dale, the love of my life:
Thank you for the precious gift of letting me be me.

To my son, Quentin, for the countless hours of brainstorming and digging.

To my firstborn, Hadley, for designing the cover of this book just like Paul wanted it.

To Bo and Sheri Farmer and Bettye Milner, for the pain you have suffered and for always being available.

To Donna Lawrence:
I am honored that you felt it was me who Paul needed to assist him with his unsolved case.

To all the team players who have kept an open mind and spent countless hours researching the Girl Scout murder case—Shaun, Cynthia, Phyllis, Kourtney, Susan, Joe, Maria, Brian, Sharilyn, Rick, Kevin

To my pastors Rick Friesen and Bill Boren for keeping my eyes focused on what really matters.

To my amazing friends who believed in me and prayed with me when the walls seemed too high and the frustrations too great.

To all my special sources for sharing your information.

To my long-suffering proofreader, Dennis, for putting up with me.

A special thanks to Kevin Weaver for the invaluable resources on girlscoutmurders.com, and to Faith Phillips for bringing Paul's story to light on Fox Nation.

To Min, Brianna and Angel:
See, I told you I would put your names in my book.

CHAPTER 1

BEST DAY EVER

The date was June 12, 1977, two weeks past Memorial Day, and the Oklahoma sun had already warmed the state's watering holes. The small town of Locust Grove, nestled in the northeast corner of the former Indian Territory, was Sunday afternoon quiet. Many of those who called Locust Grove home were enjoying the outdoors, swimming or fishing in the creeks and rivers that run just outside of town or boating at nearby Fort Gibson Lake. Some, who had the luxury of home air conditioning, were indoors napping.

Patrolman Paul Smith was lounging on a bench in the front porch shade of the Wilson-Cunningham funeral home, studying the movements of a dragonfly, as ominous screams from a lonely hawk occasionally filtered down from high in the sticky atmosphere overhead. The balding fifty-four-year-old was moonlighting at the funeral home to supplement his wages from the small town's police department. Paul had resigned his detective position with the Major Crimes Squad over in Tulsa years earlier and was now finishing out his lawman career in a less stressful environment.

A little before 3 p.m., Paul's solitude was disrupted by three chartered buses approaching from his right. They growled their way along SH-33 (known to the locals as Main Street), parading directly in front of Paul. Their tinted windows concealed the singing and laughter going on inside. The Girl Scouts from Tulsa were on their way to Camp Scott for a two-week outing in Oklahoma's beautiful Green Country. It appeared that the buses were pushing to stay ahead of the heavy thunderstorms that were forecast for that evening. What no one knew, not even the weatherman, is that the dark angel of death was also en route.

Paul's piercing blue eyes peered through his thick wire-rimmed glasses as he leaned forward and swiveled to his left to track the buses for several blocks until they reached the four-way stop at Junction SH-82. Just as they made a right turn and headed south, Paul's attention was diverted to a dark-green Dodge Super Bee that was now squarely in front of him. He was familiar with the muscle car and its driver, a local tough who went by the nickname "Bull." Paul had issued past traffic violations to the twenty-year-old and had even arrested him once on a hit and run. Bull was not alone. Paul got the impression there were at least two more individuals in the car, maybe three. The patrolman stroked his thick gray mustache and settled back after he watched the Super Bee make the same right turn onto SH-82 that the buses had made.

Minutes later and well out of Paul's sight, the buses slowed and made a jog over onto a lane that angled off from SH-82: it was affectionately known as "Cookie Trail Road." The would-be campers left the dappled sunlight of the rural highway and entered a tunnel of shadow that was the access road to their summer camp. The girls quieted. The anticipation mounted. It seemed as though they had been cut off from civilization as they drove deeper along the blacktop byway to their destination—the isolated, heavily wooded outpost known as Camp Scott. Only fifty miles east of Tulsa and a mere two miles from Locust Grove, the camp was a world away from the city life they knew. For many of the girls, this was their first-ever trip away from family and home.

Camp Scott had been active since 1928. In a mile-long north-to-south-oriented strip of land covering 410 acres, the Magic Empire Council of Girl Scouts offered outdoor activities to girls from ages eight to eighteen. These future standouts were primed in swimming, canoeing, arts and crafts, photography, fire building, basic first aid, and, of course, what to do when encountering a snake.

The campground was divided into ten large sections, known as "units," named after prominent Native American tribes in Oklahoma: Osage, Chickasaw, Creek, Seminole, Arapaho, Choctaw, Quapaw, Comanche, Cherokee and Kiowa. Each unit could accommodate twenty-eight campers and up to four counselors.

Cookie Trail Road was the main artery running north to south through the camp. After passing through the front gate, the road ran between some of the camping areas on its way to the cabins where the camp director, ranger, nurse and cook stayed. The Great Hall (also used as a dining room) and the swimming pool were at the dead-end of Cookie Trail. From there on south it was only trails and narrow foot paths.

About two-thirds of the way down Cookie Trail, the buses turned right (west) onto dirt and gravel to stop in front of the "staff house," a common meeting place for the camp employees.

The camp director and barely-adult camp counselors, all former Girl Scouts themselves, came out to greet the buses as the hiss of air brakes announced their arrival. The metal doors of the diesel giants swung open, and a counselor from each unit, clipboard in hand, climbed on board to claim the girls that were assigned to her unit. One by one, the girls got off the buses as their names were read from the clipboards.

That particular year, the leader of the Kiowa unit was a freckle-faced twenty-year-old named Dee Elder. Dee had two eighteen-year-old helpers, Carla Wilhite and Susan Emery. By the time the buses were empty, the three Kiowa counselors were surrounded by twenty-seven chatty eight-to-ten-year-olds. (One Kiowa camper was mistakenly assigned to the Cherokee unit . . . a fortunate mistake.)

The luggage would be brought to the appropriate units later: it had to be sorted first. For now, Dee, Carla and Susan led their bubbly young charges west down the dirt and gravel, also known as Kiowa Road, past the Quapaw unit, to a fork in Kiowa Road near the unused back gate of the camp. Taking a dirt trail that wound off to the right through trees, the group made their way into the Kiowa unit and assembled in what was known as the Kiowa unit kitchen. It was an open-air shelter, with a kitchen, shower and storage closet attached together along one side.

Shrieks of laughter filled the air as name games were played to get everyone acquainted. Then they got down to business. Patrol leaders were nominated and "hoppers" were selected: hoppers would set the tables for supper in the Great Hall, shuttle the meal from the big kitchen and clean the tables afterwards. Wrapping up the meeting, the counselors issued mattress covers and released the campers to go pick out a tent: the girls were allowed to choose their own tent mates—four to a tent.

The living quarters of the Kiowa unit consisted of eight large tent structures fanned out in a semicircle that cradled the unit kitchen from the west. The counselors' tent looked out toward the seven campers' tents (#1 through #7). All eight tents were constructed identically. A canvas roof was erected on a 12' x 14' raised wooden platform. Canvas walls could be rolled up or down according to weather. Two wooden steps led up to the front of each tent. None of the tents was wired for electricity. Everyone was required to pack their own flashlight, with spare batteries.

The campers who chose tent #7 were ten-year-old Doris "Denise" Milner; nine-year-old Michelle Gusé; and eight-year-old Lori Farmer. Even though they had not known each other before this trip, they decided to bunk together. The Kiowa unit was the most remote unit in Camp Scott, and tent #7 was the most remote tent in the Kiowa unit.

Kiowa counselor Dee made a chart of all her girls' tent selections. Soon the luggage arrived, and the campers busied themselves with setting up their home away from home. Lori proudly showed Denise and Michelle the brand-new camera her parents had bought her to use in photography class, which would include dark room processing this year. Then the three each unrolled their own personal sleeping bag on top of a cot in tent #7. There were two cots just inside the front of the tent (closest to the steps) and two cots in the back of the tent. It was tight quarters. One of the rear cots would remain empty for the time being. The decision was made not to move the missing camper from the Cherokee unit until after the threatening weather cleared the following morning.

When Patrolman Paul's shift ended at the funeral home, he stopped for fuel on his way home. While parked at Greg's Git-N-Split (a convenience store at the corner of SH-82 and Main), he once again observed the Dodge Super Bee: this time the occupants were outside the car. It was Bull and his usual sidekick, Buddy, and they had a Sasquatch-looking friend called "Flea" with them. The three were acting wild and crazy, almost like they were hyped up on something. They hurled hostile glares toward Paul as they got back in their car and headed south on SH-82, once again in the direction of Camp Scott.

The Kiowa campers were all moved in by 5:30 p.m. Fifteen minutes later, counselor Carla led the hoppers on the half-mile walk down to the Great Hall to set up for supper. The girls walked in lock step, their prepubescent voices filling the air with the chant, "Big red Indian, beats upon his drum, rum-tum-tum, rum-tum-tum, woo-woo-woo!" They hit their lips mimicking a war cry on the woo-woos, as ponytails and pigtails bounced in rhythm. (This was long before the days of political correctness).

Counselors Dee and Susan escorted the remaining Kiowa girls to the evening meal at 6 p.m. Salad was on the menu: it was *always* on the menu. Healthy eating was important to Barbara Day, the camp director. The Kiowa girls were joined there by the four other Camp Scott units that were in operation that session—over 100 campers in total, their counselors, plus the Camp Scott executive staff. After their first meal together, the hoppers cleared and washed the tables while everyone else sang campfire songs, complete with motions: "An Austrian Went Yodeling," "Ragtime Cowboy Joe," and "Running Bear." The singing would have normally been done out on the front porch of the Great Hall, known as "Singing Porch," but the threat of rain kept them inside that evening.

Sure enough, fifteen or twenty minutes into their melodies, large teardrops began to fall from the Oklahoma sky as it exhaled its cold breath across the camp. Ominous clouds began gobbling what little light existed. Since it was getting dark much earlier than usual, and no one had their flashlights with them, the campers were rushed back through the downpour to their living quarters.

Back in their tents, the Kiowa girls were directed to roll the canvas sides down and change out of their wet clothing into their pajamas. Dee and Susan then "buttoned down" each Kiowa tent to protect the campers from the wind and driving rain. This meant fastening canvas loops on the bottom hem of the tent walls over metal hooks anchored in the wooden platforms. The counselors were puzzled that one of the front flaps of tent #5 was missing. It looked as though it had been slashed off and carried away by someone . . . strange, since it had been fine on Friday, two days earlier, during inspection. A bed sheet was substituted to cover the opening.

Other bizarre things were going on at the camp that evening.

As Mother Nature paused to wipe her eyes around 7:30 p.m., camp director Barbara and her husband, Richard Day, drove north up Cookie Trail Road and out of Camp Scott's single entry/exit point to go into town and buy milk. It had been discovered during supper that the kitchen was running low.

The young couple observed a strange sight as they paused while Richard climbed out to open and close the aluminum gate. An unfamiliar car was parked just to their left on the west side of Cookie Trail Road against the outside of the camp's fence row. The car was facing away from them. As they passed along the rear of it, Barbara noticed two heads sticking up from the back seat. One of the car's doors was open, and the two front occupants' legs were hanging out as though they were engaged in a passionate activity. Half an hour later, when Barbara and Richard returned with the milk, the car was gone.

Meanwhile, the pajama-clad girls in the Kiowa unit were waiting out the storm in their respective tents. While they were occupying themselves, counselor Dee pulled a water-proof poncho over her head and made a quarter-mile dash over to the staff house to pick up some "Winnie the Pooh" books, hoping there might be an opportunity for story time later. From there, she went down to the Great Hall to check on the weather forecast and grab some cookies for her campers.

When Dee returned to the Kiowa unit, she dried off in her tent, then fired up a kerosene lantern and carried it to the Kiowa unit kitchen. By now the rain had stopped, and Dee decided to have another meeting with her campers. Counselor Carla went to each tent and told the girls to put on rain gear (the trees were still dripping) and meet Dee at the kitchen.

Roll was taken, camp rules were discussed, and chores were assigned. The girls were told of the exciting activities to expect the following day. Camper Denise from tent #7 doled out the cookies—Girl Scout cookies, no less. Wiping crumbs from their lips, they giggled as they played some more games to get to know each other better. They sang the always-fun musical round "Don't Put Your Dust in my Dustpan," then wound down with quieter songs: "Girl Scouts Together" and "Moon on the Meadow." Lastly, they joined in a big circle and held hands with right hand over left as they closed with "Taps." At the end of "Taps" they said, "Goodnight Scouts" and turned out of the circle. It was off to the tents to get ready for bed. The time was past 9 p.m.

A few miles north of the sleepy little town of Locust Grove, Patrolman Paul Smith was at home in bed now, snuggled next to his wife Betty. The thunderstorm had saturated the entire area. It had not spared Camp Scott nor the Smith house. Paul was looking forward to being off work the following day: he and Betty had travel plans.

Lead counselor Dee was on "sitting hill" duty in the Kiowa unit, which meant she was in charge of watching over the Kiowa campers and getting them down for the night. This allowed counselors Carla and Susan two hours of free time, which they spent at the staff house and visiting counselor friends in other units.

Between 10 and 10:30 p.m. Dee parted the front flaps of tents #1 through #7 and personally talked to every girl under her care. Dee was there to encourage anyone who might feel homesick and to make sure all her campers were warm and dry. Denise Milner in tent #7 wanted to call her mother to come and pick her up: she had been frightened by the thunderstorm and was ready to go home. Denise was assured that the next day would be better, but, if she still wanted to go home when she woke the following morning, they would call her mother then.

The girls in the Kiowa tents were still being noisy after Dee's visit, nothing unusual for the excitement of a first night at camp and making new friends. Unlike the campers' tents, the front flaps of the counselors' tent had been rolled back up when the rain had stopped—better for keeping watch over their little prodigies. Several times Dee stood at the front of the counselors' tent and yelled out for the squealing girls to quieten down. Counselor Susan was back now and sleeping soundly on her cot. Dee's yelling didn't faze her.

Ready to turn in for the night herself, counselor Carla rejoined Dee and Susan at 11:30 p.m., just as some of the girls were getting loud again. Dee started to get up, but Carla waved her back and said she would handle it this time. With flashlight in hand, Carla went to each tent with noisy campers and told them to shush. Tents #6 and #7 (furthest away) were both quiet, so she went no further than tent #5.

Sometime after 1 a.m., the talking and outbursts finally died down, and the flashlights were laid to rest. Carla, freshly tucked in bed, was just dozing off when she was alerted by a loud bang from the direction of the Kiowa latrine. The lantern-lit outhouse was to the east of the unit kitchen, at least 75 yards away from any of the eight tents. Carla jumped up, threw on her glasses and headed that way. Just steps into the pathway that led to the latrine, she was met by the four girls from tent #1 returning from there. She got on to them for making such a racket slamming the doors (which they denied) and sent them back to bed. That was the last she heard from them.

Just as a bedraggled Carla was cozying up in the covers for the second time, a burst of giggling erupted in tent #4. *Would it ever end?* She sat up, raked her fingers through her short brown hair and let out an exhausted sigh. It was 1:30 a.m. As she slipped on her shoes, she heard some sort of noise over by the fence across the road from the counselors' tent. She woke Dee, who then heard it, too. They discussed what it could be. In all their years of camping out, neither of them had ever heard anything like it. Carla pegged it somewhere between a distant foghorn, a frog or a snore, but it sounded like neither man nor beast . . . just a weird guttural sound.

Presuming it must be an animal of some kind, Carla told Dee she would try and identify the sound before going to talk to the girls in tent #4. Wearily sliding her glasses back onto her face, Carla clutched her flashlight and strode down the path toward the fence. The strange noise stopped when she flashed her light toward it.

However, it started again when she turned away and proceeded toward tent #4. She considered going back and taking a closer look, but decided it just *had* to be nothing more than a harmless four-footed creature. She continued on to tent #4 and told the girls to go to sleep, which they did.

At long last, all the campers were silent. The front gate of Camp Scott had been locked at 10:45 p.m. by the camp ranger. As the darkness congealed under a canopy of wet trees, the three Kiowa unit counselors fell into a blissful sleep. Their job was done for the night. Everyone was safe and sound.

During the chaos of the evening, the three campers in tent #7 had found time to write letters to their families back home. Lori Farmer wrote to her parents and four younger siblings:

Dear Mommy and Daddy and Misti and Joli and Chad and Kali
We're just getting ready to go to bed. It's 7:45.
We're at the beginning of a storm and having a lot of fun.
I've met two new friends, Michelle Guse and Denise Milner. I'm sharing a tent with them.
It started raining on the way back from dinner. We're sleeping on cots.
I couldn't wait to write. We're all writing letters now cause there's hardly anything else to do.

With Love
Lori

Denise Milner wrote to her mother:

Dear Mom
I don't like camp. It's awful.

The first day it rained.
I have three new [friends] named Glenda, Lori, and Michelle.
Michelle and Lori are my roommates.
Mom, I don't want to stay at camp for two weeks.
I want to come home and see Kathie and everybody.

Your loving child
Denise Milner

Michelle Gusé wrote to an aunt:

Dear Aunt Karen

How are you? I am fine. I am writing from camp. We can't go outside because it is storming. Me and my tentmates are in the last tent in our unit. My tentmates are Denise Milner and Lori Farmer. My room is shades of purple.

Love
Michelle

Michelle had begun a second letter that was apparently interrupted by the second unit meeting. The only thing that was written was:

Dear Mom and Dad

The girls had no idea that these letters would soon become some of their families' most prized possessions. By the time the murky night was driven away by the morning light of Monday, June 13, 1977, everything would be different.

CHAPTER 2

WORST DAY EVER

The loud raucous blare from counselor Carla's wind-up alarm clock pierced the still gray dawn at 6 a.m. to announce Monday morning, June 13, 1977, to the Kiowa unit. The first night of camp was in the books. The new day promised to be filled with fun games, ice cream, picture taking, nature hikes and swimming . . . all capped off with an evening campfire and story time. The promise would not be kept.

Counselor Dee had planned to go jogging that morning but was too tired from the late night. She sat up for just a moment before reclaiming her horizontal position. Counselor Susan merely groaned and rolled over. Counselor Carla yawned, put on her glasses, shook out her shoes and pulled on some shorts. Gathering soap, shampoo, deodorant and a set of clean clothes, she set out for the staff house. She wanted to be first in line at the nearest hot-water shower (the Kiowa unit shower only ran cold).

As Carla walked in the direction of the staff house, she spotted something out of place. Out in front of her was a pile of sleeping bags. They were resting under a tree at the point of the fork in Kiowa Road near the back gate. *Ranger Ben Woodward must have lost them off his truck when he was delivering luggage the prior evening.* Carla went to collect them.

As she drew near, she was surprised to see a camper there, sleeping on top of one of the bedrolls out in the open. A few steps more and Carla noticed that the girl was nude from the waist down, wearing only a pink and white flannel pajama top that was bunched around her upper body. The girl's open eyes and lifeless stare finally registered with the eighteen-year-old counselor.

Within two minutes after leaving Dee and Susan asleep in their tent, Carla was back and in a panic. She yelped at her tent mates to wake up, that she had seen a dead girl in the road, and they needed to do a head count of their unit. Dee scrambled off her cot, slid into her shorts and sprinted to the far tent, #7. Susan hurriedly donned glasses and rain boots and joined Carla at the closest tent, #1. Susan and Carla planned to meet Dee in the middle.

As soon as the counting began, Dee had a problem. There were no girls in tent #7! In a frenzy, Dee motioned over to Carla and Susan, and they rushed to join her at the empty tent. It was hard to see inside the tent, since it was still buttoned down, but, lifting the left front flap, the three counselors spotted some blood on the corner of the nearest mattress. *Had one of the girls had a nosebleed? Or started menstruating? Had they moved to another tent during the night and crowded in with some other girls?* All the counselors knew for sure was that all three girls and their sleeping bags were gone from tent #7. Even their mattress covers were missing.

Carla had ridden to camp that weekend with another counselor, so she sped off on foot to Cookie Trail Road and made a right turn: she had to notify the camp director and the nurse ASAP. An inquisitive Susan headed in the direction of the body. Dee continued to count the girls in the other six tents . . . she was not finding any of the three campers from tent #7 anywhere. She had counted and recounted three or four times when she heard two blood-curdling screams.

Dee recognized that the screams had come from counselor Susan, who had come running back to stand near the counselors' tent and was wildly slinging her hands. Dee raced to the petite counselor and smacked her, telling her to be quiet, that she would scare the other girls. Susan had seen up close and personal what Carla had seen, but it was even worse. Susan hysterically told Dee that she had tried to pick up one of the other sleeping bags and had discovered it was not empty . . . neither was the third sleeping bag. The bags were zipped closed, and Susan had left them that way and retreated. She was unglued.

Dee had heard enough to recognize this was, indeed, a situation that needed to be handled by the camp director. Unfortunately, Camp Scott's walkie-talkie system was in disrepair, so Dee dashed past Susan to run the quarter mile down Kiowa Road to the parking lot in front of the staff house. Shoving her white Volkswagen into gear before she even got the door completely closed, Dee tore down Cookie Trail Road toward director Barbara's cabin (Barbara and Richard lived at the camp during summer months).

Dee was met on the way by camp nurse Maryanne Alabeck, who had already been tipped off by Carla and was speeding toward the body. Maryanne waved at Dee to stop. Through their open car windows, Maryanne quizzed Dee about what was going down. Dee breathlessly declared that there were three, not just one . . . *three* children were dead.

By the time Dee reached the driveway of the director's cabin, Barbara and Richard and counselor Carla were scurrying into the yellow camp station wagon. As soon as the station wagon backed out and cleared, Dee pulled in, turned around, and followed it toward the scene. Stopping her own car at the staff house, she looked over to see Richard, Barbara, Maryanne and Carla by the bodies. Dee stayed back, as did Susan, because they were both feeling acutely unwell.

After checking for a pulse in the neck of the exposed girl, Richard Day gently adjusted the sleeping bag on which she lay to cover as much as he could of her lower body: he determined there was nothing else he could do to help her. As he tugged on her bag, he saw the name "Denise Milner" stamped on it. He noticed that Denise had fairly fresh blood on her forehead. Richard then ran his hands about the two additional sleeping bags and could identify shapes in them he knew were bodies.

Director Barbara ordered everyone not to do any further touching of anything. She instructed the three Kiowa counselors that one of them should stay with the bodies while the other two got the Kiowa campers up and ready for breakfast. It would be earlier than the normal 7 a.m. schedule, but they needed to vacate the Kiowa unit immediately. Barbara and Richard then went to wake ranger Ben. An older and wiser Ben advised Barbara to go directly and call law enforcement.

Barbara steered the camp station wagon back down Cookie Trail Road to her office and first called Bonnie Brewster, her Girl Scouts executive director in Tulsa. Next, she phoned the Oklahoma Highway Patrol (OHP) headquarters in Vinita, Oklahoma, and requested three ambulances. The OHP, in turn, notified Mayes County Sheriff Glen "Pete" Weaver, whose office was in Pryor,

Oklahoma, the county seat, fifteen miles away. Sheriff Weaver had his official photographer, Mike Wheat, summoned to the scene. The Oklahoma State Bureau of Investigation (OSBI); the local Medical Examiner (ME), Dr. Donald Collins; and District Attorney (DA) for Mayes County, Sid Wise, were also called.

Meanwhile, ranger Ben and Richard Day took Ben's truck back to where the bodies were, and Ben stayed there. Richard drove the truck to the front gate of the camp to wait for the medics and authorities to arrive. As Ben stood guard over the bodies, one of the first things he noticed was raised dirt in the ground at the soles of Denise's feet.

When Barbara re-cradled the receiver on her office telephone it was nearing 6:40 a.m. She stepped out and rang the "Great Bell" just outside her cabin to wake up everyone in the camp. She then drove to the other occupied units and used her best calm voice to notify the adults that there was an emergency in the camp. Campers were to be taken to breakfast at the Great Hall using a route that would keep them off all main roads or trails.

The Kiowa and Quapaw unit counselors were dealt the biggest challenge in getting their girls to breakfast without passing near the bodies. Kiowa Road was the avenue down which the side-by-side Kiowa and Quapaw units routinely strolled to access Cookie Trail Road on their way to the Great Hall. The counselors from these two neighboring units concocted a scheme to keep their campers innocently unaware. They told the girls they had to go inspect the latrines on their way to breakfast as punishment for having been rowdy so late the night before. This took them around a back path to the dining room.

Once the silverware began to clank against breakfast plates in the Great Hall at the back of the camp, authorities were allowed in Camp Scott's front gate. OHP Trooper Harold Berry was the first in. He lived only a quarter mile south down SH-82. He and Barbara Day were acquaintances, and she was relieved to see him.

Patrolman Paul had risen early that morning. He and Betty were making a 100-mile journey to visit Betty's sister for the day in Shamrock, Oklahoma. As they left their house and traveled south along SH-82, Paul saw flashes of red and blue in his rear-view mirror. Sheriff Pete Weaver and his two deputies were flying down the road with their emergency lights and sirens activated. As the three brown cruisers overtook and went around Paul, he wondered aloud to Betty where Pete and his guys could be going in such a hurry at that time of the morning. As Paul turned right onto Main Street to head west toward Shamrock, the three cruisers continued south on SH-82 . . . the same narrow highway onto which the three noisy buses and the Dodge Super Bee had turned the afternoon before.

The three county sheriff vehicles followed each other into Camp Scott just past 7:00 a.m. and congregated at the staff house. Local Medical Examiner Collins was the passenger in one of the three ambulances that arrived there close behind them.

Dr. Collins rushed to Denise, checked for a heartbeat and, without moving her around, examined what he could of her body. He would later write in his official report that she was "lying on her back with her legs wide apart" and "blood was coming from the perineal area" between them; "there was a very large bruise on the left side of [her] face and head;" and "there was a laceration of [her] right temple area approximately one inch long." Dr. Collins did his best to describe a "cord-towel apparatus wrapped very tightly" around

Denise's neck and the presence of an Ace bandage around her neck, as well. Denise was bound and her hands were behind her back (underneath her). "[Rigor mortis] was completely absent. The body was still warm to touch," he added. Sheriff Weaver made a handwritten note to himself: "Body still warm at 7:05 a.m."

For now, Denise was left in place, as OSBI Crime Bureau agents would need to take photographs once they arrived. Dr. Collins also left Michelle and Lori undisturbed in their still-zipped sleeping bags. His later report would include, "The two remaining bags had been observed from the time that they had been found [at approximately 6:15 a.m.] until 7:00 a.m. and absolutely no movement nor sound had come from the bags . . . they had been felt of to see if they actually contained bodies." That was good enough for Dr. Collins.

As the time approached 7:30 a.m., director Barbara took OHP Trooper Berry, Sheriff Weaver and Dr. Collins to show them the tent the girls had been sharing. Barbara watched as Trooper Berry climbed the steps and disappeared into the tent. Sheriff Weaver went around to the back and circled the tent trying to determine where the assailant(s) had entered. Barbara left them there to go and watch for Girl Scout executive Bonnie Brewster's arrival.

Photographer Mike Wheat, who also ran a newspaper over in Pryor, arrived with his camera at 7:45 a.m. At the direction of Sheriff Weaver, Wheat walked over and snapped black-and-white photos of the area where the bodies were lying. Denise's body, the two still-unopened sleeping bags, a plastic red and white box flashlight, some wound-up 1/8th inch cotton rope, a roll of black tape and a separate piece of the same black tape were captured by Wheat's lens.

At the same time Wheat's shutter was clicking, a high school student was driving north on SH-82 on his way into Locust Grove.

The young man came up on a strange sight. Bull, the driver of the Dodge Super Bee, and his sidekick, Buddy, were walking barefooted along the right edge of the road toward town. Bull was wearing no shirt. There was no sign of the Super Bee.

Back at the camp, Trooper Berry and Sheriff Weaver left tent #7 and passed by the front of all the other Kiowa tents on their way back to where the bodies were. They noticed nothing out of the ordinary along the way. Sheriff Weaver then had ranger Ben walk the perimeter of the Kiowa unit with him, checking behind each tent. They also explored both sides of the tree-lined fence on the west side of the unit, up to where a neighboring field began. Again, nothing of interest was discovered.

After breakfast, all Camp Scott campers, except for the twenty-four Kiowa unit survivors, were taken on a hike to Spring Creek (which traversed the lower southeast quadrant of Camp Scott). The hike was charted to last until lunchtime, which would keep them oblivious to the crime. The Kiowa girls stayed in the craft tent doing activities that morning. This kept them close, so they could be questioned by the authorities. Three by three, the Kiowa girls were taken from the craft tent to a screened-in porch at the nurse's cabin to be asked if they had seen anything or heard any strange noises during the night. None of them had.

The Kiowa unit and the area surrounding the bodies were both roped off with some nylon rope that ranger Ben produced. No campers nor counselors were allowed past the barriers.

At 10:00 a.m. a one-year veteran with the OSBI, Agent Cary Thurman, arrived and took charge of the investigation (agents with more experience and expertise were on their way). Agent Thurman directed photographer Wheat to enter tent #7 and take photos of the interior, including the cots. Wheat encountered a lot of blood on two of the cots and the tent floor, which he had to step through. The soles of his Hush Puppies became soaked. Wheat observed shoe prints of a "waffle"-style sole that were already in the tent when he went in.

It was not until 10:45 a.m. that the other two sleeping bags were ordered opened by OSBI Crime Bureau Agent Mike Wilkerson, who had arrived on the scene and was red-in-the-face mad that no one had already opened them to check for signs of life. The bags were carefully unzipped, and the bodies of Lori Farmer and Michelle Gusé were photographed. Dr. Collins performed a very preliminary examination on the two, leaving the bodies as undisturbed as possible.

Michelle's hands were tied loosely behind her back with a rope/cord. In her rectal and perineal area there was "either fecal material or dark blood." She was in a crouched position. She had an earring in her left ear. Dr. Collins could not see her right ear the way she was lying, but "there was blood about that part of the body." Dr. Collins did not see any lacerations. Lori was not bound. No wounds were detectable the way her body was positioned. Both she and Michelle exhibited rigor mortis.

The bags were then re-zipped. Agent Mike Wilkerson gave the order for the three little victims to be transported to the state medical examiner's office in Tulsa for autopsy.

OSBI Crime Scene Technicians Arthur Linville, Paul Esquinaldo and Larry Mullins had packed up their equipment that Monday morning and flown from Oklahoma City to Pryor. They had been picked up at the Pryor airport by OHP Trooper Charlie Newton and driven to Camp Scott, arriving there a little after 11 a.m. Trooper Newton had filled in his passengers during the ride that the crime fit the M.O. of a twice-escaped local fugitive known as Gene Leroy Hart. The thirty-three-year-old Cherokee was a convicted rapist who had broken out of the Mayes County jail for the second time four years earlier and was known to have been in the area. It sounded like the perfect lead.

After a briefing by Agent Thurman, the three crime scene technicians set about doing their work—identifying, documenting and securing all physical evidence left at the scene. Agent Linville took on the responsibility for the collection of anything and everything that might relate to the case.

The exterior of tent #7 was first photographed and then closely examined. No fingerprints could be found. The flap at the back of the tent was found to have been unhooked. Tent #7 was the one tent in the Kiowa unit that could not be seen from the counselors' tent: the Kiowa unit kitchen obscured the view . . . a possible reason it had been chosen by the killer(s).

All the remaining flaps of tent #7 were then unhooked, and its four cots were carefully moved outside. The two belonging to Michelle and Lori were saturated with blood. All four of the cots were sprayed with fingerprint powder. Only one fingerprint was lifted by Technician Mullins (a fingerprint expert), and it, ultimately, could not be matched to any known individual.

Technicians Linville and Esquinaldo began to examine the inside of the tent, including the wooden floor, with Esquinaldo photographing everything as they went. Blood spray on the inside of the tent walls indicated that Michelle and Lori had been struck with a blunt instrument while still on their cots. Technician Linville saw the waffle prints seen earlier by photographer Wheat and instructed

Technician Esquinaldo to take more photographs of them (in color). Curiously, when the technicians took a break and then returned to the tent a little later, the blood on the floor had been wiped of all shoe prints, except for two. The partially-smeared bloody print of a jungle-type boot was still there: it bore a military-type tread and heavy lugs on the sole. The fact that it was smeared made it impossible to calculate what size it was. A smaller sneaker print (approximately size seven) was also discovered on *top* of the smeared blood. NOTE: The news media reported that the killer(s) had attempted to clean up by wiping the tent floor.

Numerous hairs and fibers and all other items on the floor were packaged and labeled. Then a complexly filtered crime scene vacuum was hooked up to a portable power source, and the floor was sucked clean of debris. The contents of the vacuum bag were sorted into manila envelopes. Finally, ranger Ben loaned his chain saw to Technician Linville, who cut out a 4'x 4' piece of the wooden tent floor where the bloody boot and shoe prints were. The piece of the floor was hauled to the OSBI crime lab in Oklahoma City by Trooper Newton in his pickup truck.

The red and white box flashlight found with the bodies peculiarly had a piece of dark green plastic over the lens, held there by masking tape. A tiny hole had been made in the green plastic, allowing for a sliver of light to shine through.

Three items were found strewn along an imaginary line running southeast between the back of the counselors' tent and the bodies: 1) A guitar capo was found on the ground five feet north of the trail leading out of the Kiowa unit; 2) a pair of women's eyeglasses were discovered on the ground two feet further north from the capo; and

3) a red vinyl/leather-looking eyeglass case with silver-gold trim was found on the ground sixteen feet north of the same trail.

An elastic ponytail holder with blue glass balls, ultimately determined to belong to Denise Milner, was found in the center of the Kiowa unit, 108 feet from the front opening of tent #7.

Technician Esquinaldo made plaster casts of a shoe print that was fifty to sixty feet from the bodies and a tire track found in the area of tent #1. He found nothing distinguishable about either.

Sheriff Weaver gave Technician Linville a spool of rope to add to the haul of evidence that he would transport back to Oklahoma City that evening. Technician Linville accepted it without knowing exactly where it came from.

When the girls from the other four units arrived back from their hike to Spring Creek, a Quapaw counselor reported that one of her campers, Christie Jones, might have some useful information. Christie repeated to the interviewers that she thought she had heard some male voices behind her tent during the night, "about six trees back." She had not been able to understand anything they had said, though.

Parents in Tulsa were notified that all the Girl Scouts would be arriving back by bus that afternoon and that the parents should be there to pick them up. The parents were not told the truth about why this was happening, but by the time their daughters arrived they had heard that three still-unidentified girls had been murdered. The local media had learned from Trooper Berry and spilled the beans. Each of the anxious parents/families had to await the arrival of the buses—which seemed to take an eternity—to see if their Girl Scout was still alive. The campers were told only that camp was being canceled because there was a problem with the camp's water supply. They were understandably disappointed.

The parents of the three victims were called and told by Girl Scout executive Bonnie Brewster that their daughters had died during the night in an accident. It was only after turning on their television sets that these parents heard the word "murder" uttered. They were furious with the Girl Scouts organization, not surprisingly.

After all the girls had vacated the camp and headed back to Tulsa, the Camp Scott staff and counselors were retained for preliminary interviews. Their fingerprints were taken, and their footwear was checked by the OSBI. By 3 p.m., the OSBI had set up a mobile command post (a converted travel trailer) toward the back of the camp, near the director's cabin.

At 6 p.m. Jack Shroff, a man who owned a small farm a mile west of Camp Scott, called Sheriff Weaver's office to report that his farmhouse had been burglarized between 3 p.m. Sunday, June 12, and 3 p.m. Monday, June 13, a window of time during which the Girl Scouts were killed. Shroff believed the two events might somehow be related, and he wanted to be helpful.

Shroff did not stay at his farm full-time, he explained: his main home was in Tulsa. Most of his time at his farm was spent taking care of some cattle he pastured there. On occasion, he and his wife used the farmhouse as a weekend retreat.

Shroff recounted that he had left his farm at 3 p.m. on Sunday, then returned twenty-four hours later, at 3 p.m. on Monday with a friend he had talked into helping him load up some fattened calves to take to the slaughterhouse. By the time the stock trailer was vibrating with the stomping of hooves, the two men were drenched with sweat and very thirsty. Shroff drove his rig up to the farmhouse to fetch them a couple of cold beers from the refrigerator. He saw that a sliding glass door at the front of his house had been pried open, apparently with a crowbar. Much to his dismay, all of his beer was gone—someone had made off with two six-packs of bottled Pabst Blue Ribbon that had been there the afternoon before. He and his friend used a chain and padlock to secure the door before continuing on with their load to Tulsa.

Out on the road, Shroff turned on the radio in his pickup and heard, for the first time, about the bodies being discovered at Camp Scott that morning. He pulled over in Inola, Oklahoma, to make the 6 p.m. call to the sheriff's office. After hanging up the pay phone, Shroff went on to Tulsa.

He had no more than gotten in the door of his Tulsa home, when his phone began to ring. He was requested by law enforcement to return to his farm that same evening. He made it back to the location, south of Locust Grove, just before 10 p.m. He was met there by Mayes County Sheriff Deputies A. D. David and Al Boyer, plus DA Investigator Beverly Hough. Shroff unlocked the gate to his farm and led the three up the long drive to show them the sliding-glass door that had been pried open. He then pointed out the empty spot in his refrigerator where the beer had been.

Shroff's ranch was a frequent target for break-ins, he told the investigators: it had happened at least five times before. He had lost a stove, $1500 worth of tools (including six or seven crowbars), a complete set of butcher knives, small appliances and a lot of food items during the string of break-ins. He had never reported any of the burglaries before now.

The investigators told Shroff to look and see if anything other than the beer was missing this time. Following their instructions, Shroff noted that some Spam, pork and beans and a loaf of Bond bread were absent from his kitchen cabinets; some Bama pies had been taken from the refrigerator; and some meat had disappeared from his deep freeze. Shroff's wife had made him some salad spread: someone had eaten a sandwich out of the spread and left the lid off. A roll of black duct tape that had been lying on top of a window air conditioning unit and a coil of 3/8" nylon rope were gone. To make it clear what type of rope, Shroff took Deputy Boyer out and showed him a rope hanging from his dinner bell that had been used from the same coil. Deputy Boyer asked if he could have a sample piece of the rope to take with him: Shroff cut off a twelve-to-fourteen-inch piece of it and gave it to Deputy Boyer.

A waffle-style jungle boot print could be easily made out on a light-colored entry rug by the sliding-glass (front) door of the farmhouse. Three more prints that matched it were found in the freshly-rain-soaked dirt around the house, but not a single print was found inside the house. Nor had footprints of any other type been left on Mr. Shroff's property. Pieces of board were propped over the prints by the investigators to protect them until the OSBI could come to the scene the following day. Before the three officials left, Shroff mused to them that his 'squirrel gun,' a .410 single barrel shotgun sitting by the front door, and a box of shells in the cabinet were not touched.

By the time Patrolman Paul and his wife, Betty, returned to Locust Grove from Shamrock that same night, the town and much of the state had been swallowed up in horror. Word was going out. Three little Girl Scouts had been found murdered. No one was talking about anything else. It was the kind of news one has to hear repeated a few times before it sinks in.

    Patrolman Paul Smith did not know it yet, but his life had just been forever altered.

CHAPTER 3

THREE LITTLE ANGELS

Around noon on Monday, June 13, 1977, the same day they were discovered, the bodies and sleeping bags of Lori Lee Farmer, Doris "Denise" Milner and Michelle Heather Gusé were loaded together into a single ambulance for a solemn trip back to Tulsa. As the coachman from Jim Green Funeral Services steered their carriage onto northbound SH-82 from Cookie Trail Road, he cemented history for the three princesses. The girls would forever be together, not only in heaven, but in every mention of their names.

Lori Farmer was born June 18, 1968. Lori was the youngest camper at Camp Scott on that fateful night. Her parents were planning to surprise her at camp with a birthday party on the following Saturday, when she would be turning nine years old. Mature for her age, Lori had skipped a grade in school, which made her the youngest in her class. She enjoyed reading and learning. But more than anything, she loved being the big sister to her four younger siblings.

Denise Milner was born February 5, 1967. She was described as a kind and brilliant 'straight-A' student. She was an introspective young girl who thrived on talking to people, but never bothered anyone. She enjoyed tap dancing, going to the library, and she sang in the church choir. Denise sold cookies to pay her way to her first ever camp. Incidentally, Denise's father was an officer with the Tulsa Police Department.

Michelle Gusé was born February 23, 1968. It was Michelle's second year at Camp Scott. She was an active and athletic child. When she was not busy playing with her soccer team, she was growing African violets. She made her mother promise to water and take care of her plants while she was away at camp.

In Tulsa, Assistant Chief Medical Examiner Dr. Neil Hoffman received the bodies of the girls from the ambulance a little after 1 p.m. Dr. Hoffman was considered an expert in his field. He supervised all the medical examiners in the entire northeastern portion of Oklahoma.

By 3:30 p.m. Dr. Hoffman was joined by OSBI personnel who attended and assisted him with the autopsies of the girls—Agent Larry Bowles; Chief Fingerprint Technician Paul Boyd; and Chemists Janice Davis and Dennis Reimer. All those who were present watched and listened as Dr. Hoffman probed the totality of the evidence in front of him and spoke his findings into a recording device.

Dr. Hoffman first examined the outside of the sleeping bags for the possibility of trace evidence. He removed any foreign items he discovered. His next step was to free the girls from their sleeping bags and any bindings that had been placed on them by their slayer(s).

Dr. Hoffman observed Denise lying "on top of a red, yellow and blue-green sleeping bag." She was dressed in a white flannel nightshirt with "a pink floral pattern," which was gathered up across her chest. Across the front of the nightshirt was shiny black tape. Dr.

Hoffman described the 2-inch-wide tape as a "black, somewhat-rough-surfaced adhesive tape, similar to book binding." The knotted end of a spiral-stranded, approximately 1/8-inch light-colored rope/cord was trapped under the tape. The cord passed up and around Denise's neck and was knotted at the left front side of her neck. The cord was so tight around Denise's neck that Dr. Hoffman had great difficulty inserting his finger behind it to cut it loose with his scissors. Also around Denise's neck was an Ace-type bandage with a rolled up piece of towel flattened inside it.

The same tape that was on Denise's nightshirt was used to tape her wrists together behind her, with the left wrist being completely encircled twice by the tape. Partially entrapped by the tape on her wrists was more of the same 1/8-inch cord, which was tied around each wrist in a single loop and knot. Three foreign hairs were also found stuck between the two layers of the tape . . . most likely her killer's.

After carefully clipping—then ultimately reattaching with evidence tape—the cord and tape from around Denise's wrist, Dr. Hoffman made a vertical cut down the center back of Denise's pajama top and slid the top and everything attached to it forward over her arms. One additional foreign hair was retrieved from her pajama top.

All items removed from Denise's body, in addition to her sleeping bag, were placed into labeled sacks and given to Chemists Davis and Reimer.

Next, the zipper of a red sleeping bag with a red, blue and white plaid lining was opened. Michelle was inside, wearing a flannel nightshirt with a blue-and-red-floral pattern. Her panties were down between her thighs with the left leg opening of the panties still around her left thigh. Also in her bag were a blood-soaked pillow, with an unzipped pillow case and other undergarments. A 1/8-inch, light-colored rope/cord ran across Michelle's back with an end tied to each of her wrists: both of her wrists were at her sides. Her wrists were tied tightly with a double-half-hitch knot, then the free ends of the cord were tied again, this time in a single-overhand knot. Michelle's body and all the items of clothing and evidence were removed from her sleeping bag. Dr. Hoffman removed the cord from Michelle's body in a manner that left the knots in the ends intact. He then cut away Michelle's nightshirt and panties. The clothing and other items, and even the inside of the bag, were fumed for fingerprints, then placed in labeled sacks and passed off to Chemists Davis and Reimer.

Finally, the zipper was opened on "a blue sleeping bag with a pattern of red and white checked hearts and colonial figures." Little Lori Farmer appeared as though she was sleeping. In the bag with her were "a portion of a tan blanket, a green corduroy pillow, and an apparent air pillow wrapped similar to the external surface of the sleeping bag." Lori was wearing a white "BENTON STATE BANK" T-shirt with "a dark blue collar and sleeves" in addition to her white size-six panties. "A black flashlight with a yellow switch [was] resting on [her] right forearm." Lori's body and all the aforementioned items were removed from her bag. Her T-shirt and panties were then removed from her body. All her possessions and the interior of her sleeping bag were fumed for fingerprints before being placed in labeled sacks and relinquished to Chemists Davis and Reimer.

In an experimental technique using iodine fumes and a silver plate, an attempt was made to lift fingerprints from the skin of the three girls. It was unsuccessful. A black light was used to look for the presence of seminal fluid on the girls' bodies. There was none.

All three bodies, oldest to youngest, then took their turn on the autopsy table for a set of procedural tasks common to all murder victims. The three little angels silently communicated to Dr. Hoffman the horrors they had suffered.

The first task Dr. Hoffman was required to perform was to acquire two swabs from the vagina, two from the anus and two from the mouth – six in total –from each girl. Every swab separately was then smeared on a clean glass slide which was immediately sealed with an alcohol fixative. Afterwards, the swabs were broken into glass tubes which were held in the hands of Chemist Davis. The slides were retained by Dr. Hoffman to later test for the presence of sperm. Hair samples, nail clippings and blood were collected from each of the girls by the OSBI chemists.

Denise's cause of death was listed by Dr. Hoffman as "Asphyxia by Ligature Strangulation," but she also had other injuries besides the damage to her neck muscles and the petechial hemorrhages about her face and scalp [tell-tale signs of strangulation]. The left side of her skull had a massive bruise and a sunken-in fracture. The right side of her skull was broken into fragments in a circular area and sunken in. "Both eyelids [were bruised] and swollen." And there were patterned abrasions on her right face.

A black light revealed orange fluorescence in a multi-ribbed pattern on the outside of Denise's left hip. The pattern was in two phases, both angled with the center end pointing toward the back of her body. The pattern consisted of ribs measuring between 1/4 and 3/8 inches in width. Bruises measuring up to 1/2 inch in diameter were present over the outside surface of both of her lower legs. She had blunt force trauma to her external genitalia, as well as lacerations and bruising around the opening of her vagina. "Blood [was] present about the vaginal introitus. Fragments of apparent leaves and other debris [were] seen [there] as well. The hymenal ring [was] markedly [bruised] and lacerated."

Michelle's official cause of death was "Blunt impacts to [the] head with lacerations and contusions of [the] brain." Michelle had six blunt impacts to her head, to be exact, with multiple skull fractures. The shape of three of the fractures, two on the left side of her head and one on the right side, were described by Dr. Hoffman as "crescentic" (crescent-shaped). There was blood in her nose, mouth and ears. She had blunt injury to her perineal region, with superficial lacerations of her anus and vaginal introitus.

Lori's official cause of death was "Laceration of brain due to blunt impact to head." She was also found to have a non-bleeding laceration of the vagina, meaning it was inflicted after death. She had 'resolving' bruises on the front of her left leg, measuring up to 3/4th of an inch in diameter.

The public anxiously waited to hear the name(s) of the demon(s) incarnate that had robbed the world of these three beautiful, innocent little beings with such extraordinary potential. Oklahoma Governor David Boren sent a stern edict to the OSBI to find the killer(s) NOW.

CHAPTER 4

CASE SOLVED?

The following morning, Tuesday, June 14, 1977, Tulsa Medical Examiner Doctor Neil Hoffman reported the cause of death for each of the victims to Ted Limke, Chief Inspector for the OSBI, now in charge of the case. In layman's terms, Lori and Michelle had died from blows to the head, and Denise had been strangled. Using basic scientific methodology, it was Dr. Hoffman's estimation that the girls had died between 4 and 5 a.m. Monday morning—at the latest 6 a.m. (obviously).

That same day Dr. Hoffman also tested the slides made from the oral, vaginal and anal swabs he had taken from the victims the day before. He used the time-tested "H and E" (hematoxyline-eosine) stain technique to look for the presence of sperm: he could detect no sperm on any of the slides. Since the case was of such magnitude, Dr. Hoffman had a fellow forensic pathologist, Dr. Fred Jordan, review his work. Dr. Jordan (who was with the medical examiner's office in Oklahoma City) concurred with Dr. Hoffman that no sperm had been deposited into the body canals of any of the girls. The media blasted all the medical examiner's findings to the public. The headline that seemed to grab the most attention was the absence of sperm.

Also on Tuesday, the twenty-four surviving Kiowa campers were returned by bus to Camp Scott from Tulsa, and, together with their counselors, they were taken back into their tents. OSBI, OHP and DA escorts accompanied counselor and camper alike. Twenty-four hours after the Kiowa residents had been unceremoniously whisked away, they were back and on a mission to inventory their possessions to see what, if anything, was missing.

Counselor Susan discovered her blue-denim purse was gone. The tall, sandy-haired teen had personally pieced and stitched the purse together from some of her old cut-up jeans and fashioned it with a handy shoulder strap for carrying. She had tucked her masterpiece under the edge of her cot (at the front of the counselors' tent), almost directly beneath her pillow. Inside the purse were a pair of sunglasses in a tan plastic case; a comb and a brush; and a billfold containing some pictures and money.

Counselor Carla's spare eyeglasses, with the red-with-silver-gold-trim case that held them, were no longer in an orange crate next to her cot. The crate was sitting up on its side, also at the front of the tent, and Carla had inserted a make-shift shelf into the center of it. On that shelf had lain the spare eyeglasses next to a guitar capo (which was also MIA).

Counselor Dee's things were all there and undisturbed, at the back of the tent, where she had been sleeping. The cargo of all twenty-four Kiowa campers was found intact in their tents, as well.

A light-colored towel that belonged to counselor Susan was still draped over the front edge of the counselors' tent floor, immediately in front of Carla's cot. The towel had been wet when it was placed there: the counselors used it to dry off during the Sunday-night rainstorm. After that, it had served as a doormat where they had placed their dirty shoes whenever they were inside their tent. In addition to dried mud, the towel now appeared to have a small amount of blood on it. DA Investigator Beverly Hough noticed the blood and pointed it out to the OSBI, who seized the towel as evidence . . . puzzling, since it had been of no interest the day before. Somehow a rumor escaped from the camp that a towel used to wipe up the murder tent floor had been located.

The Kiowa counselors were put through much more intensive—even intrusive—interviews while they were there that day. The questions thrown at them spanned their backgrounds and even their sexual preferences. *Had the counselors entertained boyfriends during camp? Or perhaps, since no sperm had been found, were the perpetrator(s) female? Could it be the counselors themselves?* There was much to find out. Investigator Hough learned from the Kiowa counselors that Kathy Elder, a counselor in the neighboring Quapaw unit, was also missing her purse.

A trunk that belonged to Karen Mitchell, a counselor in the Choctaw unit, was hauled into the Locust Grove Police Department and placed on a bench for safekeeping. In Patrolman Paul's presence, a fellow police officer, Gary Shamel, pried open the lock on the trunk, then was unable to re-lock it. NOTE: The trunk later disappeared. Paul assumed it had been picked up by an OSBI agent or someone from Sheriff Weaver's office.

A wider search was conducted throughout the entire 410 acres of the Camp Scott property. No luck locating the purses of counselors Susan and Kathy. What *was* found were some scraps of green plastic and masking tape, lying together with a crowbar and three Pabst Blue Ribbon beer bottles next to the perimeter fence, about 200 yards southwest from the Kiowa counselors' tent.

Ranger Ben's cabin and property were scrutinized. Both he and his wife were given lie detector tests, which they passed. Blood, hair samples and fingerprints were also taken from the couple. They were quickly cleared of any wrongdoing.

Meanwhile, back at the Oklahoma City crime lab, OSBI Technician Mullins meticulously took apart the red and white box flashlight that had been nestled with the bodies. Inside he found a partial fingerprint on the reflector, which ultimately could not be matched to anyone: no other prints could be found on or inside the flashlight. A piece of folded newspaper, later determined to be from pages 5 through 12 of Section C from the April 17, 1977, issue of *The Tulsa World*, was behind the battery of the flashlight. Technician Mullins treated the newspaper with anhydron and silver nitrate (a common practice), but could detect no fingerprints anywhere on the newspaper. Mullins then checked the green plastic that had been taped over the lens of the flashlight—no fingerprints there, either. The masking tape that was used to secure the green plastic was not checked for prints.

The hairs that had been removed from the tape around Denise's left wrist at autopsy were microscopically examined by OSBI Chemist Ann Reed, who was a hair comparison expert. Reed compared the hairs to four hairs that had been swept from tent #7. Three of the four hairs from the tent floor were microscopically similar to the hairs from Denise's wrist. All of the hairs had Mongoloid characteristics, meaning they were from "an Oriental or an American Indian." This should have come as no surprise, since the murders were committed within the borders of the Cherokee Nation.

That afternoon, Technician Linville took a couple of investigators with him to the burglary scene at Jack Shroff's farm. Shroff took Linville to the sliding glass door that had been pried open. Linville removed the boards that the previous investigators had placed over the waffle-style jungle boot prints the previous night. Shroff assured Linville that the prints were not there when he had left his farm at 3 p.m. Sunday afternoon: Shroff felt they had been made sometime after the Sunday night rainstorm.

Technician Linville curled his index finger around his chin and listened intently as Shroff once again described what all had been stolen. Linville was suspicious of Jack Shroff. He saw Shroff as a possible suspect who may have accidentally dropped his flashlight and tape with the bodies and was now worried that his fingerprints on those items would identify him. *Was feigning a robbery the perfect way to cover his crime?* After all, he had never reported any of the previous burglaries.

Shroff, a former construction worker, was questioned as to whether he kept masking tape around his place. His answer was that he *always* kept "paint" masking tape around. It was then verified that green plastic garbage bags were present at Shroff's farmhouse, as well. Investigators felt they had identified the most likely source of the plastic and tape found over the lens of the red and white box flashlight.

Technician Linville ordered plaster casts be made of one of the boot prints behind Shroff's house, and the seasoned agent also seized the entry rug with the muddy boot print. The Shroff property was then dusted for fingerprints. NOTE: All prints were eventually accounted for. Shroff's phone records were checked at Southwestern Bell to see if any calls had been made from his house between 3 p.m.

Sunday and 3 p.m. Monday: none had. The damaged portion of the door frame was subsequently removed and taken to the crime lab so that 'tool marks' could be compared to the crowbar that had been found with the beer bottles near the camp fence. Shroff did not yet realize that he had moved into first place as the OSBI's chief suspect.

Upon request, Shroff went over to Camp Scott to see if he could identify any of his stolen items in the agglomeration of crime scene evidence that had been amassed at the mobile command center. While he said the black duct tape was similar to his, Shroff denied recognizing the red and white box flashlight. His fingerprints were taken so they could be compared to any unknown prints.

A day later, on Wednesday, Director Barbara Day sat for a long session with investigators. She was quizzed about all the personnel inhabiting the camp at bedtime on Sunday, June 12, 1977. *Had she vetted them well enough before hiring them? Had any of them mysteriously disappeared from where they were supposed to be at any time?* Barbara was confident that not a single member of her staff was capable of such savagery, and she assured her inquisitors the camp workers were all present and accounted for at all times. She and Richard were then exposed to the same protocol as ranger Ben Woodward and his wife had been: lie detector tests were administered and blood, hair samples and fingerprints were collected. The Days, like the Woodwards, were also cleared as suspects.

While the OSBI was trying to rule out farmer Jack Shroff as the killer, they got a "reliable" tip that escapee Gene Leroy Hart and another man were living in a cave three miles south/southwest of Camp Scott. Sheriff Weaver was requested by Agent Cary Thurman to order aircraft flyovers of the area using heat-seeking technology. Sheriff Weaver obliged, but no one was spotted.

That same Wednesday afternoon three tracking dogs arrived from Pennsylvania, along with their trainer, Don Lakin. Harras, a Rottweiler whose specialty was tracking on asphalt or blacktop roads, and two German Shepherds were billed as "the wonder dogs" by Lakin. He boasted that he had created the best team of canine crime solvers in the country, and he guaranteed they would lead authorities to the killer(s) within forty-eight hours. A Pennsylvania Highway Patrolman, who owned one of the dogs, was also in tow. NOTE: By the following week, Harras had been hit by an automobile and killed while being returned to his home in Pennsylvania, and one of the other dogs had died from heat exhaustion. Some folks believed an Indian medicine man had placed a curse on the dogs.

The following morning, Thursday, there in the camp, one of the dogs was scented on the muddy entry rug that had been taken from farmer Shroff's porch. The dog was then taken in the direction of the Kiowa area, and he tightened the leash, meaning he had picked up a scent and was trailing. Sheriff Weaver watched as the dog went to tent #7, sat down at the front step, then stepped up onto the front step, sniffed inside the tent and sat down again. Sitting down was the dog's way of signaling he had located the scent. After being scented on the entry rug again, the dog went to where the bodies had been found and sat down there, as well.

The canine tracker was next taken to the perimeter of the Kiowa unit behind tent #7. Scented on the rug one more time, the dog first proceeded west, then made a half-circle and turned north through the woods and into the area of the Arapaho unit. From there he went east until he reached Cookie Trail Road. Going north and out through the front gate of Camp Scott, he continued on Cookie Trail Road until he reached the section line that ran east/west perpendicular to SH-82. Turning left (west) the dog sniffed his way down the asphalt over to Cavalier Road, a county road named after John Cavalier, who owned much of the property that butted up against the west side of Camp Scott. The dog had difficulty following the scent at that point, almost as though he could smell it on both his right and his left. He eventually chose left and headed south down Cavalier Road until he reached the gate of Jack Shroff's farm on his right. Going through the metal gate, the dog went to Shroff's front porch and sat down.

Based on the dog's actions, Sheriff Weaver and one of his deputies crawled on their hands and knees looking for tracks along a 150–200-yd trail that extended northeastward from the Kiowa unit over to the Arapaho unit. The two lawmen observed the same jungle boot print that was found in tent #7 and at Schroff's farm: the toe was pointed in the direction of the Kiowa unit. The boot print inside the murder tent had been too smeared to estimate a size, but the one discovered on the trail appeared to be a size ten or eleven.

A straw cowboy hat thought to have been left at Shroff's farm, perhaps by the killer(s), was the next item put under the dog's nose. Taken to a starting place deep in the woods of Camp Scott, the dog traveled west out of the woods and under a fence, which put him onto John Cavalier's property. The dog followed a fence that ran west, then wound past Cavalier's barn to the driveway that led further west past Cavalier's house. Reaching the blacktop of Cavalier Road, he turned left and went south, returning to Shroff's farm, where he again sat down. Jack Shroff's stock as a suspect was rising exponentially.

John Cavalier told the authorities he had been home the night the girls were killed. He said his dog, Hooley, had never barked that night, and Hooley always barked if someone came down the driveway. Cavalier described hearing two unusual screams coming from the camp at 6 a.m. on Monday morning, June 13, 1977, but, despite having served as undersheriff to former Mayes County Sheriff LL "Slim" Weaver, Cavalier made no effort to go check things out. Unlike the Woodwards and Days, no Cavalier family members were considered or cleared as suspects, even though their land was directly connected to the camp by a simple wooden gate.

One of Cavalier's neighbors told investigators that he had heard "quite a bit" of vehicular traffic on a remote road near the camp between 2:30 and 3 a.m. the night of the slayings.

OSBI Agent Dick Wilkerson (Agent Mike Wilkerson's brother) placed a call to Mr. Shroff, requesting that he come to the DA's office in Tulsa the following day (Friday) for a lie detector test. The agent assured Shroff that it was purely routine . . . that everyone was being given lie detector tests . . . that it would remain private. Mr. Shroff agreed to the test, and told Agent Dick Wilkerson that he would be there at 11 a.m. on Friday.

It had now been three days since the bodies had been found, and back in the town of Locust Grove, Patrolman Paul Smith had his detective hat figaturively out of storage and squarely atop his head. His days spent with the Tulsa Police Department had taught him a cop should always develop informants in the area where they worked. During his two years patrolling Locust Grove, he had done just that. Now his informants were whispering to him that three names were floating the streets as being those of the killers . . . Bull, Buddy (the two the high school student had witnessed walking along SH-82 toward Locust Grove that first morning) and Flea (the third passenger in the Super Bee that Paul had seen with them at the Git-

N-Split). This mostly came from school kids, who inhabited the homes and carried the heartbeat of the small community. Paul had made special overtures with these kids during his stint in Locust Grove, having learned they overheard a lot of chatter from their parents and were willing to divulge good information to him. In return, he went soft on them for immature acts of speeding and tire-squealing that other patrolmen would ticket them for. Paul regarded informant tips as invaluable to crime solving, so he passed on the three names to Trooper Harold Berry, who had been the first on the scene and was still actively working with the OSBI on the investigation.

A fifteen-year-old girl named Janice, along with her boyfriend, Donald Trammell, contacted the Locust Grove Police Department (where Paul worked) and told Police Chief Kenneth DeCamp that Janice's brother had killed one of the little girls. Even more remarkable was that Janice's brother just happened to be Flea—one of the three young men named by Paul's informants. Janice said Flea had come home with blood on his shoes and clothing early the same morning the girls were found: Flea claimed to have killed a deer, but had brought no deer home with him. Astonishingly, according to Janice and Donald, Flea had then helped push Bull's prized Super Bee into the Neosho River.

Paul took it upon himself to drive to Oklahoma City and obtain the VIN number of the car from the Oklahoma Tax Commission, and he passed the number on to Trooper Harold Berry. Paul was disappointed that, for whatever reason, no search was done for the Super Bee. And, as far as he could tell, none of the three suspects were questioned. Bull's much-older brother, who had the same legal first name as Bull, was asked a few questions while he was in a drunken state, but it produced nothing useful.

On that same Thursday, a couple of Mayes County men went squirrel hunting—Johnny Colvin and his brother-in-law, WR Thompson. They were hunting on land owned by Colvin's parents. Their hunting dogs drew the two west off the Colvin property and onto adjacent land. After passing through a dry creek bed, they just happened to come upon the cave that, unbeknownst to them, Sheriff Pete had been searching for with his airplane. The hunters saw signs that someone, as had already been reported, was living there. There were two bread sacks containing flour sitting at the mouth of the cave, and a pile of human excrement was down in a nearby ravine with two pieces of wadded newspaper someone had obviously used for toilet paper. The hunters got an eerie feeling they were being watched. Their dogs bristled. They quickly gathered the bread sacks and hurried to Thompson's pickup truck.

Right away, the men drove around the road to the front gate of Camp Scott, where some Oklahoma Highway Patrol troopers were stationed to keep trespassers out of the camp. They gave the sacks to Troopers Charlie Newton and Leon Rice and explained where they had found them. Troopers Newton and Rice received instructions from the OSBI command post to accompany the two men back to the cave and determine if there was anything that might be relevant to the murder investigation.

When the lawmen arrived at the cave area with the hunters, they observed several items lying out on the ground. Trooper Newton's eyes immediately locked onto a tan plastic eyeglass case. A pair of green cotton gloves were next to the cave entrance. Thirty yards up a slope from the cave was an old root cellar. To the left of the cellar entrance was a partial roll of masking tape with some green plastic stuck to it. Next to the tape was a "bean flip" (sling-shot). Scattered around the immediate vicinity were pieces of rubber tubing and different kinds of cans—Vienna sausage cans; an orange juice can; and a Prince Albert tobacco can with Bandaids and matches in it. There were also larger cans that appeared to have been utilized as campfire cooking vessels. A white sack, which had the appearance of a pillow slip, was holding some canned goods and parts of old food containers. And, of course, on the ground down by the stream bed, was the pile of feces with the wadded newspaper that had been used as toilet paper.

Lying on the ground next to the roll of masking tape were two photographs printed on a single sheet of photo paper. Colvin would later testify that he picked them up, despite "don't touch anything until we clear it" instructions from Trooper Newton. It was Colvin's opinion that, even though the photos were dried, they had been rained on. Trooper Newton would later testify that it was he himself who initially picked up the photos. He described them as folded face to face with the appearance they might have been carried in a pocket. He made no mention of them looking like they had been rained on.

Trooper Rice remained at the site with the hunters while Trooper Newton returned to the camp to inform the OSBI what they had seen. Trooper Newton was given some boxes and sacks and was told to return to the cave/cellar: he and Trooper Rice were to retrieve all the items.

By the time the scene was cleared, a pair of red ladies' panties that were discovered inside the cellar had been added to the collection. The pile of feces was even retrieved, having first been placed on a "Pete Weaver for Sheriff" campaign sign. Everything was taken back to the camp and handed to Technician Linville, who inspected all the items. The one thing that was not found at the cave/cellar area was any sign of other squirrel hunters, despite Colvin and Thompson describing the area as a good place to hunt squirrels. There were no ammunition boxes or shell casings, for instance. NOTE: It was rumored that the cave was used by individuals who guarded a nearby marijuana crop.

Technician Linville's heart almost skipped a beat when he saw the wadded newspaper was from *The Tulsa World. Could it be from the same issue as the newspaper found inside the flashlight that had been left with the girls' bodies?* The OSBI veteran also quickly connected the masking tape and the piece of green plastic stuck to it with the materials that had been used to cover the lens of the red and white box flashlight. Best of all, he studied the photographs and thought he recognized someone in one of them . . . Patricia (the ex-wife of the escapee Gene Leroy Hart), who he had interviewed a couple of days earlier. Linville went to the home of Hart's mother, Ella Mae Buckskin, and asked her for a picture of Patricia. Linville did not have far to travel: Ella Mae lived only a mile from the front entrance of Camp Scott. She willingly provided him with the picture, but the lady in the cave photo was not Patricia.

Tom Jordan, the OSBI's tool mark expert, took the partial roll of masking tape (from the cave) to the crime lab and microscopically matched the ripped end of it to the end of one of the pieces of tape on the red and white box flashlight.

Meanwhile, it was learned that the old root cellar next to the cave had once had a house standing above it . . . the boyhood home of escapee Gene Leroy Hart.

On Friday, farmer Jack Shroff arrived at the DA's office in Tulsa to fulfill his promise to take a lie detector test. He had been told by Agent Dick Wilkerson on Thursday that it would only take twenty minutes. He arrived at 11 a.m., as scheduled, but was not allowed to leave until 12:45 p.m. He passed the test, but by then the fact that he was a suspect had been leaked to the press and was already on the newsstands.

He returned to his farm to find his house ransacked, with all of his furniture stacked in the kitchen. The press got up in his face, while the authorities were busy dragging his farm pond. Ugly phone calls and vicious comments thrown his way cost him a stay in the hospital: on Sunday, he had a stroke and then melted down into a nervous breakdown.

Tuesday, June 21, 1977, eight days after the murders, OHP troopers came to the OSBI command post to report a robbery. The owner of T & H Grocery, one of two grocery stores at Sam's Corner, a country marketplace on SH-33 just outside Locust Grove's western limits, had reported they had been broken into the same night the little girls had been slain. Food items, beer, cigarettes, insect repellent, a flashlight and some batteries had been stolen. Incredibly, the cash drawer had been left with cash in it. Fingerprints were taken from the owner and all employees to compare with other prints lifted throughout the small market: some matched, as would be expected, but others were not identified. Photographs were taken outside the store of a military-style boot print with lugs on the sole. They now had this same boot print in four places: 1) the death tent, 2) near the Arapaho unit heading toward the Kiowa unit, 3) at the Shroff residence and 4) at Sam's Corner.

Tracking dogs were dispatched to Sam's Corner, but after going to the back side of the store, they lost the scent, indicating the suspect(s) had probably left in an automobile. The dogs messed up the boot print before a plaster cast could be made, but photos of the broken glass from the back window of the store were captured.

The sunglasses in the tan case found at the cave were soon identified by counselor Susan as having come from her stolen denim purse (which tied the cave dweller to the murder scene), but the two photographs found on the ground were not Susan's. To try and identify them, the media was brought in. The photographs were shown on the 10 p.m. news Tuesday, June 21, 1977, and were also printed in local and area newspapers. The OSBI's phone rang.

A high school teacher from Byng, Oklahoma, recognized the pictures as having been taken at his wedding. A man named Louis Lindsey from Granite, Oklahoma, was named as the photographer. Lindsey was a records officer that had retired from the Granite Reformatory and moved to Westminster, California. The Westminster Police Department ran Lindsey down and instructed him to call the OSBI immediately. Once Lindsey was given the date the wedding photos had been taken—May 28, 1968—he said whoever was on record as being his darkroom technician at the time would have processed the film. The OSBI looked it up . . . the photos were developed by none other than the escapee Gene Leroy Hart.

On June 23, 1977, exactly ten days after the murders, DA Sid Wise held a press conference and announced, "We have our man!"

An arrest warrant was issued for Hart on triple murder charges. Now they just had to find him.

CHAPTER 5

SONNY

Sheriff Pete Weaver, the Oklahoma State Bureau of Investigation and the Oklahoma Highway Patrol proceeded ahead with their theory of the crime—that the perpetrator was the two-time Mayes County jail escapee, Gene Leroy Hart.

Hart did have a colorful history. World War II was rocking the globe when a little boy whose birth certificate bore the name "Gene Leroy Sullateskee" was born at the Claremore (Oklahoma) Indian Hospital, two days after Thanksgiving 1943. His teenaged mother, Ella Mae, nicknamed him "Sonny." Sonny never knew anything of his father, Walter Hart: Walter was married, but not to Sonny's mother. Lydia, Walter's wife of six years had just given birth two months earlier to a daughter, Ethel Lorene "Rene" Hart. Rene was the third child for Walter and Lydia—they already had a four-year-old son, Homer, and a two-year-old daughter, Zelma. There seemed to be no room in Walter's life for little Sonny. Two more Hart siblings, Donald and Maxine, arrived after Sonny's birth.

Ella Mae decided to get herself a husband. She married PFC Jesse Buckskin, nine years her senior, and he fathered the beginning of Sonny's Buckskin siblings. Just weeks before Sonny's third birthday he got a baby sister, Alice "Millie" Buckskin. The Buckskin family continued to grow as two more children—Jimmy, then Nancy—were born. Sadly, Ella Mae's husband, Jesse, died in 1950 at the age of thirty-three, when Ella Mae was only three months pregnant with Nancy.

Ella Mae was once again a single mother, and now she had four small children—ages six and under—for which to provide. It didn't make things any easier when she continued to have children. She gave birth three more times in the seven years following her husband's death, as Millard, Thurman and Tammy joined her brood. Even though their parents never married, the three youngest went by their father's last name, Johnson, throughout school. NOTE: Mr. Johnson was not a Native American.

Things were predictably tough in Ella Mae's household. She had trouble feeding and clothing her four boys and three girls. She even worked for food, slaughtering animals on the Cavalier family farm/ranch. Sonny, being the oldest, took it hard. He grew an anger towards his father, Walter. Sonny wanted to be a son, but he had no one around who wanted to be his father. *He* had to be the 'man of the house.' Sonny was hard on his little brothers, and they resented him for it.

When Sonny got to high school, he found he could vent his emotions on the football field. Wearing jersey #39, the Locust Grove Pirate was someone who garnered respect, playing both offensive and defensive positions. His coach, Roger Morris, liked him and gave him opportunities that regularly landed the name "Hart" in the sports sections of area newspapers. Coach Morris described Sonny as "the best boy I ever coached." For the first time in his life, Sonny was somebody. He was voted "Best Athlete" by his senior class. He was finally *seen* by people who had clout.

Feeling handsome and confident in his 'letter' jacket, Sonny was unmistakable, especially when he sported a pretty girl on his arm. However, when he graduated as one of fifty-six students with the class of 1963, he took an action that would rip up any promissory note to an affluent life for himself. Instead of going to college on a football scholarship, he opted to marry his fellow classmate and high school sweetheart, Patricia Pratt (who was pregnant), that June.

Almost immediately, Patricia gave birth to a son. Technically, Sonny was now a father himself . . . but in reality, he was an overwhelmed kid who was ill prepared emotionally or financially to be the head of a family. He had begun his marriage with the best of intentions, affectionate and loving, but the old demons of his early life sat heavily upon him, and he buckled beneath the weight. The bright star from the Friday night lights was sucked into a black hole. His pent-up anger towards his father now morphed into bitter hatred, and he was downright mean to his younger brothers.

On the Friday night of June 3, 1966, during the month of his third wedding anniversary, Sonny decided to ditch his graveyard shift at the Flint Steel Company in Tulsa. By the following morning, Saturday, June 4, 1966, the entire trajectory of his life was pointing sharply downward. The Fondalite Club was a BYOB (Bring Your Own Bottle) establishment, which meant patrons brought their own liquor, and the bartender would open the bottle and mix a drink into a glass for them. The club, located at 11th and Denver, was a popular Tulsa nightspot, and, well before the days of Tinder, it served as a place where one could find a hookup, if they were so inclined.

Two young ladies, a tall nineteen-year-old with dark hair named Kathy, six months pregnant, and a petite eighteen-year-old blond named Marjorie, four months pregnant, had brought a pint of vodka to the club at 9:30 that evening. Kathy was newly divorced with a toddler already, and Marjorie, newly married, was fighting with her husband already. The Fondalite Club was a place the two friends had visited a few times before. It represented a fun night of 'freedom' for them.

The lives of Sonny, Kathy and Marjorie were on a collision course.

In a preliminary hearing held just over two weeks later, June 20, 1966, before Mayes County Judge Creekmore Wallace, testimony was presented against Sonny, who was being charged with "Rape, First Degree (Force & Fear)." Only two witnesses took the stand—Kathy (from the Fondalite Club) and Mayes County Sheriff Joe Faircloth. NOTE: The following passages in quotation marks are from the official court record.

Sheriff Faircloth went first. He testified that he received a call a little before 7 a.m. on the morning of Saturday, June 4, 1966, which caused him to go immediately to the residence of Riley Wishard, the City Marshal of Chouteau, Oklahoma (a town twelve miles due west of Locust Grove on SH-33). Arriving there, Sheriff Faircloth interviewed four individuals: Kathy and her friend, Marjorie, along with two men who lived between Locust Grove and Tahlequah. The men explained that, in an act of compassion, they had taken a shaken-up Kathy and Marjorie to City Marshal Wishard's home after picking them up walking along SH-33 that morning. Kathy and Marjorie said they had been kidnapped, raped and left in the woods.

After making notes on a yellow legal pad, Sheriff Faircloth took City Marshal Wishard and the two young women and spent a couple of hours in a wooded area between Chouteau and Locust Grove in back of what was the burned-out remains of Foreman's Mountain View Bar-B-Que. This is where Kathy and Marjorie said the unthinkable had happened.

While searching the woods north of a pond, Sheriff Faircloth picked up what became State's Exhibit 2. Faircloth explained that "underneath a small bush or tree on a hillside . . . in the general area north of a pond" was some black friction tape and some olive drab tape, both bunched together with some pieces of cotton rag, braided nylon cord and cotton cord. Kathy and Marjorie identified the tape, rags and cord as the instruments that had been used by their abductor to bind and gag them. Kathy provided a partial license plate number she had memorized from the '58 Chevy that the rapist had been driving: "ME80."

Sheriff Faircloth, who had OSBI Agents Leo Albro and Al Jones in his car with him, first saw Sonny that same Saturday around 3:30 to 4:00 in the afternoon. Sonny was sitting in Trooper Charlie Newton's Highway Patrol car at the entrance of Earl Ward Park near Locust Grove. Patrolman Newton and Sheriff Faircloth's deputy, T. J. Summerlin, had already spotted the partial license plate number and description of the Chevy and had taken Sonny into custody.

The accused was transferred from Newton's Highway Patrol car over to Sheriff Faircloth's cruiser to join Faircloth, Albro and Jones for a ten mile ride to the Mayes County Jail. Sonny sat in the back with Albro.

Sheriff Faircloth put Sonny in his office as soon as they reached Pryor. Sonny was surrounded by Faircloth, County Attorney

Longmire, the two OSBI agents Albro and Jones, and the Pryor Chief of Police LL "Slim" Weaver. Slim Weaver had been the Mayes County sheriff for three consecutive terms from 1953 to 1965, having left that office only a year earlier. Sonny made no request for an attorney, according to Faircloth's testimony.

Sonny's defense attorney, Tony Jack Lyons, rose to ask questions about a statement Sonny was said to have made.

Lyons: "Now it has been reported in the newspapers that he did give a statement. Was a statement signed in your presence?"

Faircloth: "No."

Lyons: "Did you ever see the accused write anything?"

Faircloth: "No."

Lyons: "The statement you are referring to is purely an oral utterance on behalf of the accused?"

Faircloth: "Yes."

Sheriff Faircloth was of the opinion that Sonny was not under the influence of alcohol nor drugs when his rights were stated to him. Sonny was "very quiet. He didn't have a lot to say. There seemed to be – I don't know what – fear or what – but he didn't appear brazen or he didn't show any great signs of fear that I could detect." After a while, with no luck getting Sonny to spill anything, all of the lawmen left the office . . . except for one: Chief Slim Weaver.

Lyons: "Let me ask you this, if this is not true, that up to the time that this defendant or accused was left alone in the presence of L. L. Weaver, the Chief of Police of Pryor, Oklahoma, he had not manifested any indication whatsoever of any intention to cooperate or make a statement or thing of that nature. In other words, up until this point of time the officers had been completely stalled in their interrogation of the accused, is that right?"

Faircloth: "He had denied it up until that point of time."

After Sonny had spent his alone time with Chief Weaver, however, he had suddenly begun talking, and he was saying all the things the interrogators wanted to hear. Sheriff Faircloth recounted the following:

"He told us that - uh - he told us that he had picked [Kathy and Marjorie] up out at the Fondalite Club [around 2 o'clock in the morning] and that he had put them both in the trunk [of his car] to start with from there. That he went over to west Tulsa to a service station. That he bought some gas at a service station, that before he got to the filling station he had taken one of the girls, uh – out of the trunk and she was in the seat with him. They bought the gas, that he came back to somewhere along 33 highway in the neighborhood of Inola and that he took the other girl out of the trunk and put this one that was in the seat with him back in [the trunk]. That he parked behind a service station in Inola and had relations with the girl that was in the car with him and then that they came back over to this area around Foreman's [Bar-B-Que] and then that he got the girls out and took them up on this hillside and that he started to have relations with one [Kathy] and that she said it hurt and he quit and then he had relations with the other girl."

Sheriff Faircloth said that he could not recall if Sonny made any statements about the tape/rag/cord item found under the tree north of the pond: Faircloth knew they had talked about it, but he was not taking notes at the time and could not remember what exactly it was that Sonny had said. What Faircloth *could* remember was that Sonny told them he left the girls tied up there with gags in their mouths, and he went off and intended to come back.

Following a two-hour noon recess, Sheriff Faircloth's memory was much improved. He came back and testified that Sonny had told them the tape/rag/cord item included the tape and rag Sonny had used to tie the 'girls' and gag them: he had also used the rope to tie them. In addition, Sonny had divulged where both kinds of the tape had come from, as well as where he had gotten both the rope and the "shop" rag.

Defense Attorney Lyons began his cross examination of Sheriff Faircloth with observations about State's Exhibit No. 2.

The cotton rope, produced in court, was estimated by Lyons to be thirty inches long. No length was estimated for the approximately 1/8-inch nylon cord, which Lyons noted had a knot right in the middle of it and had both its ends sealed with some sort of fire or heat source. The shop rag was two pieces of yellowish woven-type heavy cotton or coarse cloth, with some printing on it.

Lyons next revisited Sonny's statement with Faircloth.

Lyons: "You say you never heard any threat made to [Sonny] in your presence?"

Faircloth: "That is right."

Lyons: "And you never heard him promised anything like hope of reward or lenient treatment?"

Faircloth: "That is correct."

Lyons: "Did anybody in your presence while he was there tell him that if he didn't cooperate he was going to get in trouble?"

Faircloth: "No sir."

Lyons: "Let me ask you if you ever heard Mr. Longmire make this statement that 'if you don't cooperate with me I am going to see that you get the electric chair?'"

Faircloth: "No sir I did not hear that statement."

Lyons: "All right, did you ever hear Mr. Longmire say 'if you hadn't have cooperated with me I was going to qualify the jury for the death penalty?'"

Faircloth: "No, I do not recall any penalty mentioned at all."

Lyons then turned the court's attention back to the morning that Sheriff Faircloth had first met with Kathy and Marjorie at the Marshal's house in Chouteau.

Lyons: "Can you describe their appearance please sir?"

Faircloth: "Yes, uh – one girl had on no shoes. There was black marks around their wrists and black streaks across their face both in the area of the mouth and eyes. One girl, who had on shoes, her dress was grass stained and dirty. She still had a piece of rope around her neck and a piece of tape around her neck and both girls, had uh – their clothing was uh -"

Lyons: "Disarrayed?"

Faircloth: "Well not fresh and done up."

Lyons: "Did either one of them have on a sleeveless dress or blouse?"

Faircloth: "Yes." [Kathy was wearing a dress]

Lyons: "All right, were there any visible bruises, lacerations or abrasions upon the portions of her body that you could see?"

Faircloth: "No."

Lyons: "Now with regard to the other girl, the short blond [Marjorie], were there any bruises, lacerations or abrasions upon that portion of her body you could see?"

Faircloth: "Yes."

Lyons: "Whereabouts please?"

Faircloth: "Around the eye and nose and I believe she had another bruise up on her head."

Lyons then asked about how Sonny said he got the girls into his trunk. Faircloth said Sonny was asked if he had a gun and forced them: he denied having a gun.

Lyons circled back to statements Sonny had made to the lawmen.

Lyons: "Do you recall him making any statement to the effect that one or both of them needed to go to the ladies room and he permitted this?"

Faircloth: "Yes."

Lyons: "What did he say about that?"

Faircloth: "Well, he said he got one girl out of the trunk and put her up in the seat with him and that she needed to go to the restroom and he drove around behind the station and let her go to the restroom."

Lyons: "O.K. And she did get out of the car and go into the rest room?"

Faircloth: "Yes."

Lyons: "Did he say anything about the other girl having to go to the ladies restroom?"

Faircloth: "Yes I believe he said she needed to go to the restroom and he let her but he never did say anything about taking her out of the trunk."

Lyons: "Was he asked whether or not he let her out?"

Faircloth: "I believe he just made this statement on his own."

Lyons: "Isn't it true that he always denied that these relations that he had was with force and threats of violence and things of that nature?"

Faircloth: "Yes sir, he denied it."

Lyons: "As a matter of fact didn't he tell you or indicate in some way that this was by agreement between the parties?"

Faircloth: "He didn't say it was by agreement, he said they didn't offer any resistance, they didn't fight him or anything like that but he didn't never say that they agreed to it."

County Attorney Longmire, in redirect, refreshed Faircloth's memory that the defendant had said something about stopping for a soda pop at a Texaco Station out on Skelly By-Pass. Lyons, in his recross, asked Faircloth about this.

Lyons: "And you recall now that he said that one of these girls wanted a - a - soda pop?"

Faircloth: "And that they stopped."

Lyons: "And they stopped at a place and got it. Did he tell you whether he got out and got it or she got out and got it?"

Faircloth: "I believe he said that he got out and got the pop."

Lyons: "Did he tell you how far away from the pop that he was?"

Faircloth: "I don't - he said he was in view of the station and I believe he was asked if the man in the station saw him and he said he didn't think the man ever saw the car."

Lyons: "Did he say he tied this girl in the front of the car with him up so she couldn't get out while he was gone?"

Faircloth: "No."

At this point, it was Kathy's turn to take the stand as the "complaining witness" in the matter.

Kathy testified that on June 4, 1966, at 2 o'clock in the morning, she and her friend, Marjorie, were leaving the Fondalite Club in Tulsa. Kathy and her child were living with her parents at the time, and Kathy had borrowed her mother's '58 Dodge to go out that night. When leaving the club, Kathy and Marjorie reached her

- 61 -

mother's car, which was parked across the street, and found another car was parked next to it. It was a blue-green and white '58 Chevy, with a partial license plate number "ME80."

Kathy first unlocked the passenger's side door to let Marjorie in, and while she was doing that, Sonny, who was in the Chevy, asked Marjorie, "Is it pretty lively in there?"

"Yeah, you ought to go in," Marjorie told him, as Kathy was walking around and unlocking the driver's side door for herself. As soon as she and Marjorie were inside, she started the car. Sonny jerked the door open on Marjorie's side and said, "I'm going with you all." Marjorie tried to push him away and shut the door, but he pulled a gun out and told Marjorie to move over. She did as he said. Inside the car, Sonny instructed Kathy to turn the motor off and give him her keys. She obeyed.

Then, Kathy stated to the court, "we asked - we told him if he would let us go he could take the car and he said 'no' that we were going to sit right there for a little while. And then he told me to get in the back seat so I did and then he told us to both get out and get in the trunk."

Longmire: "In the trunk of which car?"

Kathy: "Mine."

Longmire: "And did you get out of the car?"

Kathy: "Yes and he had Marjorie pulled right up next to him and he told me to open the trunk and I opened the trunk and he told us to get in and he told us to give him our purses."

Longmire: "And did you get into the trunk?"

Kathy: "Yes and we gave him our purses and he shut the lid down."

Kathy testified that as they lay in the trunk, they could hear Sonny inside the car "rummaging around, I guess in our purses." He then came and opened the trunk and said he had changed his mind, and he told them to get in the trunk of *his* car instead, which they did. They offered to give him their money if he would just let them go. He turned them down.

Inside the trunk of Sonny's Chevy, they heard him start the engine, and they felt the car moving. After about thirty minutes of driving, he stopped and moved Kathy from his trunk to the front seat of his car. He then told her to move over next to him, that he was going to get gas: he had Marjorie remain in the trunk. Kathy described the place where he had stopped to make the switch as on some kind of graveled road, with no lights close around, only in the distance.

He then drove to a station, the location and brand of which she did not recall, but she remembered him purchasing $3.00 worth of gas. Sonny remained in the car, and the filling station attendant put the fuel in without incident.

After driving for a ways, Kathy told Sonny she had to go to the restroom. He pulled up at the side of a station and let her out. Unfortunately, the door to the restroom was locked, so he told her, "get back in, we will go someplace else." But after he drove for a few minutes more, he stopped and put Kathy back in the trunk (without her having used the restroom) and moved Marjorie to the front seat. More driving, then another stop.

Kathy: "I heard them get out of the car and then get into the back seat and he told her to either - she - if she didn't pull her - pull her underclothing off he would."

Longmire: "Did the girl say anything?"

Kathy: "No."

Longmire: "All right, the next time you were let out of the trunk was it daylight or dark?"

Kathy: "It was beginning to be daylight."

Longmire: "All right, now, up to the time you were let out of the trunk the last time had you had anything around your hands or feet or mouth?"

Kathy: No."

Longmire: "All right, now tell the Court what happened when you stopped and you were let out of the trunk the last time."

Kathy: "As soon as he opened the trunk he put tape over my eyes."

Longmire: "What kind of tape did he put over your eyes?"

Kathy: "It was black friction tape."

Longmire: "Now Kathy, we have here what has been identified as State's Exhibit No. 2, would you tell the Court if you recognize this exhibit?"

Kathy: "Yes."

Longmire: "And would you tell the Court what that is?"

Kathy: "It is what he used to tie us up with and blindfold us."

Longmire: "You say us, who?"

Kathy: "Me and Marjorie."

Longmire: "All right, this portion of State's Exhibit No. 2 is a braided nylon cord, do you recognize it?"

Kathy: "Yes."

Longmire: "And would you tell the Court what it is?"

Kathy: "It was the piece of rope or cord that he used to put around our necks."

Longmire: "Do you know which one of you had this around your neck?"

Kathy: "I think that's the one he put around my neck."

Longmire: "You think this is the one around your neck. And would you tell the Court was it tied to any other portion of your body?"

Kathy: "Yes. My feet or ankles."

Longmire: "Were your feet tied or brought up behind you or in front of you?"

Kathy: "Behind us."

Longmire: "Were your hands tied?"

Kathy: "Yes."

Longmire: "Were they tied in front or behind?"

Kathy: "Behind."

Longmire: "Then what happened after he put the tape over your eyes?"

Kathy: "He started, from what I could hear, he started tying Marjorie up."

Longmire: "Did she say anything?"

Kathy: "She asked him for a cigarette."

Longmire: "And did you say anything to him?"

Kathy: "I asked him if he was going to, if he was - he told us he was going to come back and that he was going to leave us there for awhile."

Longmire: "All right did he take you anyplace?"

Kathy: "After he tied us up."

Longmire: "Were you able to see what was going on?"

Kathy: "No, only on the ground."

Longmire: "You could see the ground?"

Kathy: "I could see out from underneath the tape."

Longmire: "Now Kathy, after your hands were tied, then what happened?

Kathy: "Then he put a piece of that rag in my mouth and taped my mouth up."

Longmire: "There are two rags here, can you tell me which one it was?"

Kathy: "This one."

Longmire: "Can you tell the difference in the two rags, if you know?"

Kathy: "Because this one has got some dirt or something on it and Marjorie picked my piece of rag up and wiped her leg with it."

Longmire: "Tell the Court what happened after that, did you go anywhere or did you stay there?"

Kathy: "Yes, the defendant grabbed hold of our arms and sort of pushed me in front of him and led Marjorie in back of him and we climbed over hills and rocks and went through trees and weeds and bushes and I don't know what all."

Longmire: "Did you hear any other noises?"

Kathy: "We could hear cars on a highway."

Longmire: "Did you hear any animal noises or insect noises?"

Kathy: "None except crickets."

Longmire: "Did you hear any frogs?"

Kathy: "Oh, heard fish jumping in the pond."

Longmire: "You knew you were around water?"

Kathy: "Yes."

Longmire: "Now, do you know how long it took you to reach your destination from the car to where you stopped?"

Kathy: "Oh, 10 or 15 minutes.

Longmire: "When you stopped was there anything said or done?"

Kathy: "Yes, that's when he - when he raped us."

Longmire: "Kathy what did he do?"

Kathy: "He uh - I fell down while we were walking and he sat Marjorie down and told her to stay there and he took me and led me on to a rock and made me sit down and then he went back and got Marjorie and led her up there pretty close to me but not exactly where I was. Then he came back and got me and took me over to where Marjorie was and he made us lay down and he took our pants and raped us."

Longmire: "Now as to what occurred to you, tell the Court, were your hands bandaged?"

Kathy: "Yes."

Longmire: "In front or back?"

Kathy: "Back"

Longmire: "Were your feet bandaged?"

Kathy: "Not 'till after he raped us."

Longmire: "Now when you arrived at this point did you still have all your clothes on?"

Kathy: "Yes."

Longmire: "You were near your girlfriend?"

Kathy: "Yes."

Longmire: "All right, after he brought Marjorie back up what did he say, if anything."

Kathy: "He told us to lay down."

Longmire: "And did you?"

Kathy: "No and he said 'well you are going to have to anyway.'"

Longmire: "Then what happened?"

Kathy: "He sort of pushed us down, we were sitting down and he just sort of pushed us on down."

Longmire: "Now could you see what he was doing to Marjorie?"

Kathy: "Yes."

Longmire: "And how could you see?"

Kathy: "From underneath the tape."

Longmire: "Now you say he took your pants off of you, were you laying on your back or stomach when this happened?"

Kathy: "Back."

Longmire: "On your back and your hands were still tied?"

Kathy: "Yes."

Longmire: "And the tape over your mouth?"

Kathy: "And eyes, yes."

Kathy then described in graphic detail how he pushed her dress up, pulled his pants down "a little ways" where she could see his white underwear and "private parts" and then stood between her legs. She said she was unable to speak, so she groaned from pain after he briefly penetrated her "private parts" with his. This caused him to leave her and go over to Marjorie, where Kathy watched as he made Marjorie roll onto her stomach.

Longmire: "Could you tell the Court what happened then?"

Kathy: "He committed sodomy."

Longmire: "How long was he in the act of committing this, how long did he commit this act in time?"

Kathy: "It was just a - I don't believe it was even a minute, but he reached a climax with her in that long."

Longmire: "How do you know that he reached a climax?"

Kathy: "You could tell from the way he acted."

Longmire: "Was there anything said by the defendant?"

Kathy: "No."

Longmire: "Did Marjorie say anything?"

Kathy: "No, she made noises like she was in pain."

Longmire: "Now will you tell the Court whether or not there was anything around her eyes and mouth?"

Kathy: "Yes, she was - she was taped and gagged exactly the same way I was."

Kathy testified that Sonny then put tape around her ankles and carried her a little ways and put her "over in these bushes or trees." He went back and got Marjorie and put her in the bushes next to Kathy, and that's when he tied them with the rope.

Kathy: "I heard him tell Marjorie 'it was - it would be all right,' she was making noises and he said 'it will be all right.'"

Longmire: "All right, how long did he stay there after he finished tying you by putting these cords around your neck?"

Kathy: "Not very long, he took my shoes off and left as far as I know."

Longmire: "Did you hear him leaving the scene?"

Kathy: "Yes we could hear him walking away."

Longmire: "All right, did you ever hear a car start?"

Kathy: "Yes."

Longmire: "Approximately, in your best judgment, how long was it from the time he left until you heard the car start?"

Kathy: "It was maybe ten minutes."

Longmire: "All right, did you do anything prior to the time you heard the car start?"

Kathy: "Yes, Marjorie said, I heard her say 'be quiet, Kathy, be quiet,' and I could hear something rustling around in the bushes and I didn't know what it was 'cause I couldn't see and she - but I knew she had got the tape off her mouth because she could talk and she came over and took the tape off my eyes and mouth and my hands and then we took the rest of the tape off. I took the tape off my feet and the rope off my neck."

Longmire: "Now, Kathy, as I understand it, both of you girls are untied?"

Kathy: "Yes."

Longmire: "At this time. Now, is it daylight or dark?"

Kathy: "Daylight."

Longmire: "Now what did you do then, Kathy?"

Kathy: "We hadn't heard the car leave yet so we just stayed there and didn't make any noise 'till we heard the car leave."

Longmire: "All right, now how long was it after you had untied yourselves did you hear the car?"

Kathy: "Just a few minutes."

Longmire: "All right, and what did you do then?"

Kathy: "We started walking towards the cars we heard on the highway."

Longmire: "Now, when you reached the highway what did you do Kathy?"

Kathy: "We tried to flag down some cars and several went by before anyone would stop, and while we were doing that we walked - we walked up the highway."

Longmire: "Did someone stop for you?"

Kathy: "Yes."

Longmire: "Where did they take you?"

Kathy: "They took us to a sheriff's house."

Longmire: "In Chouteau?"

Kathy: "Yes."

Now Attorney Lyons began his cross examination. He began by asking Kathy about her age and marital status.

Lyons: "How old are you please ma'am?"

Kathy: "19."

Lyons: "And you were divorced recently was it ma'am?"

Kathy: "Well, what do you mean by recently?"

Lyons: "Well, when were you divorced please?"

Kathy: "1963." [It was now 1966]

Lyons: "O.K. And you say you are not married at this time?"

Kathy: "No."

Lyons: "How long have you been pregnant?"

Kathy: "6 months."

Kathy then testified that she and Marjorie had gotten to the Fondalite Club around 9:30 p.m. and were there until 2 a.m. when they met Sonny. Kathy described the Fondalite as a "nice club" with a band. She and Marjorie each had two glasses of Vodka Collins. She was unsure of what time the club closed, but it was still open when she and Marjorie left at 2 a.m.

Lyons: "When you get right down to it, isn't this a place where girls who are on the prowl for men can go and men who are on the prowl for girls can go?"

Kathy: "Not necessarily no, well, I mean you can."

Lyons: "Isn't it known locally as a pick-up joint around there?"

Kathy: "No."

Lyons: "But it does happen there?"

Kathy: "I suppose."

Lyons: "Is that the purpose you went there for?"

Kathy: "No."

Lyons had Kathy describe what she was wearing that night. It was the same dress she was wearing in court—a sleeveless blue shift with embroidered yoke on the front outlined in white. She also had worn a pink half-slip and a white bra and panties.

Lyons: "All right, now when you left this place did you get your bottle to take with you?"

Kathy: "No."

Lyons: "Why?"

Kathy: "We just left it there."

Lyons: "Did you serve any drinks to anybody else?"

Kathy: "Not that I know of."

Lyons: "Do you remember serving him a drink out in your car?"

Kathy: "No."

Lyons then had Kathy describe what Marjorie was wearing. Marjorie had on a white skirt and an orange and white striped blouse with a black outline design. Kathy also described her mom's car that they were in. Only the driver's door opened properly. The other three could only be opened from the outside. Kathy stated that she and Marjorie were planning to go straight home when they left the club.

Lyons: "O.K. Now, up to this point of time had you ever noticed or seen the accused here?"

Kathy: "No."

Lyons: "Now when the accused said he was going with you all, what did you say?"

Kathy: "I didn't say anything."

Lyons: "Was it all right with you?"

Kathy: "No, but Marjorie pushed him away."

Lyons: "You saw her push him?"

Kathy: "Yes."

Lyons: "How far did she push him?"

Kathy: "Not very far because he had his hand onto the door."

Lyons: "Which hand did he have on the door?"

Kathy: (Indicating right hand)

Lyons: "You are indicating his right hand?"

Kathy: "Yes."

Lyons: "Where was it, please ma'am?"

Kathy: "On top of the door."

Lyons: "On top of the door? You mean the door or the top of the automobile?"

Kathy: "The door."

Lyons: "I thought it was up on top of the door."

Kathy: "Well, when she pushed him it was and as soon as she pushed him he pulled out the gun out of his pocket."

Lyons: "Which pocket?"

Kathy: "The right pocket."

Lyons: "O.K. Do you know anything about firearms?"

Kathy: "I know what a gun looks like."

Lyons: "Will you describe this one for me please?"

Kathy: "It was small and silver."

Lyons: "Could you see any bullets in it?"

Kathy: "No."

Lyons: "You say he pulled it out of his right hip pocket?"

Kathy: "I didn't say his hip pocket, I said his pocket."

Lyons: "Well which pocket was it?"

Kathy: "I'm not sure, just out of his pocket."

Lyons: "O.K. How long was the gun?"

Kathy: "It was a small gun (indicating 5 to 6 inches in length)."

Lyons: "You are indicating about 5 inches long, would that be a fair statement of fact?"

Kathy: "I guess."

Lyons: "If it's not you correct me because it's your story."

Kathy: "It was a small gun."

Lyons: "A small gun. All right, did you ever see it presented sideways to you?"

Kathy: "The side of it?"

Lyons: "Yes."

Kathy: "When he got into the car, yes."

Lyons: "All right, you can't describe it any more than this?"

Kathy: "No."

Lyons: "Silver?"

Kathy: "Silver."

Lyons: "Did you see the handle of it?"

Kathy: "No he had his hand on it."

Lyons: "O.K. Now, did he ever point this gun at you?"

Kathy: "Not directly at me but he kept it in Marjorie's side."

Lyons: "Well now, how close to her side?"

Kathy: "He was poking her in the ribs with it."

Lyons: "Which side?"

Kathy: "The right side."

Lyons: "Marjorie facing the front of your automobile or facing the rear of it?"

Kathy: "The front."

Lyons: "The front, well then her right side would be away from you wouldn't it?"

Kathy: "Yes."

Lyons: "And you say you saw him poke it in her right ribs?"

Kathy: "Yes, he had the gun in his hand when I saw it and he stuck it down there, in the ribs."

Lyons: "All right, now, did you hear him threaten to use the gun on Marjorie?"

Kathy: "He didn't say he would shoot it but he said if we didn't do what he said we would get hurt."

Lyons: "All right, up to this point had he ever touched you or laid a hand on you?"

Kathy: "Not me, no."

Lyons: "Then all you know he did was to poke a gun into the side of Marjorie?"

Kathy: "Yes."

Kathy recounted for Lyons how she and Marjorie had first been put into her trunk and then into Sonny's trunk. Kathy said that she never hollered or screamed, because she was scared that Sonny would hurt Marjorie.

Lyons: "Kathy, isn't it true that he wanted to take Marjorie back into the Club and you didn't want her to go?"

Kathy: "No."

Lyons: "And that you wanted him to take you into the Club?"

Kathy: "No."

Lyons: "Was there any discussion at all there about him having a date with Marjorie?"

Kathy: "A date with her?"

Lyons: "Yeah. Didn't he want to take Marjorie and leave you there?"

Kathy: "He said, he said – let's see, after we told him to take the car and leave us there and he wouldn't do it, we told him that we were sick and we wanted to go home, and –"

Lyons: "Did you tell him what you were sick on or of?"

Kathy: "And he said 'if you want to,' he said, 'you can go back into the Club.'"

Lyons: "He was talking to you?"

Kathy: "He said that 'Marjorie stays here with me for 30 minutes and if you say anything to anybody I'll kill her.' And Marjorie started crying and hanging on to me and begging me not to leave her."

Kathy testified that at that point they both got into Sonny's trunk.

Lyons: "What did you notice in the back end of his trunk, if anything?"

Kathy: "A quilt."

Lyons: "Did you see him spread it out?"

Kathy: "No."

Lyons: "Did you ever hear any discussion between Marjorie and someone else in the automobile to the effect that she wanted a bottle of soda pop?"

Kathy: "No."

Lyons: "Never heard anything like that?"

Kathy: "No."

Lyons: "O.K. When you were in the trunk after – the second time – could you see anything at all?"

Kathy: "No."

Lyons: "Couldn't see anything, all right. After the car stopped then the car took off again, is that right?"

Kathy: "Yes."

Lyons: "And how long would you say you drove then?"

Kathy: "About an hour, maybe more."

Lyons: "Could you hear any conversation during this hour?"

Kathy: "No."

Lyons: "None at all, o.k. And then you had the sensation of turning off the road?"

Kathy: "Yes."

Lyons: "And going over some gravel I believe you testified about?"

Kathy: "Uh - we backed up, I remember backing up."

Lyons: "Do you have any idea how far you backed or how long? Was it quite a back up or just a short one?"

Kathy: "It was quite a back up."

Lyons: "In other words it was not like backing out of a driveway, it was longer?"

Kathy: "No, yes."

Lyons: "All right, then the car stopped?"

Kathy: "Yes."

Lyons: "Hear any conversation?"

Kathy: "Marjorie asked me, I heard a car door slam, and Marjorie said 'Kathy' and I said 'what' and she said 'are you all right?'"

Lyons: "Then what was the next thing that was done?"

Kathy: "He opened the trunk and put the tape across my eyes."

Lyons: "Did it go clear around the back of your head? Or just patches over your eyes?"

Kathy: "Oh, around our head."

Lyons: "Around your head."

Kathy: "At first he just put two strips across eyes and then he put it around the back."

Lyons: "Do you know how many times he went around your head with it?"

Kathy: "No, I don't recall."

Lyons: "All right, up to this point of time did he ever strike you or threaten you or hurt you in any way?"

Kathy: "No."

Lyons: "In other words you were just doing what he commanded were you not?"

Kathy: "Yes."

Lyons: "If I understand your testimony, after he taped your eyes there, he taped your mouth after putting a gag in it?"

Kathy: "He taped my hands first, before he taped my mouth."

Lyons: "Did he tape your hands behind you?"

Kathy: "Yes."

Lyons: "Now, did he tell you he was going to put this gag in your mouth?"

Kathy: "No, he just said 'open your mouth.'"

Lyons: "Did you protest or make any noises or objections against it?"

Kathy: "Yes."

Lyons: "What did you tell him?"

Kathy: "He said – uh he kept telling me to open it wider and it was too much rag to put in my mouth and so he tore it up and tore a little bit off of it and stuck it in my mouth."

Lyons: "O.K. Now, what did you see him put on [Marjorie] by way of any restraint?"

Kathy: "The tape on her hands."

Lyons: "O.K. Were they in front of her or behind her?"

Kathy: "Behind her."

Lyons: "Tape any place else on her body?"

Kathy: "Her eyes and mouth."

Lyons: "Did you ever see the accused here strike or hit Marjorie at any time during the course of this evening or this morning?"

Kathy: "No."

Lyons: "In other words your testimony is that you submitted by reason of the fear you felt, is that right? Is that it?"

Kathy: "I guess you would say that. He didn't beat us up or anything."

Lyons: "Well, did he scare you in any way?"

Kathy: "Yes."

Lyons: "Were you afraid of him?"

Kathy: "Yes."

Lyons: "Did he threaten you?"

Kathy: "Yes."

Lyons: "And what did he say?"

Kathy: "He told us if we didn't do what he said that we were going to get hurt."

Lyons: "O.K. Did you believe him?"

Kathy: "Yes."

Judge Wallace found that there was enough evidence to hold the defendant over for trial. Sonny originally entered an innocent plea. Then, after the jury had already been selected to hear his case, his new attorney, Bill Thomas, who had replaced Tony Jack Lyons, convinced Sonny that, instead of going to trial, he should take a plea deal to one count of First Degree Rape and two counts of Kidnapping. Sonny actually believed he might get probation or a suspended sentence, so he followed his lawyer's advice. He got ten years. Losing his freedom was small in comparison to the true cost of his transgressions, however. Patricia divorced him, took their son away and changed his name—something Sonny would never get over.

At Oklahoma's Granite Reformatory, Sonny was a model prisoner. For the better part of a year, he was assigned a job with the prison records keeper, Louis Lindsey, who liked Sonny and saw potential in him. Lindsey was responsible for the intake processing of prisoners, including rolling their fingerprints and snapping up to twenty photos of each of them. Lindsey trained Sonny to do both tasks. By permission of the warden, Lindsey also used the prison darkroom for a side photography business he ran.

Lindsey taught Sonny how to take negatives into the darkroom and come out with photos. Lindsey once put in a request to the warden to take Sonny off prison grounds on a big wedding shoot with him: he needed the strength of the former athlete to carry the large amount of equipment required. It would also teach Sonny a trade that might benefit him post-prison. The warden refused, but Lindsey did bring many rolls of film back to the prison for Sonny to develop. What Lindsey did not catch was that Sonny created a couple of extra prints he wanted for himself. The pictures contained the image of a woman who had an uncanny resemblance to Patricia.

After twenty-eight months of incarceration, Sonny was paroled in March 1969 by unanimous recommendation of the Oklahoma Pardon and Parole Board. Sonny returned to Ella Mae's house in Locust Grove with not much more than the clothes on his back . . . and the photographs that reminded him of his lost love (two 3 ½" x 5" prints placed together side-by-side onto a single 5" x 7" piece of photo paper).

Now a convicted rapist, Sonny's chances for a job were pretty much nonexistent. Job applications always had that treacherous section where one had to disclose their prior criminal history. Sonny's pen always seemed to run out of ink just about the time he reached those blanks in the forms.

To support himself, Sonny resorted to committing burglaries. His new criminal enterprise was no more successful than his previous one. For one thing, Sonny was poor at picking victims. One night he broke into the apartment of a Tulsa police officer who had just gotten off duty. Detective Heather Campbell was still awake when she heard him jimmying her door. Pulling out a pistol from under her pillow, she scared him away. When fellow cops showed up in response to her call, unbelievably they heard Sonny attempting to break into another apartment one floor up. They arrested him and, upon searching his vehicle, they discovered items from three other burglaries that had gone unreported during the prior week. There were two wallets and a purse with drivers licenses still inside. When the police contacted the owners of the items, they discovered the owners had considered their belongings to have merely been misplaced. One of the wallets had been removed from a nightstand six inches from the head of a sleeping male victim. Sonny seemed to prefer entering occupied dwellings during the night to commit his burglaries.

Sonny had regrets about pleading guilty during his first serious brush with the law. He felt it had ruined his life, and it left him with a huge distrust of defense lawyers. He decided he would never plead guilty to anything again. He would fight and make them *prove* him guilty. So, in spite of the DA offering Sonny four ten-year terms that he could serve at the same time for all four of the robberies, he chose to go to four separate trials with four separate juries.

Once a jury in Oklahoma finds a defendant guilty, they are then told of the defendant's past criminal record before recommending a sentence. In Sonny's case, the four juries had no sympathy for a kidnapping rapist thief. They wanted him off their streets—for a very long time. They threw the proverbial book at him. The four sentences added up to a maximum of 305 years. Sonny ended 1969 the same way he had begun 1969—behind bars. This time Sonny went to "Big Mac," the state penitentiary at McAlester, OK. He would never breathe free air again, so it seemed.

Four years went by. Then, on April 25, 1973, Sonny was brought back to the Mayes County Jail in Pryor for a 'post-conviction relief' hearing on the 1966 kidnapping and rape incident for which he had served the twenty-eight months (his parole had been revoked when he got in trouble for the burglaries). Sonny was wanting to withdraw his guilty plea for the 1966 crimes and have his conviction set aside.

Two days after arriving at the Mayes County Jail, Sonny and a fellow inmate, Larry Dry, escaped by sawing through the bars on their cell (the saw blade was alleged to be compliments of none other than Sonny's mother, Ella Mae Buckskin). The pair of fugitives were caught eleven days later when a fireman noticed smoke coming out a window of an abandoned house: the fireman assumed the house was on fire. What was really going on was an ill-fated attempt to make coffee using a trashed coffee pot. Sonny and his cellmate were returned to the Mayes County jail.

A short time later, on September 16, 1973, they escaped again while being left unattended out of lockup. This time they split up. Larry Dry was apprehended rather quickly, but Ella Mae's boy was still free four years later. Now it was June 1977, and three Girl Scouts were dead. Word was put out that the strange guttural sound heard by counselor Carla at 1:30 in the morning was a sound that had been made by Sonny when he had raped Kathy and Marjorie back in 1966. Kathy and Marjorie also supposedly said that Sonny had asked to try on their eyeglasses. As far as the county and state authorities were concerned, the escaped rapist and thief Gene Leroy Hart had just added "murderous pedophile" and "odious necrophiliac" to his resumé. He absolutely *had* to be apprehended!

Patrolman Paul Smith was convinced there was more to the story—much more—but he stayed quiet and waited to see what would unfold. He had done everything he knew to do. His information had obviously been ignored or disproven by the OSBI.

CHAPTER 6
CATCH ME IF YOU CAN

The District Attorney's announcement that Gene Leroy Hart was being charged with triple murder immediately divided the small town of Locust Grove into two camps—those who thought Hart was being used as a scapegoat and those who believed he was guilty as sin. The whole of Mayes County was thrown into an uproar.

Those who believed Hart was innocent began to voice their opinions to the media: they were adamant that the DA had the wrong man. Most of Hart's classmates remembered him as the quiet, good-looking football star. A lady who had once dated him considered him to be a perfect gentleman. Jars were placed in local eateries and gas stations to collect funds for Hart's defense. The way Hart's supporters saw it, Sheriff Weaver was merely embarrassed by Hart having twice escaped his jail and was out for revenge.

The newspapers carried statements from the sheriff's critics, some of them going so far as to accuse the sheriff of planting or tampering with evidence in order to frame Hart. The Cherokee Nation rallied around their fellow citizen: they would eventually donate $12,500 to Hart's defense fund to ensure that he got a "fair trial." Hart's twenty-one-year-old half-brother, Millard, who held animosity toward the cops already, threw a verbal jab that made it into print: "Every time something goes wrong, the law always goes to [Gene]."

Wagging tongues alleged that when Hart had escaped from Sheriff Weaver's jail, Hart had left behind the photos he had developed back in 1968 at the Granite Reformatory. All personal belongings were taken from prisoners when they were booked into the Mayes County Jail, so Sheriff Weaver would have had the only access to the photos, they reasoned. Now the photos had been conveniently discovered by the squirrel hunters, Johnny Colvin and WR Thompson. Trooper Newton, who accompanied the squirrel hunters back to the cave, had been in on the arrest of Hart when Hart had committed the kidnapping and rape of the two Tulsa women years earlier: Newton was possibly still biased against Hart. Sheriff Weaver must have slipped the photos to Trooper Newton as he headed out with the squirrel hunters to search the cave area, and Trooper Newton then dropped the photos out in the open where Johnny Colvin would inevitably see and pick them up. Out in the elements was an absurd location for Hart to 'store' his valued photographs, after all.

And so it went.

On the other hand, the citizens who believed Hart was guilty began keeping a sharp eye out for a sighting of him. Not only were these folks looking for justice for three little girls, some of them were looking to pocket some cool cash. Several organizations, both public and private, had set up reward funds for the person who could lead the authorities to Hart's location and capture: the amount would eventually swell to a hulking $50,000.

Around lunchtime on the very same day that Hart was unveiled as the suspected killer, a farmer named Victor Auxier was out checking the fence line on a hill south of his residence, one mile due west of Camp Scott. Auxier spotted a male subject sitting in an overhang in a cliff: he could only see the subject from the waist down and was not able to see his shoes or the upper portion of his body. Auxier thought it might be Hart, so Auxier walked on by, pretending not to see the man, then circled around back to his residence and called the sheriff's office.

Even though the crevice in the hill where the stranger was sitting was not truly a cave, it became known as "Cave Number 2" by law enforcement. The hill that held Cave Number 2 was known to the locals as "Skunk Mountain." The original cave discovered by the squirrel hunters was now labeled "Cave Number 1."

OSBI Agents Cary Thurman, Harvey Pratt and Charlie Wellman, plus a few local officers, were led by Auxier 200-300 yards up the steep fence row to the site where he had seen the man sitting. Cave Number 2, incidentally, overlooked Ella Mae Buckskin's house from the west.

The armed band was greeted by a ghastly enemy. The area was crawling live with seed ticks. The agents were soon coated with the bloodsucking arachnids and began shedding their clothes. Their movements rivaled that of a ceremonial dance as they cried out and pulled the tiny barb-snouted leeches from their bare skin. The man who had been in Cave Number 2 would have to wait. All they wanted to do right now was get out of there!

Agent Pratt simply ignored the ticks. As a Cheyenne-Arapaho, he was a strong believer in Indian "medicine," which included rituals with smoke. Lying on the ground in front of the crevice was a cigarette butt with the filter torn off. Agent Pratt picked it up and mulled over what he was looking at. It was common for the Cherokee to tear the filter off a cigarette when using it to practice Indian medicine. Agent Pratt also observed ashes where four small fires had been built directly in front of the crevice—a significant number and tradition in Indian medicine: four fires represent the four winds and the four seasons.

Agent Pratt crawled behind the four piles of ash and into the crevice, which was markedly devoid of ticks. He was convinced that Hart had been there and was using medicine to protect himself and evade not only ticks, but his would-be captors. While in the crevice, Agent Pratt discovered more cigarette butts without filters and also some long black hairs . . . the same type of hair that was caught in the tape around Denise's wrists and on her pajama top.

Agent Thurman and the others were not so blasé about being tick bitten. Agent Thurman barked a command to evacuate.

When the team returned less than an hour later, joined now by Agent Bowles, Trooper Newton and a tracking dog, they were slathered in tick repellant. The dog was provided scent from the ledge area. Then, as soon as its leash was unsnapped, the canine tracker took off to the east, outrunning all the humans, who could only hear it barking as they perceived it turning back west onto the top of Skunk Mountain. After a little while, the dog returned defeated. The dog handler's explanation was that the subject must have doubled back. Whatever the case, the dog never delivered up the intruder.

Various items were strewn on the ground about the area of Cave Number 2. Agent Thurman found a Band-Aid with Mongoloid hair stuck to it. The Band-Aid was checked for blood, but Agent Thurman would later testify he could not remember the results.

Little tabs from Band-Aids, various tin cans hidden beneath leaves and rocks, a broken quart mason jar, candy wrappers and butts from at least two different brands of cigarettes were seized as possible evidence. A Vienna Sausage can was determined to have come from the grocery store that had been robbed at Sam's Corner. Euwell Tharp, co-owner of the store, recognized the unique price marking on the can.

Agent Wellman made plaster casts of some prints of a military-style boot with lugs in the soles. These boots that had left tracks at the murder tent, between the Arapaho and Kiowa units, at Shroff's house and at Sam's Corner were now making their fifth appearance on Skunk Mountain.

It was getting into the evening, so, as the light was fading, a four-mile square area encompassing Cave Number 2 was surrounded by law enforcement and hundreds of local volunteers, who stayed through the night. A SWAT team was brought in. Automobile headlights were used to illuminate the search perimeter. Nearly two dozen dogs were employed to try and detect the subject. No suspicious person was ever spotted.

When morning came, a manhunt station was set up at Sam's Corner. The search area was expanded to a ten-square-mile area. A small army of lawmen and citizen volunteers spent the entire day braving the rugged terrain and ticks in an all-out effort to apprehend the suspect. Still no luck. OSBI Agent Leo Albro, who had handled Hart during the 1966 rape incident and knew his mother, spent part of that day going to Ella Mae's house to try and convince her to give Hart up. The short-and-sassy Ella Mae ran Agent Albro off her porch with a shotgun. So much for that.

On June 26, 1977, thirteen days after the crime, the Federal Bureau of Investigation (FBI) joined the manhunt. They came bearing a warrant for Hart for "Unlawful Flight to Avoid Confinement," which had been issued October 29, 1973, following Hart's second escape from the Mayes County Jail. The OSBI was not happy to see the FBI. Up until then, the OSBI had been in complete control as the top cops on the case . . . and they liked it that way.

On Monday, July 4, 1977, precisely three weeks after the crime, a seventeen-year-old juvenile delinquent, Darren Creekmore, was released from Sequoyah School, a boarding school run by the Bureau of Indian Affairs in Tahlequah, Oklahoma, some thirty miles south down SH-82 from Locust Grove. By the following week, on July 13, 1977, Darren was being held in the Mayes County Jail as a run-away. While in Sheriff Weaver's jail, a wide-eyed Darren told an amazing story. He recounted to Sheriff Weaver that he had seen Gene Leroy Hart at a cave on the land of frequently-robbed Jack Shroff. The cave was near the home of Darren's grandmother, where he had been living since his release from the boarding school. Strangely, Darren could not provide much detail of a conversation he had supposedly had with Hart. However, the third time he repeated the story, Sheriff Weaver told him they would go look, and, if Hart was there, Darren would receive $700 in reward money that had been collected so far. Young Darren was excited by the thought: he began mentally envisioning all the things he would be able to buy for himself. Sheriff Weaver and a couple of uniforms took Darren with them and went to the southeast section of Jack Shroff's ranch.

Depending on who you believe, they either located the cave that day or they did not. Darren's version of the story was he pointed to the cave up in a ridge, and Sheriff Weaver and the deputies went up and checked it out. Then they came back and told him that no one had been in or around the cave anytime lately. Darren insisted to the sheriff that he knew better, because he had personally been to the cave the very day before he had been detained in Weaver's jail: he had seen where a fire had been built in the four-foot-tall by two-foot-deep opening and had observed footprints in and around there. The prints looked to Darren like they had been made by "combat boots" with "smooth soles" (no mention of lugs). Sheriff Weaver scoffed at the truthfulness of Darren's story and later testified in court that the cave was *not* discovered that particular day.

However, shortly afterwards, on July 29, 1977, Sheriff Weaver, OHP, OSBI, FBI and a dog handler went back out to 'look' for the cave a second time. This time they found it. It officially became "Cave Number 3." There was a titillating message written just inside the front wall of the cave. The message read, "77-6-17 THE KILLER WAS HERE BYE BYE FOOLS" with the word "FOOLS" underlined twice. Sheriff Weaver scraped some of the 'magic marker' ink from the wall of Cave Number 3 and put it into an envelope. The sheriff later testified he never even wrote up a report about the whole ordeal with Darren Creekmore, but head and pubic hair and a saliva sample were taken from Darren.

Darren never made mention of any writing on the wall of the cave. If the date of June 17, 1977, was truly when the message was written there, Darren should have seen it: he could have only been there *later* than June 17, 1977, since he had not been released from the boarding school until July 4, 1977.

More rumors flew about Sheriff Weaver creating evidence against Hart. Sheriff Weaver responded by taking some reporters to see the message at Cave Number 3. As the sheriff pointed out the impossible terrain to the newsmen, he was quoted as saying, "Why would someone come way up here to write a message that was only found by chance? . . . I think the killer wrote it, I'm sure of it . . . he's taunting us." NOTE: Cave Number 3 had a direct line of sight to the back gate of Camp Scott, where the bodies were discovered.

While Sheriff Weaver was busy fielding questions from reporters, the OSBI began to turn their attention to Larry Dry, the Cherokee who had twice escaped from the Mayes County Jail with Hart. Unlike Hart, Dry had been caught following the second escape and, therefore, was back in prison and easy to find. OSBI Agent Tom Puckett went to the Granite Reformatory to interview Dry. Agent Puckett questioned how Dry and Hart had survived while they were on the run together. Dry explained that they had gotten help from Hart's family, especially with food. When asked about the pictures that had been published in the paper—the prison-processed pictures that had been discovered in front of Cave Number 1—Dry said that Hart did not have the pictures with him in the Mayes County jail, that Hart must have left them at the home of a family member back in 1969 when he was paroled from his kidnapping/rape sentence. Dry *had* seen the pictures in Hart's possession following their September 16, 1973, escape, though.

Dry recalled some of Hart's habits to the OSBI, such as committing burglaries for food and supplies and putting socks over his hands to avoid leaving fingerprints. Going against all statistical odds, there had been no meaningful fingerprints found at any of the crime scenes, save the one partial print inside the red and white box flashlight, and it was not a match to Hart. Rope and tape were always a hot property to Hart, Dry said, because they made it easier to bundle and haul supplies, especially small sticks that served as kindling for fires. Hart always collected any rope or tape that he came across, Dry assured Agent Puckett.

Of great interest to the OSBI was how Dry and Hart had traveled at night. Dry explained that they would cover the lenses of their flashlights with pieces of plastic from a dark-colored trash bag, then punch a little hole in the plastic. This would allow them to see their path, while at the same time preventing the light from shining brightly enough where it could be seen by others, who might report them and get them captured.

Dry offered the OSBI a deal: he promised that if they would release him from prison, he would be able to find Hart. He hoped, if he was successful, it would gain him parole. Eventually, with Governor David Boren's permission, Dry was set free to help hunt for Hart. Dry was allowed to roam free as long as he reported in once a day. He never provided the OSBI with any useful information as to Hart's whereabouts, but he did get paroled by the governor for his effort.

The OSBI kept piecing together a timeline of Hart's movements since the date of his second escape four years earlier. They placed undercover agents at some of the more public places where he reportedly had been seen. They learned that one of the most recent places Hart had stayed was in a community known as Lost City, roughly fifteen miles south of Locust Grove. Hart had shown up at his cousin's house there at the end of 1976 and had stayed through the first three or four months of 1977, then had disappeared just weeks before the murders. His cousin pleaded ignorance to the fact that Hart was a prison escapee: the cousin claimed to have believed that Hart had been newly discharged from the Army. The cousin and his wife did concede that neither of them had ever been asked by Hart to take him out anywhere, and that was a bit odd.

Another cousin of Hart's, Norman Carey—who was a minister—admitted to the OSBI that he and a fellow minister and friend, Jimmy Beck, had gone to Ella Mae's house at 7 a.m. on a Saturday morning, May 28, 1977, two weeks before the murders. They had seen Hart there. The pair of visitors had borrowed a rod and reel from Carey's aunt Ella Mae and then returned a little later to dig some worms from Ella Mae's yard. Carey knew his cousin was wanted by the law and that he spent a lot of time at Ella Mae's house, but Cherokees do not tell on each other. It's a code of honor. On the first trip to the Buckskin matriarch's humble abode that Saturday morning, Jimmy Beck remembered meeting her eldest son for the first and only time. He saw Hart emerge from a back bedroom with Carey after Carey had gone into the bedroom and spoken with Hart for fifteen or twenty minutes. Hart was wearing only black horn-rimmed glasses and blue jeans. No shirt, no shoes. Minister Beck was introduced to Hart at Ella Mae's breakfast table as they all sat down together to eat. When the fishermen returned later to dig the worms, Beck saw no sign of Hart.

Hart's eyesight was poor and seemingly getting worse. He was known to wear anyone's glasses that could help him see better . . . even those belonging to females. An individual on the lam cannot go into an optometrist's office for a checkup without the risk of being turned in, so Hart had to make do.

After several more weeks of investigative frustration, Agent Larry Bowles approached the OSBI agent in charge, Ted Limke, with some electrifying news. He had a goose in his possession that was ready to lay a golden egg . . . he had someone who could absolutely, positively lead them to Gene Hart. There was only one condition: no one other than Agent Bowles could ever know the person's name, not even other members of the OSBI. Letting an informant remain eternally anonymous was something that went against OSBI protocol, but Agent Bowles insisted that was the only way the informant would help them: if his name were to be mentioned, it would endanger his life.

Agent Bowles guaranteed the OSBI executives at the Oklahoma State Capitol that the informant had unimpeachable information—Bowles bet his job on it. The informant was from Hart's inner circle. He spent most of his time in Ella Mae's house. He had been there the day Agent Linville had come to get the photo of Hart's ex-wife, Patricia. He had quietly watched as Agent Albro had encountered the barrel of Ella Mae's 12-gauge the day after Hart was announced as the DA's "man." He was in on all the private conversations Ella Mae had with her family. Who better to compromise?

It seems the informant had been at a Cherokee stomp dance in late August 1977 when a medicine man, William Lee Smith, had sidled up next to him to stand by the ceremonial fire. Smith had divulged to the informant that an old man wearing overalls, who was currently standing over on the other side of the fire from them, was harboring Hart at his home. 'Mr. Overalls' lived in the Cookson Hills near Tahlequah. Medicine Man Smith assured the informant that Hart was safe and was being well taken care of . . . Smith had made the arrangements with the fellow medicine man himself.

Even though the informant was a Cherokee and supposedly loyal to Hart, the OSBI was delighted that his head was turned by the $50,000 in the reward fund. That was quite a wad of legal tender in 1977, especially for a poor Indian. The OSBI acquiesced about keeping the informant's identity anonymous, and Agent Bowles was allowed his never-to-be-named informant.

It took some time for the informant to get specific information, as he never asked questions . . . he just listened. He was patient, played it smart and never aroused any suspicions among Hart's family that he was in almost-daily contact with Agent Bowles. The informant eventually overheard Ella Mae mention that Mr. Overalls sold firewood. The OSBI did some research, but were never able to come up with the name of the man. They finally resorted to catching Medicine Man William Lee Smith's wife, Eva, at home alone and threatening to throw her and her husband in jail if she refused to take and show them where Mr. Overalls, whose real name was Sam Pigeon, lived. Eva Smith was scared and complied.

The three-room shack where Medicine Man Sam Pigeon was harboring Hart was at the top of a hill, up behind the home of one of Pigeon's brothers. The shack was invisible from the road because of all the blackjack trees and the distance. Eva Smith had to point out the nearly- impassable ruts that led up to the shack. With Mrs. Smith still in the OSBI van, agents surrounded the shack, as Agent Jack Lay kicked open the front door. Agent Lay came face to face with Hart, who was the only one present in the shack. Hart attempted to flee out the back door: he was given the choice to either surrender or die. The next thing he knew he was face down on the ground in front of the shack wearing handcuffs. "I didn't kill those little girls," he said, as he squirmed to breathe.

Gene Leroy Hart was captured on Thursday, April 6, 1978, ten months after the Girl Scouts were murdered, deep in the Cookson Hills in Cherokee County, Oklahoma. Agent Bowles had his informant there, hiding in the backseat of a car, in order to identify

Hart. The informant had just earned himself a fistful of reward money: the remaining jackpot would be paid out upon Hart's conviction. Over two million dollars had been spent capturing Gene Leroy Hart, but if not for the informant, they would have never located Hart. The informant had been *everything* to the investigation. On April 20, 1978, Agent Bowles took a sheet of paper and, in his best handwriting, made out a receipt to Sheriff Weaver for $5,000 of the reward money, which Sheriff Weaver, in turn, placed in the hand of Agent Bowles to be passed on to the informant in cash. The informant had earned every dime.

Patrolman Paul Smith believed the OSBI had made a mistake, but Paul lingered in the background and held his tongue . . . for now.

CHAPTER 7
TRIALS AND TRIBULATIONS

Gene Leroy Hart was lifted from the ground by OSBI agents and put on his feet. He had gained a good twenty pounds while living with the medicine man. Hart's usually short-cropped hair had grown to cover his ears. After ten long months of the most sensational manhunt in Oklahoma history, the OSBI finally had their trophy, and they were practically giddy. Agents grabbed their cameras: it seemed everyone present wanted to be in a souvenir photo with Hart. The OSBI wanted to make sure the public knew that it was *them* who had captured the fugitive, not Sheriff Weaver and *certainly* not the FBI.

Hart was plucked from the same woods where famous outlaws had hidden in bygone years, including the famous bank robber, Charles "Pretty Boy" Floyd. Hart was first taken to the OSBI's Tahlequah office for official identification through fingerprinting, then to Grand Valley Hospital in Pryor, where two blood samples, a saliva sample and hair from different parts of his body were extracted. (Chemist Janice Davis personally transported the samples to the laboratory in Oklahoma City. Davis ran a secretor analysis on the saliva. She found Hart to be a secretor of blood group substance "O."

No big revelation there, as at least 80% of the U.S. population are secretors and, according to the National Institute of Health (NIH)'s National Center for Biotechnology Information, "Native Americans are nearly exclusively in the O group.")

Hart was driven from the hospital to the state penitentiary in McAlester to be held on Death Row for security purposes. It was a fitting place, in the estimation of the OSBI, because, once Hart was convicted of the murders (and he was sure to be), he would spend his final days on Death Row before his rightful execution. Might as well get used to it.

Agent Larry Bowles was on Hart's right and Agent Bud Ousley was on his left for a dramatic longer-than-necessary perp-walk-of-shame that was orchestrated by Agent Mike Wilkerson. Agent Wilkerson instructed Agent Bowles not to park at the entrance door of the McAlester prison, but rather out in a parking lot 200 yards away. This would give the media plenty of time to shoot their tabloid-worthy footage. Sheriff Weaver and his deputy, A. D. David, were allowed to follow behind, in their rightful place—second in pecking order to the OSBI. It was quite the show.

Hart was dressed in a blue-and-white-striped tank top, Levi's cutoffs, multi-colored crew socks, tan lace-up suede boots . . . and a pair of women's eyeglasses. His outfit was accessorized with shackles around his wrists and ankles. Once inside the prison, agents collected the clothing, shoes and glasses, and these items were transferred to the OSBI Laboratory in Oklahoma City. Hart was provided with fitting prison attire.

The authorities had been able to say anything they wanted about Hart while he was still out on the run. Now that they had him in their custody, they would have to prove all their accusations in a court of law.

Medicine Man Sam Pigeon signed a search waiver for his tar-paper shack. OSBI Agent Roger Chrisco and OSBI Chemist Dennis Reimer went in and took anything and everything that looked like a murder weapon or an item that could have come from Camp Scott. They also stripped all the linens from the beds, hoping to find hairs or semen stains.

The medicine man and his brother, Freeman Pigeon, who lived in the house down on the road in front of Sam's shack, were hauled in for questioning by the OSBI. Sam Pigeon, who bore the most guilt for personally hiding Hart, told the OSBI that he only knew Hart as "Drum." Sam Pigeon was a short, plump, devout Cherokee who put his Cherokee ways above white man's law. When his own medicine man, William Lee Smith, had told him to take care of Drum, he took care of Drum. Sam Pigeon had come to know that Drum was wanted for the murders of the three Girl Scouts—Drum had told him why he was needing to hide out. Both Sam and Freeman Pigeon told the OSBI that they had asked Drum if he had killed the girls, and Drum had assured them he had not. They had taken their fellow Cherokee at his word.

Later, during a second search of Sam Pigeon's shack (following the preliminary hearing), a mirror and clay pipe were found. The mirror and clay pipe were identified by camp counselor Karen Mitchell as having been taken from her trunk in the Choctaw unit of Camp Scott . . . this was the same trunk that Patrolman Paul had witnessed Officer Gary Shamel break into while it was at the Locust Grove Police Department. Karen had not received the trunk back from law enforcement until two weeks later. Sam Pigeon swore he had never seen the mirror or clay pipe at his place.

Chemist Davis went to the Mayes County jail twelve days after Hart had been captured and retrieved a pair of his used underwear that were handed to her in a paper sack by Sheriff Weaver. Davis ran some tests on the underwear and found sperm, including "deformed and decomposed sperm," which she attributed to a vasectomy Hart was reported to have had. *Perhaps the vasectomy had gone bad and caused his sperm to morph.* Davis created slides from the swabs she had received from Medical Examiner Hoffman back at the time of the girls' autopsies. She observed what she believed to be "decomposed sperm" on Denise and Michelle's anal slides and Lori's vaginal slide, as well, which convinced her that Hart had raped the girls before killing them.

Larry Oliver, the first attorney to represent Hart against the murder charges, was rumored to have quit after one day on the job because of Hart's reply to a question about the fingerprint inside the red and white box flashlight. When Oliver asked Hart if the fingerprint might turn out to be his, Hart took a long pause, seemingly to search his mind in a review of his actions, before blurting out, "[it] couldn't be." Hart, interestingly, did not outright lie about it as one might assume he would, and his lack of a resounding "no" had lost him his first legal defender. Larry Oliver had let out a sigh as he had thrown his legal pad in his briefcase and got up and left. It all sounded rather damning (if you believed the rumor).

Fellow Native American Gary Pitchlynn took over Hart's case. Pitchlynn was relatively inexperienced in criminal law, so he invited a white thirty-something, scraggly-haired lawyer named Garvin

Isaacs to come and take the lead. Isaacs was a former public defender in the Oklahoma District Court and a colorful figure in the courtroom. According to Isaacs, the first words out of Hart's mouth to him were, "I want you guys to know something—I didn't kill those little girls." Isaacs believed him.

The preliminary hearing took two full weeks. The Honorable Jess B. Clanton, Jr. presided. Judge Clanton was grumpy about Isaacs using up so much of the court's time for a preliminary hearing. Normally, the prosecutors are the main ones presenting witnesses and evidence in a preliminary hearing, all in order for the judge to decide whether to send the defendant to trial or dismiss the charges. But in Hart's case, Isaacs treated the preliminary almost like a full trial. He put on a slew of witnesses, challenged evidence and tried to convince Judge Clanton that the charges against Hart should be dismissed. At times he yelled. Regardless, Hart was bound over for trial.

A team of lawyers joined Isaacs and Pitchlynn on the top floor of a two-story dental office across the street from the courthouse in Pryor. Citizens brought by food and donations, and twenty souls lived there around the clock, including some volunteer college students. It became known as "Hotel Hart." A white paper sign with large block letters written in black was put up on the wall, displaying the provocative name.

Attorney Isaacs asked for more time over and over. Every request for a delay was denied. His team was given less than a year after Hart's arrest to piece together a defense. Meanwhile, the $5000-richer informant continued to give Agent Bowles intelligence from within Hart's defense pool. The OSBI knew things ahead of time that Isaacs was going to do on Hart's behalf.

Jury selection began March 5, 1979, in the courtroom of District Judge William J. Whistler. At the prosecutor's table, the Mayes County DA, Sid Wise, had been replaced by the DA of Tulsa County, S.M. "Buddy" Fallis, Jr., due to an unfortunate discovery that Sid Wise had already been shopping a personal book deal about the case. A jury expert named Cathy "Cat" Bennett, from Santa Barbara, California, sat at the defense table with Isaacs and Pitchlynn and helped them with their choices. One hundred potential jurors were questioned. Two full weeks later, on March 16, 1979, six men and six women had been seated. None of the jurors were from Locust Grove, and none of them were Native American.

The notorious trial began Monday, March 19, 1979, with opening statements from DA Buddy Fallis and Defense Attorney Garvin Isaacs. The parents of Lori, Denise and Michelle came from Tulsa, saw the Hart defense fund jars in restaurants where they ate and were sickened. They felt as though they had entered enemy territory: at the very least, they were "outsiders." To them, the trial was a bad movie at best and a carnival at worst. The lawyers put on a performance that would garner Isaacs a "contempt of court" conviction afterwards. The Milners, Gusés and Farmers were not amused.

After it was established *how* the girls were killed, the prosecution set about proving *who* had done it. They presented a 'circumstantial evidence' case. 1) They tied Cave Number 1 to the Girl Scout camp through counselor Susan's sunglasses plus the roll of masking tape that was used in the dimming of the red and white box flashlight found with the girls' bodies 2) They tied Cave Number 1 to Gene Leroy Hart through the photographs that he had developed at the

Granite Reformatory. They felt those two facts cinched it for a guilty verdict.

Since no fingerprints matching Hart had been found at the murder scene nor on any of the evidence, the prosecution put great emphasis on the Mongoloid hairs that had been found. However, under cross-examination, Chemist Ann Reed admitted that no two hairs could be positively matched to one another, nor could any single hair scientifically identify an individual. This stung the prosecution. NOTE: Matching one hair to another hair is still not considered to be scientifically conclusive and is no longer allowed to be entered as evidence in U.S. courtrooms. Newly developed mitochondrial DNA testing, however, *can* now match a hair to a unique individual.

Dr. John MacLeod, a seventy-three-year-old fertility expert from the Cornell University Medical College in New York, was called to testify about the "deformed sperm" found by Chemist Davis in Hart's dirty jail underwear. Dr. MacLeod testified that it would not be unreasonable to conclude that the sperm taken from Hart's underwear was a match to the semen found in the bodies of the little victims.

Chemist Davis's partner, Chemist Reimer, had seen no such sperm. Evidently, it came down to one's eyesight and opinion as to whether they could distinguish the head or the tail of a sperm in seminal fluid. If the crown in the head, collar and tail could not be seen clearly through microscopic examination, the examiner could opine the sperm were decomposed (swollen beyond recognizable features of intact sperm). Dr. MacLeod and Chemist Davis, being the only two who could see the deformed sperm, also put together a statistical analysis and claimed that only .002 percent of the U.S.

population could have deposited the sperm. The jury was unconvinced. NOTE: According to the Mayo Clinic, "Typically, only around 4% to 10% of the sperm in a semen sample are normal, meaning that the vast majority don't look perfect under the microscope." Janice Davis testified that out of the "high thousands" number of tests she had performed looking for sperm during her three years as an OSBI chemist, this was her first time testifying that she had found what appeared to be decomposed or deformed sperm. The quality of Janice Davis's work fell under grave suspicion in later criminal cases; she was involved in numerous convictions of individuals who were later exonerated, and was fired from the Oklahoma City Police Crime Lab. Sadly, she died by suicide in 1988 at age forty-one.

The prosecution had other problems. Something that served Hart well was when OSBI agents took the witness stand and testified under oath that they had never taken any pictures of themselves with the accused. Garvin Isaacs was more than happy to display the photo line-up of grinning OSBI agents with Hart in front of Sam Pigeon's shack. It cost the OSBI a good amount of credibility.

As they had worked on Hart's defense, Isaacs and Pitchlynn had been frustrated that the OSBI had repeatedly refused to turn over many investigative documents to them, items to which the defense attorneys felt entitled by law. They believed that there was exculpatory evidence the OSBI had discovered that would help Hart. The OSBI claimed the documents were their "work product" and refused to budge. A suit was filed on behalf of Hart to *force* the OSBI to turn them over: it was unsuccessfully appealed all the way to the Oklahoma State Supreme Court. The attorneys were left very suspicious of the OSBI's stubborn concealment of their paperwork.

Ella Mae was the only member of Hart's family that testified on his behalf. She was the first defense witness to take the stand. She had an attorney present to protect her from charges of harboring a fugitive.

Hart's defense centered on the notion that the evidence against him had been planted by Sheriff Weaver. Medicine Man Sam Pigeon repeated under oath, through a Cherokee interpreter, that he had never before seen the mirror and clay pipe that the OSBI had seized from his home during their second search. Tom Kite, a Vietnam veteran who had experience with jungle terrain and had helped in the search for Hart in treacherous woods, told the jury that Sheriff Weaver had made disparaging remarks about Native Americans, had told Kite that Hart's fingerprints had been found at the scene (not true) and that Hart was armed and dangerous. Kite even testified that Sheriff Weaver had supposedly told his deputies if they brought Hart in alive, they would lose their jobs. (Sheriff Weaver's response was that he remembered making no such statements).

Allen Little, a former jailer that Sheriff Weaver had fired, threw a gut punch to the prosecution when he testified in the closing salvo that he had seen the now infamous 'cave photographs' in *Sheriff Weaver's* possession after Hart escaped the second and final time in 1973 from the Mayes County jail. This contradicted Larry Dry, who had sworn that he had seen them in *Hart's* possession after he and Hart had escaped the second time.

Hart was acquitted after a mere six hours of deliberation. One juror, who requested anonymity, claimed they had their minds made up after five minutes but did not want to appear non-serious. When the words "Not Guilty" were uttered three times—first on the Denise Milner count, second on the Lori Farmer count and lastly, on the

Michelle Gusé count—by Court Clerk Eloise Gist on Friday morning, March 30, 1979, Garvin Isaacs beat the table with his fists, and Hart cried as Gary Pitchlynn put his arm around him. Ella Mae was not there when the verdict was read over her boy. She had left the courthouse, expecting deliberations to take much longer.

"OSBI - 0 [zero]" was added with a magic marker to the left top corner of the Hotel Hart sign, and "Indians 1" to the bottom left corner (the "1" was written backwards). Garvin Isaacs framed the sign and kept it as a memento.

Those who had accused Hart were *not* happy. OSBI Chief Inspector Ted Limke, DA Buddy Fallis and Sheriff Weaver all declared publicly that the investigation would not be reopened. They had the right man, and the jury had gotten it wrong. It was as simple as that. There was no need to look any further. The girls' personal belongings that had been collected from their tent were returned to the girls' families—which is against the law since the case was still officially unsolved, but OSBI Agent Joe Collins did not seem to care.

Sheriff Weaver began to visit jury members and harass them about their verdict. One juror, Lela Ramsey, who had given a television interview was called by Weaver and threatened in such a manner that she felt afraid. She granted no more interviews.

Isaacs and Pitchlynn had received threats during the trial that had caused Isaacs to put in a request to the OHP for security. It was denied. The attorneys had resorted to packing weapons to protect themselves. At least one of the threats had come from one of Sheriff Weaver's deputies. Evidently, Mayes County law enforcement was not fond of Isaacs and Pitchlynn looking for alternative suspects in their county.

Sheriff Weaver returned Hart to the penitentiary in McAlester to continue serving his 300+ years of prior sentences, plus some more that had been tacked on for his two jail breaks. Sheriff Weaver and Hart were met by a trusty at Big Mac, who asked the sheriff if Hart "did it." Sheriff Weaver declared to the trusty that Hart *absolutely* did it. "We'll take care of him," the trusty said, with a sly grin. Hart was placed on Death Row for his protection, but within weeks, by his own request, he was moved to the prison's general population.

On Friday, June 1, 1979, Hart, joined by Isaacs and Pitchlynn, gave an exclusive interview to the tribal newspaper The Cherokee Advocate, where Hart announced his intention to sue Sheriff Weaver. As part of the interview, Hart made some mysterious statements, indicating that he believed the person who had 'planted' his photos at Cave Number 1 was one and the same as the informant who had enriched himself by cooperating with the OSBI to effect Hart's capture. Hart went even further, saying he and his attorneys were almost certain they knew who had done it, but they would wait until they could find a witness to verify it before naming the person.

By Monday, June 4, 1979, nine weeks and three days after his acquittal, the former football star was in a routine to get back in physical shape. That particular day he lifted weights, then went for a jog in the prison yard. Suddenly he collapsed and was rushed by ambulance to McAlester State Hospital, where he was pronounced dead. The shocking event was placed in bold print at the top of the nation's newspapers, as television reporters on every major network informed their dumbfounded audiences. The man that had been charged with the brutal murders of three little Girl Scouts was now himself dead. Once again, the town of Locust Grove was divided. Those who believed Hart had killed the little girls were satisfied that a greater power had punished him. Those who believed Hart was innocent suspected foul play.

The following morning, Tuesday, June 5, 1979, at 10 a.m. Oklahoma Offender #79547 was presented for autopsy to Dr. A. Jay Chapman at the Office of the Chief Medical Examiner in Oklahoma City. Gene Leroy Hart came wearing blue denim shorts, size 34-36 white Fruit of the Loom briefs with fecal staining and yellowish stains in the genital area, white socks and red striped Adidas jogging shoes. His size 42-44 white Fruit of the Loom T-shirt had been cut off by Emergency Room personnel and was now stuffed into his shorts.

Hart had an abrasion above his left eye and another on the bridge of his nose from planting his face on the ground when he fell. He apparently went down on his left knee, because that kneecap was scraped, as well.

Dr. Chapman opened Hart's chest cavity and wrote the following:

"There is a significant degree of atherosclerosis involving particularly the left circumflex branch and the right main coronary artery. Streaking is observed in the left anterior descending coronary artery but in the right main coronary artery there is ca. 98% occlusion proximally, and throughout most of this artery there is a significant degree of occlusion. The left circumflex branch is occasionally somewhat diminutive and is also involved by atherosclerosis with ca. 85 to 90% occlusion focally. The myocardium is reddish brown throughout, save for an area ca. 2.8 cm in greatest dimension in the posterior left ventricular wall which is characterized by whitening and firmness."

In layman's terms, Gene Leroy Hart had died from a heart attack caused by almost complete blockage of two of the main arteries that supplied blood to his heart. Scar tissue on the lower left back side of his heart indicated Hart had suffered a prior heart attack that had gone undetected at the time it had occurred.

One point of interest was Hart's left spermatic cord was completely intact and undamaged . . . not what one would expect to find in a man who had undergone a vasectomy, successfully or otherwise. Hart was still perfectly capable of producing normal sperm.

Hart's attorneys hired an independent pathologist, Dr. Murlyn D. Bellamy, to do an additional autopsy. Dr. Bellamy ordered a comprehensive toxicologic evaluation of the tissue and fluids retained from Hart's body. Lidocaine (used by medical personnel trying to revive him) and caffeine were the only substances found. No other drugs nor chemical agents were present, including the following:

Alcohols including Ethanol, Methanol and Isopropanol; Acetone; Carbon Monoxide; Chloral Hydrate; Cyanide; Propellants including Butane, Isobutane, Dichlorodifluoromethane and Trichlorofluoromethane; Solvents including Benzene, Toluene, Methylene Chloride and 1,1,1-Trichloroethane;

Arsenic; Mercury; Acetaminophen; Barbiturates; Salicylic acid derivatives; Amphetamines including Dexedrine, Methamphetamine and Phentermine;

Benzodiazepines including Chlordiazepoxide; Clorazepate, Diazepam and Flurazepam; Cocaine; Hydroxyzine; Methapyrilene; Methaqualone; Opiates including Codeine, Meperidine, Methadone, Morphine and Pentazocine;

Phenothiazines including Chlorpromazine and Thioridazine; Phencyclidine; Propoxyphene; Strychnine and Tricyclics including

Amitriptyline, Desipramine, Doxepin, Imipramine and Nortriptyline;

Carisoprodol; Ethchlorvynol; Ethinamate; Glutethimide, Hydroxyphenamate, Meprobamate and Methyprylon.

Dr. Bellamy made the following findings when examining Hart's body:

Hart had "arteriosclerotic cardiovascular disease, severe:

    A. With occlusive coronary atherosclerosis, left circumflex and right main coronary arteries.

    B. Myocardial infarct, posterior, age greater than 3 months

Vasectomy, no apparent ligation site demonstrated in left vas deferens."

In other words, Dr. Bellamy found exactly the same conditions that Dr. Chapman had found.

Despite the extensive testing for poisons in Hart's body tissue, blood, urine and stomach contents, some folks would never let go of the idea that he had been poisoned by someone in prison. Someone had gotten to him . . . they just *knew* it.

Over 1,000 mourners packed the Locust Grove High School gymnasium for Gene Leroy Hart's funeral, making it the largest funeral crowd in Locust Grove history. It was standing room only. Hart's six siblings sat on the front row with Ella Mae, who cried bitter tears into a white handkerchief. A somber Garvin Isaacs and Gary Pitchlynn were there. Hart was dressed in a dark-blue three-piece suit, his favorite 'trial suit.' Sam Pigeon wore a pair of new overalls.

After the nearly hour-long memorial service, including some eulogies spoken in Cherokee, Hart's steel bluish-gray casket was opened for viewing. The coffin was then driven to Ballou Cemetery for burial. The hearse was followed by a three-mile-long procession of vehicles. Afterwards, Hart's family, close friends and defense counsel had congregated for a meal, when a terrible thunderstorm moved in. Garvin Isaacs commented on the fierceness of the storm. "You know what that means?" one of Hart's relatives asked Isaacs. "That means the spirit of Gene Leroy Hart got to where it was intended to go."

The time had come for former detective Paul Smith to step forward with what he knew.

CHAPTER 8

SON OF A PREACHER MAN

Warren G. Harding was the President of the United States when Paul Dean Smith cried for the very first time on April 22, 1923, in Wagoner, Oklahoma. There was plenty to cry about. The world was still reeling from the deadliest war in history when Paul arrived just in time for the Great Depression and the Oklahoma Dust Bowl. Paul entered the world carrying a gift that he would grip tightly throughout his life—a remarkable ability to recall details.

Mrs. Florence Smith had given birth eight times before: Paul was her ninth child. There would eventually be two more. Paul's dad, Rev. Bill Smith, was an old time Pentecostal preacher, who worked various other jobs to make ends meet for his large family. Rev. Smith had lost both legs to a railroad accident, but he walked so well with his artificial limbs that most people never noticed. The Smith family ate a lot of fried potatoes and wild rabbit, trapped by Paul's older brother, Don, but they never took money from the government . . . a fact that brought an enduring sense of pride to them.

In the opening days of Paul's life, the family lived in Tuxedo, Oklahoma, a wide place in the road between Dewey and Bartlesville. Rev. Smith worked at a shoe repair shop in Bartlesville owned by

John Flores (Paul never forgot names). An old Dodge touring car with wooden running boards got the reverend to work every day. When the car was home, it served another purpose. The kids would often entertain themselves by lining up at the back of the yard, listening for someone to holler "go," and then, along with their nanny goat, they would race to the Dodge's running boards. The goat always won.

In 1929, when Paul was six years old, the Smith family moved to Locust Grove. Rev. Smith ran a shoe shop, a harness shop and did a little preaching. Paul's recollection was that they "still practically starved." Then Paul's father was elected mayor of Locust Grove, and countless memories of the little town were forever seared into Paul's mind.

The town folk had begun trading in their horses, wagons and buggies for automobiles. An old Indian man named Tood Harlow bought a big, brand new Pierce Arrow car that he never really learned how to drive. He lived up over the hill going out of town. Tood never mastered shifting gears on the hill, so he always went up the hill as far as he could go in high gear, then would come back down at full speed. One day Tood lit in the creek. Paul and his siblings laughed until their sides ached. Luckily, Tood was uninjured.

It was during Rev. Smith's stint as mayor of Locust Grove that Paul's contempt for crooks began to stir, seemingly inborn in him. With no movie houses in town to entertain the people, minstrel and medicine shows would set up in an empty lot between Rev. Smith's shoe/harness shop and Stevenson's Drug Store. The shows were required to operate by a permit from the mayor's office. A certain 'snake-oil salesman' would occasionally visit Locust Grove to pedal his potions. The chubby fellow would obnoxiously call out to passersby and lure them in with a loud, well-rehearsed pitch for his latest cure-all. If they bought anything from him, he would make a big show of placing their name in a hat for a drawing that would be held at the end of the show. Paul overheard the man quietly ask his father for his wife's first name the day Mayor Smith was filling out the man's permit. When it came time for the big drawing, a member of the audience came up and pulled a piece of paper from the hat. Paul saw the man make a maneuver, before conspicuously crying out, "Florence Smith!" Paul's mother had 'won' the coveted prize, an ornate comb-and-mirror dresser set. Even at his young age, Paul discerned that the slight-of-hand was merely to get the salesman in favor with the mayor, so he would be able to continue getting permits to operate in Locust Grove. It bothered Paul that the man got away with it. Paul never forgot it.

Mayor Bill Smith only lasted one term. The increasing number of automobiles caused the diagonal-style parking along Main Street in Locust Grove to become so crowded that it became difficult to navigate the thoroughfare. Mayor Smith solved the dilemma by replacing the diagonal spaces with parallel parking slots. None of the citizens knew how to parallel park and were dissatisfied by the decision. Come election time, they showed just exactly *how* dissatisfied they were by stripping Mayor Smith of his worldly position. But the reverend continued on with his heavenly mission.

The family moved to Bartlesville, where Paul's dad took a church to pastor on the west end of town. There was no bridge on SH-33 at the time, so they had to take a ferry across the Grand River (since renamed to Neosho) to get from Locust Grove to Bartlesville, where more memories collected in the lockbox of Paul's brain.

A man Paul deemed to be an unsavory character attended Rev. Smith's church there in Bartlesville. One Sunday, Paul was both shocked and enchanted to learn from the unsavory character that a stranger who had sat on the back row and deposited a twenty-dollar bill in the offering plate was none other than the famous outlaw, "Pretty Boy Floyd," from Sallisaw, Oklahoma.

A lady who owned the Landram Grocery Store in Bartlesville would daily walk up the well-known mound in the western part of the city for exercise. Paul and another boy would walk with her, and she would gift them with candy. That was a "sweet" memory for Paul (pun intended).

From Bartlesville, the Smith family moved to Tulsa and rented a two-story house at 2509 E Fourth Place for $12.50 per month from a family named Watters. At Eighth and Elgin was an artificial limb and brace shop, owned by a Dr. Sisler. Paul's dad and three of his older siblings all worked for Dr. Sisler at one time or another.

William Shakespeare got Paul into trouble at Central High School in Tulsa. One day Mrs. Douglas, the English Literature teacher, read from a Shakespearean play, then slowly took off her glasses and sighed, "Isn't that a beautiful passage?" Paul burst out laughing and put his head down on his desk to hide his face. Mrs. Douglas caught him after class and scolded him harshly, making a negative comparison to his "smarter" older sister, Ollie, who Mrs. Douglas had taught five years earlier. Mrs. Douglas apparently tied intelligence to an appreciation for the arts: Paul was not buying.

After staying in Tulsa for a few years, Paul's dad began to suffer from asthma. Rev. and Mrs. Smith packed up and moved to Colorado Springs, Colorado, hoping the high altitude would help Rev. Smith breathe more easily. Once the couple got settled, they sent for their three youngest sons. Paul, Jack and Joe rode a bus, driven by Bob Loving (yes, Paul remembered his name), from Tulsa to Colorado Springs, making a stop in Amarillo, Texas. Joe had his guitar, and the Smith brothers serenaded the bus riders all the way to the Amarillo stop. Hours later, just as daylight broke, they spotted their mom standing in front of the Colorado Springs bus station. She walked the boys several blocks to a house they had rented on Pikes Peak Avenue.

Before long, the Smith family began moving around again, crisscrossing the state of Colorado. The first move from Colorado Springs was 150 miles northeast to Fort Morgan. From there it was to Olathe, located out on the Western Slope. It was while living in Olathe, on December 7, 1941, that they turned on the radio and heard about the attack on Pearl Harbor (which drew the U.S. into World War II). Soon afterwards, the Smiths returned to the northeast corner of the state, to Sterling, for a period, then back to the Western Slope, where they settled in Rifle, Colorado for many years.

As Paul was growing up, he had always had one thing on his mind—becoming a cop. It was his dream from the time his cognitive memory formed. To him, policemen were "dragon slayers." Paul was fascinated by the men in blue. But, first he was required to wear a uniform of a different color . . . Army green. He had gotten the feeling he was going to be drafted, so he left Colorado and went back to Tulsa. He wanted to avoid being sent to the Pacific, and being drafted in Oklahoma would ensure his spot in the type of unit that would deploy to Europe instead.

Paul was nineteen when he received the letter that would end his innocence. It was from the U.S. government and began with,

"Greetings." The simple instructions that followed were matter-of-fact. Paul was to report on March 15, 1943, to be inducted into the military, pending a physical examination. He went to the Flower Hospital on North Boulder Street in Tulsa and took his physical. He passed.

When he got his clothes back on, he was directed down the hallway where there were three booths clearly marked "NAVY" -- "MARINES" -- and "ARMY." The Navy recruiter liked the looks of Paul and tried to get Paul to join the Navy, but Paul declined and moved to the "MARINES" booth. A big, ugly sergeant looked at Paul's skinny little body and, without saying a word to Paul, moved his eyes to the line behind Paul and called out, "Next man!"

Paul was given two options: 1) he could be transported to the Army base at Fort Sill, Oklahoma, that very same day, or 2) he could first take two weeks to set his affairs in order. Paul chose to depart without delay. He spent what was left of the night in a barracks in Ft. Sill, Oklahoma, a very scared young man. Fort Sill served as a clearing station for hundreds of new soldiers, who received their immunizations and assignments on their way to World War II. Paul arrived in Fort Sill between 2 and 3 a.m. during the unseasonably cold night.

At first light, a sergeant entered the barracks where Paul was sleeping. The sergeant was yelling at the top of his lungs and pulling mattresses out from under the new recruits, rolling them out onto the floor. Paul jumped out of bed before the sergeant could get to him: he managed to suppress a wry smirk of victory. After several days of orientation and multiple shots, Paul was ordered to Camp Robinson, Arkansas, for training as a front-line combat medic.

After many weeks of intensive training at Camp Robinson, Paul was ordered to appear at the camp commander's office. The commander gave Paul a corporal's rating and classified Paul as a surgical technician, then ordered him to Kennedy Hospital in Memphis to make orthopedic braces. Making braces was practically the Smith 'family business,' so Paul did well. He did *so* well that he was ordered to Marine General Hospital in Palm Beach, Florida, to set up a brace shop there . . . but it never happened.

Because of Paul's neat printing and drawing skills, he instead got put on detached service, working for Military Intelligence under a Major Collins and an Agent Abel Wallinsky. As Collins and Wallinsky interrogated released POWs or other individuals who had recently left Germany, Paul made notes and drew descriptions of locations they described inside the Nazi nation. Major Collins told Paul, "Don't make any mistakes: no one touches these maps after you are through." Paul suspected his maps were being used for bombing missions. One day he got a call from his worried dad back in Colorado. The FBI had come to the family home and asked all kinds of questions about Paul. His dad thought Paul was in trouble. Paul laughed and explained that they were merely doing a required background check for Paul's top-secret security clearance.

Eventually Paul was ordered to Camp Grant in Rockford, Illinois, to help organize the 101st General Hospital and prepare for overseas duty. As soon as it was organized, the 101st left for the Boston Port of Embarkation. Paul's unit boarded a huge ship, the USS West Point, along with more than ten-thousand other soldiers and sailors. They sailed the North Atlantic where German submarines had sunk many ships. The West Point was speedy, and it traveled all the way to Liverpool Harbor in England in a mere six days, without the escort of a 'destroyer' ship. The West Point's crew zig-zagged the ship, changing directions a lot (every seven minutes, to be exact), because the Navy had calculated it took ten minutes for an enemy submarine to sight, aim and fire. Most everyone on board got seasick . . . not a pretty sight.

Paul and company arrived in Liverpool, England, July 26, 1944. They were put on a train in Liverpool and traveled all night to Taunton, England. There they set up the 101st General Hospital using quonset huts: each ward was a different hut.

If Paul had not personally seen horrid things before then, he certainly would see them in the war. As a medical technician, he treated almost six thousand battle casualties and still recalled some specific cases, including some of their names, when he was an old man.

One day as the ambulances were unloading the wounded, Paul saw among them an older man who was wearing blue bib overalls. Paul learned it was a French railroad engineer whose train had been attacked by German planes. Paul assisted a Captain Meridith in removing both of the engineer's lacerated eyes. It was almost more than Paul could bear.

An orthopedic surgeon, Major Kenneth Duff, once sent Paul to see a young soldier in the orthopedic hut. Entering the hut, Paul called his name and told him Major Duff had sent him to see if he could help. The young man raised his bandaged, bloody forearms: both hands had been blown off. He said, with tears in his eyes, "I don't want my mom to know." He asked if Paul could make something to lace around his wrist with a pencil in it: he wanted to write a letter to his mom. Paul cut up a combat boot to get the lace portion and used it to attach a piece of wood with a pencil secured to it. He laced his creation on the young soldier's tender wrist, and though the kid tried hard, it was too painful to write. Paul felt like he had failed him. Sometimes, all the way into his nineties, when Paul was awake during the night, he would still think of his "hero and his mom."

Late one evening, a Jewish kid from Brooklyn named Ralph Kabelin was carried in. Ralph's throat had been slashed by a piece of shrapnel, severing his trachea tube and dropping it into his chest cavity. Paul and the surgeon (a captain) laid him on the table with his head lowered off the end of the table, supported by Paul's left hand. The captain had a long narrow instrument that he inserted into the wound to retrieve the trachea and re-attach it. As Paul bent over the wound, Ralph heaved and coughed a big gob of phlegm and blood, which stuck on Paul's face mask. Paul stood there "until the room went around about twice." Then he hit the floor. The captain successfully completed the surgery by himself, but he never let Paul forget it. That was the only time Paul ever passed out in surgery . . . not bad for "a kid who used to get sick at the sight of blood."

Paul held poignant memories of Christmas 1944. Christmas Eve was cold that year, with a heavy mist falling. Paul sensed that his fellow soldiers felt lonely: many of them were far away from home for the first time, in a foreign country and in the middle of a hard-fought war. Everyone was quiet and seemed lost in their own thoughts.

Paul and a buddy of his, Bob St. Claire, walked to a nearby hill, where they found a small evergreen tree that they cut down with their pocket knives. They took the tree to the 'cast room' (where broken bones were set). They stood the little tree on the counter and used plaster of paris dust for 'snow' on and around the tree. Then they cut the fingers out of rubber gloves and blew them into balls and tied them. One of the guys found some small bottles of poster paint to color the balls, and they became ornaments for the tree. Even though no such plans had been made for Christmas Eve night, every one of the surgical team showed up, including the orthopedic surgeon, Major Duff. They all stood quietly, admiring the tree, when a member of the team took a harmonica out of his pocket and started playing "Silent Night." Paul looked over at Major Duff, who was crying un-ashamedly, as was everyone else.

No one ever knew it then, but Paul lived in fear that the next casualty would be one of his own brothers, three of whom were serving in the war. Joe was stationed nearby and once came by to see Paul. Together they went into a little shop in downtown Taunton, bought a postcard and wrote on it, telling their parents where they were. They left it for the shopkeeper to mail. Their parents were elated to hear from them, knowing that they were alive, together and safe. All they could write in their letters to their parents was "somewhere in England."

Joe later got caught up in the Battle of the Bulge, which was Germany's final major offensive against the Western Front of the Allied forces (December 16, 1944 - January 25, 1945). The surprise attack began on a foggy day and turned into one of the most important battles of World War II. The million-man-strong Allied forces prevailed and put Germany on the run for the remainder of the war, but not before 19,000 American soldiers were killed. Joe was pinned down and dared not stick his head out of a foxhole for three long days: he had to soil his own pants to relieve himself. When Joe later recounted this experience to Paul, it brought Paul to tears.

As the Allied troops moved up through France, Paul's unit was ordered there, as well. They closed the hospital in Taunton and crossed the English Channel to Le Havre, France. From there, they rode in small boats all day in the bitter cold up a river that deposited them in Verdun, France. From Verdun, it was to Brussels, Belgium, where the young soldiers observed the Manneken Pis, a two-foot-tall bronze fountain statue of a boy peeing in a basin, which they found whimsical. The next thing they noticed were slate walls placed along the sidewalks, where men would walk up, unzip their pants and pee right in public view. Paul and his buddies decided they would do it, too. They thought it was funny and laughed so hard that some of them almost peed on themselves.

Once Hitler's Third Reich had been finished off, Paul was picked as one of twelve men who comprised the 'advance' party to go into Berlin. The party loaded up in two 6x6 trucks and were accompanied by their colonel in his Jeep. After driving through France, they had no trouble getting into Germany, but not long after crossing the border, they came up against a Russian roadblock.

Someone in Paul's party knew how to speak a little Russian. Paul's colonel took the guy with him to talk to a Russian sergeant who appeared to be in charge. Before Paul knew it, the Russian sergeant—who was clearly drunk—began jabbering and waving his arms. Paul watched as the Russians took the logs down and let the Americans pass. A little way up the road, Paul's band ran into some British soldiers, who were laughing. It seems that British General Monty Montgomery had been ahead of the Americans, had never gotten out of his vehicle, but had opted instead to radio for a light tank which had blown up the Russian roadblock.

Paul's party traveled on to the outskirts of Berlin, where they were again stopped by Russian troops. This time they had to set up camp for quite a long time before being allowed to proceed. During the wait, Paul found a big sword with a swastika in the handle, and later brought it home as a reminder of the worldwide agony that could be caused by one barbarian with a supportive audience. A more positive finding was when Paul discovered some big cans of sardines. He had never been served sardines in the service, so he eagerly consumed the lot of them.

Once inside Berlin, Paul saw Russians, their trucks lined up as far as the eye could see, loaded with all the pianos, furniture and appliances they could steal. They were headed home with their loot to Mother Russia. Paul realized that was why the Russians had argued to be the first to go into Berlin when Churchill, Stalin and Roosevelt had met at Potsdam to map out the post-war balance of power. The Russians stripped Berlin.

Paul's advance party commandeered a city block of buildings in the Zellendorf area of Berlin for a hospital and living quarters and awaited the rest of their unit and equipment to arrive. As additional American troops and allies poured into Berlin, the advance party turned the hospital over to them and moved to the Neukolln district, where they set up a smaller hospital right on the border of the "Russian zone." Paul took notice that Russian men and women worked together. They came to the hospital and tried to get treatment for venereal disease. They were refused. "We were as good to them as they were to us," Paul would reminisce many years later.

Soldiers got points for being overseas, and Paul spent more time overseas than he did stateside. When he had racked up enough points to enter the pipeline to start working his way home, the Russians had all the roads blocked around Berlin, and there was no rail traffic available. Paul was taken to Tempelhof Airport and flown from there to Frankfurt. Despite his fear of flying, he climbed aboard an old bomber that had been repurposed. Paul and a "bird colonel" strapped themselves to a wooden bench mounted to the side wall and took off in a heavy mist to Frankfurt. During the flight, a wide-eyed Paul watched through the window the plane's wing tips going up and down. The colonel could tell that Paul was frightened by this and explained to Paul that the wings had to have flexibility or they would break off. Paul felt better. They landed on strips of steel with holes, making an awful noise, but it was a beautiful sound to Paul's ears.

After staying at the 97th General Hospital in Frankfurt for several months, Paul was transferred to the 130th Station Hospital in Heidelberg. U.S. General George Patton and his wife were staying nearby. Patton went pheasant hunting one day, and his driver had a car accident, which left Patton paralyzed from a broken neck. Patton was taken to the 130th Station Hospital, where he lingered for a few days before he died. Paul was present in the hospital when Patton passed, but Paul worked on a different floor than where Patton's room was located. Paul was aware, however, when Patton's wife brought brand new cigarette lighters to all the nurses and medics who had taken care of her husband. NOTE: Paul, always a stickler for the truth, would later write to Bill O'Reilly to correct him about how General Patton had died when O'Reilly published *Killing Patton* in 2014, claiming Patton had been murdered . . . Paul never heard back.

Paul was impacted by how hungry the German people were during his time there. He and his fellow soldiers always ate outside and, when they were finished, they threw their mess kits and leftover coffee into garbage cans. The Germans would reach into the slop to get any fat that had been left from the meat, squeeze it out and put it in their buckets.

German families were kind to the Americans. Several of them asked the troops over and fed them kartoffelsuppe (potato soup). Paul went home with them a couple of times.

Another example of German starvation that Paul never forgot was when a man who worked around the Heidelberg hospital rolled up his sleeves and smeared butter as thick as he could get it onto his arms (a pound or two), trying to get home with it. Even though he rolled down his sleeves to hide it, the man was caught.

On the way back home to the United States from Heidelberg, Paul's unit first sailed to the weakened port of Le Havre, France, which was one of the most destroyed European towns during the war, having endured 132 bombings. From there, they headed home to America. Near the Azores (nine volcanic islands in the North Atlantic 870 miles west of Lisbon, Portugal) they hit a horrible storm. The front end of their ship would come up and shiver a little, then bang back down: they could hear the props coming out the back, chopping air. It got pretty scary. Paul remembered intimate details of the ordeal, including a man of color going down and putting on all his clothes plus his overcoat and his life preserver, with "his eyes about as big as a half dollar." All of a sudden, a bunch of guys went to one side of the ship and the black man said, "I wonder does they see land yet?"

After several days, they could finally see the Statue of Liberty. A small fireboat, shooting out a stream of water, met them to give them a salute. The boat pulled up next to them with three girls (sounded like the Andrews sister) singing "We Love You Soldier Boy." Paul would never be able to recount that story without getting choked up.

Paul's unit landed in the heart of New York, then were loaded on a train and taken to Fort Dix, New Jersey. For the first time in his Army life, he was asked what he wanted to eat. He ordered steak. Nothing had ever tasted so delicious. He was then put on a train to Fort Leavenworth, KS, where he received his discharge in April 1946. He immediately went to Sterling, CO, where his dad had once pastored a church, and, from there, he traveled west across the state to pay his mom and dad a visit in Rifle. Four Smith brothers had fought in World War II. Florence Smith had hung four blue stars on the glass pane in the front door. Fortunately, none of them had ever turned gold . . . but the Paul that had left never came home.

After he visited with his mom and dad, six years of hell began. Paul had trouble fitting back into civilian life from the regimented life he had gotten so used to in the military. He became a prodigal and wondered about, going from job to job and town to town. He drank and did other things he knew would break the hearts of his father and mother. It did not help that he was suffused by an awareness that his country had changed, and not for the better, in his estimation.

Paul got a job hauling oil shale down the side of a mountain on the Western Slope. One day, on his way down the mountain in his Euclid diesel dump truck, he was buzzed by a small airplane. He did not recognize that there was a photographer aboard the plane, until his picture ended up on the front cover of *Life* magazine. He recognized his rig, most notably by the deer antlers he had mounted on the front of it. It was a real kick for him. At the time, he thought that would be the front-page story of his life, but, boy, was he ever wrong.

CHAPTER 9

I FOUGHT THE LAW . . .

Paul eventually began to frequent a certain small diner every evening to eat supper, taking his meal at one end of a U-shaped counter. He took notice of a young lady with big brown eyes that would come in each evening and sit directly across from him at the opposite end of the 'U.' Paul would gaze past his comfort food at the alluring beauty, who would give him a soft smile, and soon the sight of *her* became his comfort.

Paul began to move one seat closer each evening until, finally, fourteen moves and two weeks later, he was sitting right next to his dream girl. He found out her name was Betty Matthews. She was the single mother of a seven-year-old son, Jimmy. Paul walked Betty home that night. It was the beginning of something beautiful that would bring great happiness to his life.

One evening Paul and Betty left the diner and strolled over to the nearby Zale's jewelry store. Together, they picked out a small diamond ring for Betty. Paul purchased it on the store's installment plan. He sat Betty down and made her promise that she would never raise her voice at him, and he vowed to do the same in return. They agreed that anytime they had a difference or a problem, they would sit down at the kitchen table and work it out together. Paul petitioned the court and adopted Betty's little boy. He and Betty never had children of their own.

In 1952, after his wedding, Paul went to the Tulsa Police Department to try and finally fulfill his lifelong dream. He had always considered himself too small, but he filled out an employment application and was pleasantly surprised when he was accepted. He entered the Tulsa Police Academy and put his whole heart into it.

One day he found himself sitting in a class about sex perverts. The instructor told a story about a rooster that was kept in a cage and starved for a while. Just before the famished fowl was turned loose, chicken feed was set on one side of him and a hen on the other side. As soon as the door of his cage was opened, the bird went right straight for the food. Paul thought out loud in class, "I hope I never get that hungry." He, at first, was afraid he would get demerits, but was met, instead, with laughter. Whew!

Paul got "excellent" written on his notebook by the professor on February 19, 1953, the day he graduated from the police academy and became a member of the fraternity for which he had always held such a deep respect. He was excited and proud to finally carry a badge and wear that magical uniform: he was now officially a dragon slayer.

Paul's first assignment was a foot beat at Third and Boston Streets. After several months, he was assigned to the Patrol Division, working the western part of the city (Red Fork, Carbondale and west Tulsa). For his first night of patrol training, he was put in a car with an older cop named Leroy. Several blocks from the police station, Leroy pulled into an alley and blinked his spotlight a couple of times on the third floor window of an apartment building. A lusty blond opened the curtain and waved. Leroy slid out of the car and said,

"Pick me up at the end of the shift." Paul noted that the officer was married . . . and he and the woman in the window weren't wearing matching rings. So, Paul had to patrol alone until 6 a.m. That was the beginning of a "real education" for him.

After three years in the Patrol Division, during which time he received several commendations, Paul was promoted to the Detective Bureau. He would find being a detective was his true calling. He lived and breathed working and solving cases. He possessed an innate ability for investigation, and his photographic memory was a great asset to him. He first served in "General Assignments" and later with Captain Harry Stege, Sr, in the Major Crimes Squad. Paul was the recipient of an "Officer of the Month" trophy and certificate for solving the most burglaries (twelve) in a single month. He never threw away the picture of himself standing on the courthouse steps holding his prize.

Later, Paul was assigned duty in the Vice Squad under Sgt. Bob Bevins. After being there a while, Paul happened to spend a shift riding with an older officer. They stopped a bootlegger and took his whiskey. The older partner said nothing, just turned around and drove up an alley, where a guy came out: it was another bootlegger. Paul watched as his partner gave the second bootlegger a lug of whiskey in exchange for some money. His partner then threw a five-dollar bill into Paul's lap: Paul tried to give it back, but his partner refused to take it. When they returned to police headquarters, Paul took the five-dollar bill to the sergeant's desk and told him what had happened. The sergeant chuckled and said, "Aw, don't worry about it, if you never do anything worse than that, you'll be alright." Paul was stunned.

As time went by, Paul began working with three other officers, Carter, Bruner and Spybuck in a squad that had been formed to control bootlegging, prostitution and gambling. The squad soon learned that several of their fellow lawmen, all the way to the top brass, were taking payoffs from underworld players, who had formed a crime syndicate. All four members of the squad went together to B. Hayden Crawford, the US Attorney in Tulsa, and related to him all the dirt they had uncovered. Crawford, in turn, formed a federal grand jury, who indicted nineteen people, including the police commissioner, the chief of police and three detectives. The four honest cops testified against the dirty ring, sixteen of whom were sentenced to a federal prison.

The fiasco, complete with seedy pictures, was published by *True Detective* magazine in an article entitled "Tulsa's Kingdom of Vice." The article displayed a picture of Police Chief Paul Livingston, who got twenty percent of the syndicate's profits, with the words "some could be bought—" under his picture (Police Commissioner Jay Jones got forty percent). On a subsequent page were pictures of Paul and Officers Carter, Bruner and Spybuck, with the words "—and some could not." Paul and the rest of his squad became hated men in the world of law enforcement. They had violated the infamous "blue line."

A letter soon arrived on the desk of a new Tulsa police chief, George O'Neal. Paul always referred to it as the "letter that ended my [law enforcement] career."

United States Department of Justice
UNITED STATES ATTORNEY
Northern District of Oklahoma
Tulsa 3, Oklahoma

June 11, 1957
Chief George O'Neal
Tulsa Police Department
4th and Elgin
Tulsa, Oklahoma

Dear Chief O'Neal:

It is the intention of this letter to commend Officer Paul Smith for his outstanding assistance and performance of duty in conjunction with the recent federal grand jury investigation and liquor conspiracy trial here in our district. At a time when so many individuals were reluctant to stand up and be counted on the side of truth and justice, it was particularly gratifying to work with a man who displayed the devotion to duty and sincerity demonstrated by Officer Smith.

As you know, after several weeks of investigation, an indictment was returned by the grand jury alleging violations of federal laws on the part of some 20 defendants, 16 of whom were convicted after a trial covering a period of almost two weeks.

I was particularly impressed with the moral courage and complete truthfulness exhibited by Officer Smith, in spite of the possibility of retaliatory measures which were indicated against him. He could not be intimidated and he did not waiver from his responsibility as an officer and a citizen.

The people of Tulsa are fortunate to have a man of Officer Smith's caliber as an officer of the City of Tulsa Police Department and, consequently, it appears appropriate for me to advise you by this letter of the exceptional devotion to duty on the part of Officer Smith and his very commendatory conduct throughout the entire undertaking.

Sincerely yours,
Hayden Crawford
United States Attorney

Unfortunately, most of the convicted officers left behind relatives in the department with whom the honest cops had to work. Officer Spybuck was transferred to the dog pound, picking up stray animals, and Paul, too, was told he would go to the pound. Paul firmly refused the new assignment, so, instead, he was demoted back to the Patrol Division, working back in Red Fork and west Tulsa.

Paul's wife, Betty, began receiving threatening phone calls. It was before the days of "Caller ID," so she had no way to identify who it was that was threatening to kill her, Paul and even their son, Jimmy. Betty was petrified. When Paul would come home after serving a shift, he would find Betty crying or with still-red eyes. It was not worth it to him to put his family through the terror, so Paul resigned from the Tulsa Police Department and walked away from the career that he was made for. He glumly went to work with his older brother, Don, working in an artificial limb factory until October 1975, when he returned to the little town where his father was once mayor—Locust Grove, Oklahoma. He took a lowly patrolman's position with the Locust Grove Police Department and worked part time for the Wilson-Cunningham Funeral Home. It was there where he was sitting on the afternoon of June 12, 1977, when he watched the Girl Scout buses go through town on their way to camp.

Paul had learned pretty early who had committed the murders of the three little girls, but Sheriff Weaver, the OSBI, the OHP and Pryor PD had all worked together to convict one Cherokee man named Gene Leroy Hart. While Paul knew that Hart did not have a good record, he also knew that the State of Oklahoma had not convinced a jury that Hart was responsible for the killings. As far as Paul was concerned, the case was still open and needed further investigation. Since no one else was going to do it, he felt he needed to act. He knew he had the training and experience to take on the job. The year after Hart was acquitted, Paul raised $1600 and ran for sheriff of Mayes County. On September 16, 1980, he won handily over Sheriff Pete Weaver's re-election bid. Paul had no idea the brutality that awaited him.

CHAPTER 10

... AND THE LAW WON

In January 1981, Paul Dean Smith was sworn in as the seventeenth individual to hold the office of Sheriff of Mayes County, Oklahoma. The outgoing sheriff, Pete Weaver, did not honor Paul with the usual transition meeting to orient him to the office. Paul found this to be unprofessional, but that was just the way it was.

Since Gene Leroy Hart had been acquitted of killing the three little Girl Scouts, Paul began his tenure as sheriff with an open triple murder case to work on. Eager to get started on bringing justice to Lori, Denise and Michelle, the first action Paul took was a dive into the office file cabinets. He was looking for the case file on the Girl Scout murders, as well as the file on Hart. Paul was dismayed when he came up empty. Hart's file contained a single sheet of paper with a case name listed that wasn't even Hart's. The Girl Scout file was nowhere to be found. Sheriff Weaver had shafted Paul.

Paul walked across the street to the office of Fred Sordahl, the Assistant District Attorney in charge of Mayes County, to request help in locating the missing files. Paul did not get the reaction he was expecting. Mr. Sordahl came out of his chair, shook a finger in Paul's face and said, "I've got all those files locked up in my office, and you are *not* getting them. As far as I'm concerned, the man who killed those Girl Scouts is in his grave, and that's where he belongs. And furthermore, if you are going to work on the Girl Scout case, you'll get no help out of this office."

Paul knew that he himself, as Sheriff, would never be able to personally file charges against any suspect—only the District Attorney's office could do that. Paul, in essence, had just been informed by Assistant DA Sordahl that it would not matter what kind of evidence Paul presented, no one else would ever be charged with the murders. In Paul's words, "my first day in office was my worst day in office." Many years later, Paul looked back on this day and assessed, "If I had had any sense, I would have immediately gone and resigned as Sheriff and announced to the public why." But, Paul Smith was not a quitter.

So, instead, he drove to Oklahoma City, to the office of the Oklahoma Attorney General, and reported how the former Sheriff and the Assistant District Attorney were obstructing justice. The Attorney General told Paul that there was nothing he could do about it. Paul was confounded.

Since he could not obtain any investigatory records, he decided, while he was in Oklahoma City, he would pay a visit to the Chief Medical Examiner. Paul explained his problem and asked for a copy of the autopsy reports on the little girls. The ME stated to Paul that he was glad someone was continuing to work on the crime, that he would be happy to give Paul copies and wished him luck.

Paul was heartsick as he read over the details of the injuries to the helpless little victims. One thing puzzled him, though: there had been much talk about semen and deformed sperm at Hart's trial, but nowhere in any of the three autopsy reports could Paul find the presence of semen mentioned.

Although the drawings made by Dr. Hoffman in the girls' autopsy reports were good, Paul wanted to get a better look. He went to the Tulsa Office of the Medical Examiner to view the colored slides of the victims' head wounds. After close observation of little Michelle, Paul drew the conclusion that she had been bludgeoned by two instruments: 1) an abraded-faced hammer-type instrument, and 2) what appeared to Paul to be a crowbar, indicated by crescent-shaped injuries. It was Paul's opinion that one blow on the left occipital region of Michelle's head had been made by the nail-pulling end of the crowbar, leaving a "V" type injury. Dr. Hoffman, who had performed the autopsies, told Paul the only injuries for which he had been unable to determine a cause were the small bruises on the legs of Denise and Lori.

When Paul returned to his office in Pryor, he was visited by OHP Officer Harold Berry (who had been the first on the scene) and Private Investigator Ted LaTurner. Paul told the two men his belief about what weapons were used against the little girls. Officer Berry appeared rather shocked when Paul mentioned a crowbar: Berry said "I've been waiting to see if anyone mentioned a crowbar." Berry then told Paul, in the presence of LaTurner, that he had been with OSBI Agent Limke searching the area around the crime scene, when Agent Limke had reached into the bushes and picked up a crowbar. Agent Limke had said to Berry, "I wonder if this is some of Pete's planted evidence. Let's keep quiet about it and see what develops." Paul found Trooper Berry's account to be stupefying: it cemented in Paul's mind the same theory Hart's attorneys had used to defend their client at trial . . . that all the evidence against him had been strategically placed by a vendetta-carrying Sheriff Weaver.

A trusty currently serving time in the Mayes County Jail came to Paul and shared that he had been ordered by Sheriff Weaver to burn a "bunch of papers" out behind the sheriff's office the last day that Weaver occupied the office. Paul assumed that meant anything that was not presently under lock and key in Fred Sordahl's office had already been destroyed by fire. One way or another, Paul was not ever going to see the case files that were rightfully owned by the taxpayers of Mayes County and should have been readily available to the sheriff they had overwhelmingly elected (Paul had won all but one precinct).

Paul contacted the OSBI, and they sent Agent Leo Albro to Paul's office. Agent Albro came in angry and refused to help Paul pursue the case. He accused Paul of "playing Indian."

After Paul was in office a few days, a young man by the name of Donald Trammell came into his office and stated, "Sheriff, my wife's brother had a part in the killing of those little girls." Donald stated that his wife, Janice (who had been his girlfriend at the time of the murders), had told him that her brother, "Flea," had come home about daylight the night of the crime and was really "high" on something like she had never seen him before. Janice said Flea had blood on his tennis shoes and clothes, and, when asked what had happened, he said he had killed a deer . . . but no deer was ever found. Flea later sat in the floor with two pie pans and used a spoon to dip water from one pan to the other, all the while mumbling about "those poor little Girl Scouts." After sobering up, he had told his sister he would kill her if she opened her mouth. She believed him: Flea had a reputation for being big and mean . . . he had once fired a .357

through a carload of kids at Twin Bridges (fortunately he had not hit any of them). NOTE: Twin Bridges was an area where Snake Creek and Spring Creek merged and each had a bridge, side by side. Twin Bridges was approximately 3.5 miles down Spring Creek from the Girl Scout camp.

Paul had heard this story before. He was around when Donald and Janice had come and told Locust Grove Police Chief DeCamp the same details back in 1977. Paul still had the VIN number of the car Flea had allegedly pushed into the river following the murders. Donald did his best to estimate for Paul exactly where the Super Bee had gone in.

A little later, Donald Trammell came back into Paul's office with a roofing hatchet that had a rectangular rasp-type face and said, "I think you want this, Sheriff—it belonged to Flea, and he gave it to me." When Paul saw the shape and abraded face of the hammer and compared it to the autopsy description and drawings of Denise's wounds, it happened to be approximately the same size. Paul took the hammer to a Dr. Hemphill in Tulsa and viewed the slides again. Dr. Hemphill could not say it was or was not the instrument used, so the hammer was sent to the OSBI who reportedly said the hammer was definitely not the instrument used. Noticeably, the name of the expert who had drawn that conclusion was not provided. Paul learned, while there with Dr. Hemphill, that Dr. Hoffman had resigned because of his disagreement with the OSBI about Janice Davis's 'deformed sperm' findings, among other misdeeds of the OSBI that were intolerable to Hoffman.

Through informants, Paul received information that, following the crime, after Bull's Dodge Super Bee had been put in the river, Bull and Buddy had come to town barefooted, where they made contact with a Native American woman by the name of "Bird" and had her take them to Tulsa to the home of a friend by the name of Chris Elliott (Elliott denied this). Bull obtained a pair of shoes and was then taken to the airport, where he caught a plane to Monterey, California. He stayed there with a Native American family by the name of "Chunestudey" [Bull's mother was a Chunestudey before marriage]. This was the third time Paul was hearing the Super Bee had been put into the Neosho River.

Paul contacted the Oklahoma Tax Commission again, gave them the VIN number and learned that Bull's Super Bee had never again been licensed since the crime had occurred four years earlier. Paul tried to get help searching for it in the treacherous, rolling Neosho River, but the OSBI and even the military refused his requests for divers or technology. Nowata County Sheriff Mike Bird had a dive team, and he sent them to try and find the car for Paul, but they were ill-equipped and unsuccessful. Paul knew that, with the roaring current of the Neosho, the car most likely would have rolled before it sank. So, the amateurs, with their limited equipment, did not represent a meaningful search, but that was the only assistance Paul was ever offered.

His informants further told Paul that a day or two after Bull flew out to his kinfolks' house in Monterey, California, Buddy had gone back to Locust Grove and borrowed $179 from his dad, Floyd, and also flew to Monterey. Both Buddy and Bull stayed in California until Gene Leroy Hart was arrested and charged with the triple murder. As far as Paul could ascertain, Flea had remained in the Locust Grove area during this time.

Paul, when not following up informant leads, attempted to rebuild a file on Gene Leroy Hart: he set out on a mission to become as educated as possible about Gene Hart. He made visits to Hart's family and asked many questions. They were very helpful, except for Hart's brother, Thurman. Paul attempted to talk to Thurman twice: Thurman had nothing to say.

Paul also tried to recreate an official file on the Girl Scout murders. As in the case of Hart, Paul figured the most accurate information he could get would come from the girls' families. Herb Hartz, a personal friend of Paul's, who happened to be the Assistant Tulsa Police Chief, tried to set up a meeting for Paul with Denise's police-officer father, who worked for Hartz. Officer Milner refused to meet with Paul. Paul twice visited Lori's parents in their home: they were cordial, but he could tell they did not believe his story. He was not allowed to take pictures of Lori's belongings that had come from the camp (which were there illegally, thanks to the OSBI).

Buddy was eventually convicted of another crime and sentenced to Stringtown Prison. While Buddy was there, one of Paul's informants, "Baby Joe," was convicted of an unrelated crime and landed in Stringtown, as well. In 1983, Paul drove to the prison to ask Baby Joe if he would talk to Buddy and find out all he could about the Girl Scout murders. Baby Joe said, "I'll do better than that: I know his cell mate [Abe Garcia], who is like a father to him, and as soon as I know something, I'll call you."

After some time elapsed, Baby Joe called Paul and said, "Come on down, I've got it."

When Paul arrived at Stringtown, Baby Joe related to him the following:

Buddy said that he, Bull and Flea had been doing drugs and drinking beer for three days. They had run out of beer and had no money to buy more, so they decided to go to the Girl Scout camp and rob the adults. They drove out early in the evening, and too many people were up and around at the camp, so they went to Sam's Corner and stole some more beer (no mention was made that the cash drawer had been left with cash in it). They came back to the camp later that night and parked on a nearby dirt path that was still soft from the rain the day before: they were worried about getting the car stuck. Proceeding in their plan to rob the adults, they went to the far tent (they did not expect girls to be that far out into the woods by themselves) and found the girls there, and one almost got away from them (Paul understood it to be Denise). Buddy said they carried them away from the tent, and two of the boys held up victims by the upper extremities and were swinging them in a circle until their legs hit a tree (Paul felt this explained the mysterious bruises on the legs of Denise and Lori, and Buddy had just given information that only the killer(s) would know). Sticks were pushed up their privates (Denise had dirt and leaves in her vagina at autopsy). Upon leaving the scene, they agreed they should put the car in the river. They [took Cavalier Road south] and headed to Cooper's Bridge to clean themselves up as much as possible. In addition to the girls' blood, Bull's hand was cut (perhaps by barbed wire as they made their exit from the camp), and they had to wait for him to stop the bleeding. Next, they drove on south to Flea's house, where Buddy said he stayed in the car. When they left Flea's house and went to push the car in the river, the Super Bee high-centered on the bank. They needed a pickup and had to get somebody who had one to come and finish the job.

After listening to Baby Joe, Paul pulled Buddy out of his cell and let him know that he had enough information to get him charged with first-degree murder. Buddy swore to Paul that he had no personal part in the killing, that he had been sent to move the car. Paul informed him that it would not matter—he was with the others and that meant he was equally guilty of murder. Buddy was terror-stricken and told Paul that, if Paul would promise to take the death penalty off the table, he would tell Paul everything. Paul pointed out to Buddy that, as Sheriff, he could not make any deals with him or promise him anything, but that the DA could. Paul asked him if he would talk to the DA, and Buddy agreed.

Instead of driving to Pryor to have to deal with (appointed) Assistant DA Sordahl again, Paul went straight to Claremore, OK, to the elected DA, Jack Graves. Paul filled Graves in about Buddy's story and let Graves know that Buddy was willing to tell him everything that very afternoon if Graves would just go back to the prison with Paul. Paul was so desperate to get Graves's help that he even gave up the name of his informant (something he had never done before in his law enforcement career). Graves's reply was, "Hell, no, I won't go, but I'll call the OSBI." NOTE: Some of Paul's deputies, along with a member of the Oklahoma Highway Patrol, had raided a club in Langley for liquor (it was a dry county at the time), and during the raid one of the deputies had thought he recognized one of the patrons as Jack Graves. It was not Jack Graves, but that got printed, and Jack Graves held Paul responsible for it. Jack Graves held a great deal of malice toward Paul.

Paul drove to Oklahoma City to the Attorney General's office and spoke to Mike Wolfe, who promised to get back in touch with Paul. NOTE: Paul never heard back from Mike Wolfe.

Paul then went to the FBI and talked to an Agent Hamilton, who told Paul it was out of the FBI's jurisdiction.

A despondent Paul returned to his office, where he later got an angry phone call from Baby Joe, who informed Paul that two men [Graves and Agent Albro] had come to Stringtown and taken Baby Joe into a room where they pounded the table and said, "What did Sheriff Smith promise you to get you to tell that crap?" Baby Joe said he simply got up and walked out of the room. His two visitors had no interest in hearing Buddy's confession.

Helpless to do anything else, Paul kept up with the "Trammell kids." Donald and Janice had gotten married. Donald related to Paul on several occasions the stories his wife had told him about Flea's involvement in the murders. Each time, Paul would attempt to question Janice, and she would tremble visibly and say she had lied. Finally, Donald took Paul aside and said Flea had whipped Janice and threatened to kill her if she talked to the sheriff again. Janice quit her job at a clothing factory and disappeared. By late winter she was located in Baytown, Texas. Paul took money out of his own pocket and gave it to Donald to go get his wife. Donald then moved them to Anadarko to get Janice away from Flea.

One day, Paul took a deputy and drove to Anadarko, where he caught Donald and his father out on the bank of a fishing hole. Paul began running a mini-cassette recorder and captured a fascinating conversation. Donald asked Paul if he had been able to locate the Super Bee in the river. Paul answered negative. Donald tried to clarify for Paul where he thought the car might be, based on the location of a couple of docks. Then Donald told Paul that Janice had agreed to join her family in lying to protect Flea: Flea's family had made a pact that they would all swear Flea had never left the house that night. Paul asked if Janice had agreed to this because she was afraid of Flea. "I think it is to protect their mother," Donald explained. The family had even hired an attorney to advise Flea: they were expecting Flea to be arrested.

Several days after the fishing hole conversation, Paul arrived at his office one morning to a ringing phone. It was Donald calling: he informed Paul that Janice's family was coming to Anadarko to get her, that they were going to hide both her and Flea. When Paul hung up, he immediately dialed the Tulsa PD and asked Herb Hartz if he could borrow Herb's plane and pilot. In short order, Ted LaTurner was dropped off in Anadarko and, together with a female officer from the Anadarko PD, persuaded Janice to do the right thing and come back to Pryor to tell Paul her story. LaTurner got into Donald and Janice's VW with them to drive the 200 miles from Anadarko to Pryor. In a peculiar turn of events, Paul got a call from LaTurner later that same day, stating that when the Trammell car had reached the Turner Turnpike toll gate near Tulsa, two OSBI agents, wearing dark suits, had exited a black car and taken Donald and Janice into their custody. LaTurner, still in the Trammell car, followed the OSBI vehicle to the OSBI's offices on Skelly Drive, where he overheard one of the agents telling his secretary [about Paul], "Hon, he's trying to make fools out of us." Paul believed the OSBI had bugged his phone: there was no other way they would have known Donald and Janice were heading toward Pryor.

The two agents each took one of the Trammells and split off into separate offices and closed the doors. Paul jumped in his car and headed that way. The agents were still questioning the Trammells when Paul arrived. After about ten minutes, Janice walked out as white as a sheet and visibly shaking. Paul got the impression she was about to vomit or faint. She never made eye contact with Paul. Donald and Janice Trammell drove back to Anadarko, packed up their things and left for a destination unknown (supposedly somewhere in Arizona). Paul never heard from them again.

Paul's health crashed with the stress he was under. One day, when he was out in the county, his bowel ruptured, and he came very close to leaving this world. When he collapsed in pain, a helicopter was sent to bring him back to Pryor. The surgeon was standing at the door waiting for him. After a quick x-Ray, Paul found himself in surgery. After he watched the anesthesia tube being placed in his arm, he was suddenly riding in a long train-like tube. Way up front, he could see a bright light. They were going at a terrific speed. Then Paul heard the 'tube' start to slow down. He looked out and saw what he would describe as "a pasture or a lawn, and it was the most beautiful, brilliant green" he had ever seen, "like a perfectly manicured lawn." There stood Joe (Paul's brother) and Woody (Paul's brother-in-law), both deceased. Joe's sleeves were rolled about half-way up, like Paul had always seen him wear them, and a big smile covered Joe's face. Just as the thing Paul was riding in was almost to a stop, Woody raised his hand for just a bit and motioned them on. They began rolling again and got up to a high speed. The next thing Paul knew, he woke up in surgery, put his hands on his stomach and asked the nurse if it was over. She said, "Yeah, you had a rough one." Paul always cried telling the story: it was a very real thing in his life.

He left office at the end of his four-year term, in January 1985, a sick man, broken in every way. He moved to Bristow, Oklahoma, to his sister's 500-acre ranch and began to work cattle and repair fences. And heal. The fight for justice was put on hold . . . but it was not canceled.

CHAPTER 11
JUSTICE FOR TRUTH

While watching the autumn leaves blanket the ground in 2009, Missouri author JD "Jennifer" Morrison received a phone call from a librarian in Bristow, Oklahoma, near Tulsa. Donna Lawrence had an offer for Jennifer. Donna wanted Jennifer to come and feature her book *Justice for Truth* at a meeting of the Bristow Library Club. The day would include an early-morning interview with a Bristow radio station.

Flowing through the pages of *Justice for Truth* was Jennifer's narrative of how her son, Richie, had died from injuries sustained in a minor automobile accident. There had been nothing noteworthy about the wreck itself. The real potboiler was that Jennifer had been double-crossed by the billion-dollar corporation whose delivery vehicle had run out in front of Richie. Jennifer had abandoned her computer programming career to find the truth. She had gone on a crusade to learn why the office of the Jackson County Medical Examiner had ruled Richie a "suicide" after initially ascribing his death to whiplash trauma. Jennifer had squared off against a worldwide company who had compromised one of the most powerful agencies of the government, and she had found the stone that landed the giant. It had taken four long, gut-wrenching years and a two-week court trial, but she had walked away as victor.

Librarian Donna had a bit of an ulterior motive in inviting Jennifer to come visit. What Jennifer was not told was that she was about to meet Paul Smith, the former Sheriff of Mayes County, Oklahoma.

Paul was now eighty-six years old and an avid reader. He was one of Donna's regulars, in and out of her library loading up on books every two weeks (the longest the library allowed a reader to keep them). Often, during his visits, Paul spoke to Donna of his angst regarding a case he had never gotten solved back in his days as Sheriff. It seemed to Donna that whatever topic she and Paul would initially be talking about, their conversation always reverted to Paul's unsolved case.

Donna had come to understand that Paul's every waking moment was never far from the murders of three little Girl Scouts at a summer camp near Locust Grove, Oklahoma, in June 1977. Donna had learned all the details of Paul's woe by heart. At the time of the slayings, he had been a Locust Grove policeman and had lived only five or six miles from the scene. Believing he could bring the killers to justice, he had successfully run for sheriff three years later. He had gathered personal informants' tips and even a confession that amounted to what he believed was strong enough evidence to make arrests and get justice for the little victims. Then he had been blocked by his own DA and law-enforcement colleagues. Paul had never gotten past it. Donna worried about Paul. It seemed his existence was trapped in 1977 and the unresolved atrocity. Paul was pressing Donna to help him write a book, hoping if his story got to enough people, someone out there would open a new investigation. Donna wanted to help Paul, but did not feel qualified to write the book.

One day Paul came to check in his books at the library and pick out his next bundle to take home with him. Donna surprised him by placing *Justice for Truth* at the top of his stack. She expressed to him that the author was someone who might be able to help him tell his story. Donna felt the two of them might even pair up and solve the case. When Donna had first read *Justice for Truth*, she had turned the last page optimistic that she might finally have something/ someone to offer Paul other than her own kind and listening ear.

Jennifer Morrison arrived in Bristow the following month as planned. After finishing her radio interview and her 'book report,' and even singing *Glad You Came Along* (a song she had written to her lost son), introductions took place at the library. Jennifer met Paul and his now-adult son, Jimmy. The men invited Jennifer to the Bristow Pizza Hut for lunch. She was delighted.

If Jennifer had not been through her own agony with dirty government officials, she would not have been prepared to believe what she began hearing over pepperoni and sausage. But she did believe. Paul's soft but commanding voice relayed Paul's own saga of betrayal. It triggered feelings Jennifer had experienced during the wretched years she had fought for the truth in her son's case. Paul explained how he had reached out to several people to try and get help with the case. The latest was Dennis Francini, a supervisor with the OSBI. Paul had hoped it had been long enough that the OSBI agents who had disliked him back when he was sheriff would now be gone from the Bureau, and a new set of agents would take up the investigation, but so far, he had not heard back.

He wanted Jennifer to write his story in a book, and he wanted it titled *Shattered Justice*. He envisioned a red cover, with the title in big, white block letters that looked as though they had cracks in them.

Whether all of Paul's details about the Girl Scout case were accurate or not, Jennifer knew he was telling the truth about how he had been prevented from pursuing his own investigation as sheriff. His pain was still palpable. Jennifer shared Paul's passion for truth and was determined to help him in any way she could. His account could easily be proven or disproven, she figured.

Paul had never believed that Gene Leroy Hart had been in any way connected to the slaughter of the three little girls. What Paul *did* believe were the rampant rumors about Sheriff Pete Weaver planting evidence to implicate the two-time escapee. Paul did not have a lot of confidence in "Pete" to begin with and presumed that Pete had an agenda against Gene for the embarrassment Gene had caused him by escaping his jail not once, but twice.

Jennifer mused at the thought of someone being able to escape twice from the same jail. "What in the heck was wrong with that jail?" she asked Paul. Paul was not trying to be funny when he gave the answer, but Jennifer could not keep a straight face. Her sometimes-irreverent sense of humor got the best of her. She listened intently to the tale of a would-be jail break that once happened on Paul's watch.

Paul's office was on the first floor of the seventy-nine-year-old Mayes County Sheriff's office building, and the jail was on the second floor. At one time the only way out of the building had been a path that led right past Paul's office door. But the Occupational Safety and Health Administration (OSHA) had come along and demanded that a fire escape be installed on the second floor. This meant adding a set of stairs that descended along the outside of the building from a side door on the upper floor.

A trusty came down to Paul's office one day to tell the sheriff he had overheard some inmates in the "big tank" (the largest cell) plotting an unscheduled release date. Paul asked the trusty to keep his eyes and ears open and to keep the information coming. Sure enough, the time came that the trusty returned to let Paul know the prisoners were currently prying on the cell bars. Paul went into action. He stationed an auxiliary officer on the roof of the building next door to the sheriff's office. Before long, the officer on the roof observed three men bursting through the second-floor door and running down the fire escape. The officer fired off a round from his service revolver into the air. Immediately, the prisoners did a 180 and ran right back up the stairs into the building. The next thing they did was crawl back through a hole into their cell . . . a hole they had created by breaking over and bending a section of the bars with their bare hands.

"So, I had to move them to another cell and call a welder out the next day to fix the mess," Paul concluded in a dry tone. Jennifer could not hold her laughter as she pictured what Paul had just described. It was straight out of a scene from the *Andy Griffith Show* (not really, but it could have been). Jennifer would soon learn that Paul could be a jokester, but it seemed to her he was funniest when he was not trying to be.

"Well, I guess if the jail was that easy to get out of, it is no wonder Gene Hart made it out twice." Jennifer did her best to compose herself.

"Oh, the jail failed inspection every single month that I was in office, but there was nothing I could do about it. The county would never give me any money. They never even bought me a car: I had to use my own vehicle. I got a $400 per month allotment for gasoline and maintenance, and my three deputies were reimbursed for mileage."

On to more serious matters, Jennifer mentally downloaded Paul's theory about the homicides and his three suspects, and Paul loaded her up with photostatic copies of his memoirs and all the supporting documents. Jennifer drove the four hours back to her home in Kansas City with her mind racing. *Where would she begin?*

She only vaguely remembered the Girl Scout murders. She was born and raised in Oklahoma and had been as stunned as everyone else when they had occurred. What she recalled most clearly was the evening news being filled with the hunt for a fugitive named Gene Leroy Hart. As a teen at the time, the frequent news updates seemed like they would never end. Hart had become a sort of ghost figure in Jennifer's mind before they finally captured him . . . and then he was declared to be the wrong man by a jury. But that was more than thirty-four years ago. Life had gone on, and the case had faded. It spoke to Jennifer that Paul was still so affected by it.

Google was not the tool it would someday become, but Jennifer used it to find a few helpful odds and ends about the case. She spent a few months of her spare time intently soaking in details, and then she began contacting people.

Just as 2011 calendars were hung on the wall, Jennifer connected with Kyle Eastridge, a former OSBI employee who had recently resigned from the OSBI. Kyle Eastridge had been hired by the agency to create and head up a cold case unit. Once inside, he had found case file after case file containing great leads and clues that had never been properly followed up on. He began to complain about it. Loudly. He suddenly was not welcome anymore. He left after six months.

Eastridge agreed to accompany Jennifer to meet with Judy Copeland, the general counsel of Oklahoma Governor Mary Fallin, who was the 'boss' of the OSBI. Before she had moved away from Oklahoma, Jennifer had once sat on a committee hosted by Fallin, who had been an Oklahoma state senator back then. Jennifer regarded Fallin as someone who could get things done. At the end of a five-hour trip to Oklahoma City, Jennifer was met by Eastridge. He lent support as she placed all the details of Paul's investigation and mistreatment in front of Attorney Copeland. Even though Copeland showed interest at that moment, she never called Jennifer with a response from Governor Fallin.

Jennifer was disheartened when she figured out a few weeks later that former OSBI Agent Dick Wilkerson had become an Oklahoma state senator and was now working with Governor Fallin on a project to help incarcerated women in Oklahoma prisons. This was the same Dick Wilkerson who had retired from the OSBI after Gene Leroy Hart's acquittal to write a book with his brother, OSBI Agent Mike Wilkerson. The Wilkerson brothers had been devastated that Hart had not been held accountable. They were sure they had captured the right man and still wanted the public to know it.

It would obviously be a conflict of interest for Governor Fallin to side with Jennifer and Paul against the OSBI. Jennifer was learning just how long the tentacles of the OSBI reached across the state of Oklahoma. It was a huge setback. Seeing the 'front door' was bolted shut, Jennifer started scheming ways to get in the back door, with Paul urging her on.

Jennifer managed to find the name of a juror who had served as one of the twelve during the trial of Gene Leroy Hart, and Eastridge, who was now a private investigator, presented Jennifer with an address for the juror. Jennifer composed a letter and used a clothes pin to attach it to the mailbox hanging next to the front door of her red-brick home. The letter held Jennifer's request for an interview with the juror: she wanted a tour guide inside the deliberations of the six-man and six-woman panel that had acquitted Gene Leroy Hart. *Had they returned a "not guilty" verdict because they felt the evidence had been planted?* The defense had directed a spectacular show using that hypothesis.

If the jury had indeed seen the evidence as planted, Jennifer had more specific questions. How deeply had the jury delved into the manner in which the evidence got to where it was found? Was it really *possible* that every single item that had indicted Hart could have been introduced into the crime scene by someone else? *Who* would have had such an opportunity, and *when* could they have deposited it where it was discovered?

Jennifer was ripe with anticipation as she watched a U.S. mail carrier pick up her letter and disappear off down the street . . . and she was beyond ecstatic when he delivered a return letter from the juror's address a few days later. But her excitement was short-lived.

She opened the envelope to find a letter from the daughter of the juror. The letter was sent to inform Jennifer that the juror (her mom) had been deceased for years. Jennifer's heart dropped. Another dead end. She would have to search for a new avenue. Again, Paul rallied her to not give up.

Eastridge used 'skip tracing' on Jennifer's behalf to look for Donald and Janice Trammell. Perhaps they would tell her the inside scoop of the OSBI capturing them at the toll booth and stealing them away as material witnesses in Paul's investigation. And, just maybe, Jennifer could pull out all the information that Janice had buried away in her brain. Sadly, neither Donald nor Janice was still alive. After divorcing Janice, Donald had moved to Chuckey, Tennessee, where he had begun a new life. Two decades later, a Chuckey newspaper had carried the story of Donald's strange "suicide," leaving a wife and two daughters behind. His obituary had listed him as a "loving father," yet he had taken his own life in a locked vehicle parked next to the family home. He was forty-seven years old. Jennifer then discovered that Janice had only lived to be forty.

Jennifer decided to check Buddy's story about how none of the girls had been raped (other than by instrument). She put out a search for the OSBI chemist, Janice Davis, who had testified that she could see sperm in the bodily fluids taken from the girls. The news came back that Janice Davis had committed suicide twenty-three years earlier.

It was time for Jennifer to play her 'ace' card. She located Buddy, which was easy. He was in prison on a twenty-five-year sentence for indecent exposure. Seems he had felt the urge to openly masturbate and jut his genitals toward five children, ages two to thirteen, on a swimming beach at Spring Creek. Jennifer could not help noticing the "Body Marks" section of Buddy's prison record: they included tattoos on his arms and legs of "Girls," "Skulls," "Skull w/wings," "Reaper," and "Devil." Buddy had his case under appeal and was being represented by an attorney named Gloyd McCoy, author of

Tent Number Eight (a book about the Girl Scout murders and the trial of Gene Leroy Hart). Small world.

Jennifer placed a formal request to visit Buddy at Stringtown Prison. It was denied. Buddy's prison advocate called Jennifer to tell her Buddy "did not want to talk about anything like [the Girl Scout case]." Paul had felt like Buddy was their best shot.

By the end of that calendar year, attorney Judy Copeland was dead. Jennifer keenly remembered the beautiful and vibrant blond who had listened intently to her and Eastridge just outside Governor Mary Fallin's office. Now Judy had succumbed to an apparent stroke in the wee hours of Sunday morning, November 6, 2011, in the University of Oklahoma Medical Center. Tragic. She was only forty-two years old.

Seventeen days after Judy Copeland died, Buddy gasped his last breath. Cancer took him from this earth November 23, 2011.

The case seemed to Jennifer to have a darkness surrounding it. Everywhere she turned, she encountered death. She felt like she had failed Paul. It was as though a fortress had been built around the case that Jennifer could not scale. It would be ten long years before she would find a crack in the wall . . .

On the first day of Spring 2021, Jennifer stepped outside her front door and clutched a bundle of items from her mailbox. As she walked back inside and toward the desk where she always stashed anything that needed further attention, she sifted through the envelopes. Within a minute, a hand-addressed letter had made its way to the top. The letter had come from Oklahoma. Of course, it was the first piece of mail to be opened that day.

Jennifer was curious as she read the brief, typed letter that asked if she was still at this address. The writer wanted to send her something very sensitive that had to do with the Girl Scout case. It was information that had been written down by someone who had since died . . . someone who had insisted the information be mailed to Jennifer *after* the person's death. Did Jennifer still want it?

Jennifer ran straight to her computer to do a search of her files for the name of an individual mentioned in the letter, someone who was related to the mailer of the envelope. She realized that the name belonged to the daughter of the juror, the one who had answered the interview request Jennifer had sent to her deceased mother a decade earlier.

Realizing her printer was on the blink, Jennifer sat down and grabbed an ink pen to scrawl out a reply. Yes! Yes, she wanted the information! Her intuition told her that a postage stamp would fetch her something exciting. It did.

Within a few days, Jennifer was holding a different hand-written letter. It was from a Cherokee man named David Sack. Cherokees do not tell on each other, but David had suffered a pang of conscience after he found out that a lady had come looking for information about the Girl Scout murders. He wrote down what he knew, including who he thought was involved in the killings, and made a friend promise to mail the information upon his death. David named Flea, Buddy and Thurman, the half-brother of Gene Leroy Hart. David's nephew, Michael Nott (who was the same age as David), had seen them at Flea's house during the wee morning hours of Monday, June 13, 1977, and had connected the dots. Before Michael's death, he had ridded his soul of the horrible secret. His Uncle David had sat with Michael as he was dying and had become the recipient of the loathsome burden. Both of the men wanted to go to the authorities and ask them to investigate what Michael knew, but feared for their safety, and, even more so, for the safety of their families. Plus, they had no trust in local law enforcement. David pointed out in his letter that a DNA test performed in 1989 that showed a partial match to Gene Hart had convinced him more than ever that the half-brother of Hart was one of the killers.

Jennifer, unfortunately, had lost track of Paul. Her first thought was to find him, of course. Her second thought was he would be ninety-seven years old now. Would he still be alive? She took a deep breath and did a Google search for "Paul Smith Oklahoma obituary." Nothing came up. She used a different search engine. Still no result. Hope began to rise. She looked up Paul's address in Bristow, Oklahoma. He was no longer there. His name (no locating information) still showed up in voter registration records, though.

Jennifer continued to study on how she might find him. On April 8, 2021, it hit her. Property tax records. Whoever was paying the taxes on Paul's former home had probably purchased it from Paul or his son, Jimmy, and maybe these new owners would know where the Smith men had gone.

By dinner time, Jennifer heard Paul's voice say "hello" over the phone. She excitedly told him about the letter and promised to come and see him so she could show it to him in person. Paul still lived in Bristow, Oklahoma, four hours away from Jennifer. They set a date for six days later, April 14, 2021, for Jennifer to drive to Paul's apartment.

Even though Paul was frail and described himself as "wheelchair-bound" now, Jennifer could tell that he was still as mentally sharp as he had been the last time they had spoken, and he still wanted the case solved just as badly. She did a happy dance.

While they were talking, Paul told Jennifer that he had spoken to a school teacher/writer/lawyer named Faith Phillips, who was going to be bringing her school kids to meet him in three weeks, on April 29. Paul thought Jennifer ought to give the lady a call, and he passed along the phone number. Jennifer assured him that she would reach out to Faith.

Paul next told Jennifer that a new sheriff in Mayes County had sent his special deputy, Dean Majors, out to talk to Paul on December 23, 2013. At first, Majors had presented himself as a reporter. He had set a recorder on the arm of Paul's couch and had begun naming names and asking Paul questions, which Paul had refused to answer. Majors then asked Paul if he would talk to the Mayes County Sheriff or one of his deputies. Paul had replied that he would be happy to do so. Majors had then handed Paul his deputy's commission for Mayes County, stating that the Sheriff wanted "closure" on the Girl Scout case. Paul gave Deputy Majors a copy of his memoirs and a psychiatric evaluation of Hart to provide to Sheriff Mike Reed, but Paul had never heard anything back from either of them. He had been disappointed. Again.

Jennifer was sad to hear that Paul had just buried Jimmy the summer before. Paul had now outlived ten siblings, his wife and his son. Jennifer could hear the pain in Paul's voice as he told Jennifer that he had been unable to find anyone to 'preach' Jimmy's funeral and he had had to do it himself.

On April 14, 2021, as pre-arranged, Jennifer drove to Paul's apartment and placed the letter in front of him. Paul was a little troubled by the letter. He agreed with Flea and Buddy being a part of the story, but Bull was glaringly absent, and Paul had never heard the mention of Thurman from the "Trammell kids" or as part of

Buddy's confession. Paul immediately deduced that Michael Nott had mistaken Thurman for Bull (both were Cherokees and around the same age). Jennifer accepted Paul's theory of the discrepancy. After all, she was not acquainted with any of the four individuals whose names had now been raised.

While Jennifer was in Paul's presence, she took note of something that hurt her. Paul now had a feeding tube ungracefully protruding from his abdomen. He explained that he had a huge hiatal hernia that pushed against his esophagus making it nearly impossible to take food by mouth. He was able to suck on mints and small candies (just to be able to taste something pleasant), but he mostly got his nutrition by pouring Ensure into the feeding tube. He also mentioned that he had nearly died in 2015, but did not go into detail. Jennifer hugged him and told him she was certainly glad that God had left him here.

Paul and Jennifer were excited to be back on the case together. When Jennifer said goodbye to Paul that day, her heart melted with the sweet smile he gave her. She was moved by the fresh twinkle she caught in his nearly-98-year-old blue eyes. Neither of them had a clue yet how the universe was already aligning in their favor. Paul would soon get to tell his story to the world.

CHAPTER 12
YOU GOTTA HAVE FAITH

It was a fluke that Faith Phillips found herself teaching in the Oklahoma public schools from 2019-2021. Her entire family had spent their lives in various public servant capacities as teachers, nurses, police officers and military. She was proud of them, but knew that was not the life for her. She decided to go to law school. She practiced corporate law for a half-dozen years before she left to pursue her first true love—a literary career. She knew the chances of becoming successful by writing books were not good . . . in fact they were near-impossible odds. Still, it was worth the shot for her. Writing was really the only thing Faith felt good at in life. When she wrote she felt fulfilled, like she had found her gift.

She moved back home and lived off of her family at the age of thirty-two, when she took a year to write her first fiction novel. It was embarrassing to have to live a life of poverty, once again, after having made a nice living for herself as a corporate attorney. Very few in her community back home could understand it. Faith believed in herself, though, and figured it would take two years before her writing went national. After eight years of writing for a living and still no big break, with her third book, *Now I Lay Me Down*—which fell in the true-crime category—she began to get her first real taste of writing success with a measure of national media exposure. It was a very exciting time.

Not long after that, the principal of Faith's old high school contacted her to speak to the student body about writing as a career. She was happy to do so, feeling very proud of herself to be providing some measure of public service by spending a day in the schools. Then the principal said he had an opening for a senior English teacher, and he thought Faith would be great for the students. She was stunned and automatically said "no," because becoming a public-school teacher was the exact opposite of her ideas of success as a little girl growing up. Then she spoke about it to those closest to her—her best friends, her preacher, her family—and they were all unanimous in saying that she should do it. She agreed to teach for one year.

About the time she accepted the teaching job, she married a man she had first met in 2015. Their initial meeting had been rocky, to say the least, and they had gone their separate ways. Yet, somehow, they had reunited two years later, and Faith inexplicably found herself living in a new home. Not just any home, though. This house was located a half mile, as the crow flies, from Camp Scott. On winter days, when the foliage was gone from the trees, she could stand on her front porch and make out the old buildings that still stood, long-abandoned, on the Camp Scott property. It reinvigorated her interest in the three little girls who had been murdered there before she was even born.

During that first year of teaching, Faith's grandfather was dying of emphysema. She regularly went by to visit him after school. Before he got really sick, he would always raise up on one elbow and shout, "Osiyo, Wild Woman!" "Osiyo" is the traditional Cherokee way of greeting someone with deep affection. One day when Faith stopped by, her grandpa was too sick to say "Osiyo," and the Cherokee chaplain was there to pray with him. The chaplain immediately took a strong interest in Faith and wanted to know what she did for a living. She told him she was a book writer and that her most recent book was about the triple Weleetka, Oklahoma, murders that had included two young girls. His eyes shone bright and he asked, "Have you ever heard of the Girl Scout murders?" She was taken aback. The Girl Scouts were just about the very last topic she expected to hear about at her grandfather's hospice bedside. But there they were.

The two struck up an intense conversation on the topic. Faith told him her various theories based on what she had researched up to that point. He shared with her that he knew Gene Hart had not committed the murders. According to the chaplain, Gene was staying with the chaplain's father—who happened to be Gene's cousin—at the time of the murders and that although he (the chaplain) was just a little boy at the time, he remembered Gene being there with his father. Faith was stunned and filed it away, thinking she might add to her research and write a book about the murders one day. Faith and the chaplain prayed together, the chaplain invited her to his Cherokee church outside Locust Grove and they parted ways.

Meanwhile, back at school, Faith's students researched, wrote, and produced a nationally recognized podcast about the poverty, health, and environmental issues facing their hometown of Stilwell, Oklahoma. Their work caused a big stir and garnered so much media attention that the students decided to keep making podcasts. They were addicted to the act of telling their own stories and the powerful change it effected on their families and community. As their teacher, Faith let them vote on the next topics they wanted to research. The class chose to divide themselves. Half of them chose to research the topic of "Missing and Murdered Indigenous Women." The other half chose to research the "Girl Scout Murders." Excited about the prospect, Faith posted about their topics on social media in December of 2020.

On February 26th, 2021, she received a private message on social media from a close friend of former Mayes County Sheriff Paul Smith. The message read, "I know you're well-versed on the Girls Scout Murders. I'd love to chat with you some time. I met a veteran who was one of the main law enforcement investigators. It was heartbreaking. He is confident about who actually murdered the girls and says that some are still running around alive in the area. I cried the whole way home."

The attorney in Faith immediately began 'discovery' on Paul Smith. Skepticism ran high in her mind, because she believed she knew almost everything there was to know about the case, and Paul Smith's name had never even crossed her periphery. What she found made her feel even more of a skeptic. She read that Paul had campaigned on solving the Girl Scout murders, that he had run a thorough investigation and had turned everything over to the OSBI . . . and that nothing had ever come from his work. In fact, *most* of the articles she found stated that the possible evidence and leads had all been "run down" by other investigators (including the top cops in Oklahoma) and had all been dismissed.

Faith went to school the next day and told her students. They had an opposite response to the news. They demanded that she pack up their podcasting gear and go meet with Paul right away. Faith's mind was full of doubt—especially at the height of Covid, to go meet with this man in a retirement home—but her students would not relent. So, she set up a private meeting for herself with "Mr. Smith."

When she arrived at Paul's apartment, she immediately noted the medals and recognition of service he had acquired over the years. They lined the walls and window sills of his tiny apartment, along with family photos, all placed where he could see them from his giant, overstuffed recliner. Next to the recliner stood a massive magnifying glass on a stand that he could easily move in order to review documents with his failing eyesight. Faith would soon realize how much he needed that tool when he pulled out a black, bulging briefcase filled with documentation regarding the Girl Scout murders.

Faith began recording as Paul relayed the most startling story she had ever heard in her forty-two years on earth. Her head nodded and she maintained composure as he spoke over the next two hours, relaying the story of how he had come to know the actual perpetrators of the 1977 triple homicide.

Faith left the retirement home in a daze, wondering if it was time to contact authorities, unsure if it was ethical to share the information with her students, and leery that two of the three murderers might be living within miles of her new Locust Grove home. The one thing she believed to be certain was that Paul Smith was telling the truth. Perhaps all that he told her was not 100% accurate, maybe some additional information was waiting to be found, but she was convinced that Paul believed every word of what he told her that day.

Faith's students convinced her to take them on a field trip to see Camp Scott. They could not get into the actual property, but she agreed to take them down Cookie Trail Road to the main entrance of the camp. On April 8, 2021, they turned down the road that led to the gate. The drive was intimidating, with sights of old broken-down buses, houses with busted windows and desperate looking dogs along their route. When they reached the gate, an angry-looking woman stepped out on her porch and stared them down. Faith could not really blame the woman, considering all the ill-intentioned people who must have shown up over the years, looking for a gruesome thrill. Faith told the bus driver to get them out of there! The students were glad to go. They were visibly shaken just by looking at the entrance to the camp. It seemed that, through their research, they had formed a deep sense of empathy for the victims and a righteous sense of outrage for the perpetrators.

The previous year, a Locust Grove poet named Shaun Perkins had contacted Faith. The two ladies had mutual friends in the publishing world, and Shaun had taken note of some of Faith's work with the students. Shaun had put out a standing invitation for Faith to bring them to Shaun's artsy establishment, the Rural Oklahoma Museum of Poetry (R.O.M.P.) Faith thought R.O.M.P. would be a delightful place to take them now, for them to enjoy some light-hearted, imaginative fun after such a heavy moment outside Camp Scott. She was right. The kids took off and spread out through the museum, engrossed in the many exciting activities Shaun offered up. While they were thus engaged, Shaun and Faith struck up a private conversation in Shaun's office. The prolific poet explained to Faith how she had grown up in Locust Grove and that she had recently sent a new book off to her publisher. The topic? Growing up in 1977 during the time of the Girl Scout murders. Her theme centered on the casual nature of violence and *sexual* violence, in particular, against girls in the small town. The story was deeply rooted in the notorious crime that had rocked Locust Grove that year, when Shaun had been fourteen years old and careening down the backroads around Camp Scott, carefree and often alone on her bicycle. Naturally, Faith was intrigued. She mentioned to Shaun that her students had just undertaken the Girl Scout case for a research podcast. Faith told Shaun the story of meeting with Paul Smith, but did not mention the names of the three suspects Paul had revealed to her. Before Faith got out another word, Shaun said three names of local men and asked if Paul had mentioned them. Faith stopped dead in her tracks. She told Shaun that two of the names were the second and third of the suspects Paul had named. Here was a second source, completely independent of Paul Smith, who mentioned some of the same names as suspects in the murders.

Shaun went on to confide other long-held information to Faith, and Faith asked Shaun to document everything in an email to her. It read:

"Suspect 3 [Buddy] was a known animal abuser [he shot his own dog for the entertainment of some friends] and peeping tom and had a rap sheet by 19 that was already long and no telling how many juvenile ones. For years, the gossip was that it was Suspect 3 [Buddy], Suspect 2 [Bull], and another guy known as a drug dealer around town, just because we knew all three of them hung out together and were into drugs. I don't remember where that rumor started.

"BUT the real evidence is something I found out several years ago when I reconnected with a guy who was Suspect 3's age and had hung out with him a bit. This guy had brothers in California, and he flew out to see them the Monday after the murders. While he was waiting for the plane, Suspects 2 & 3 [Bull & Buddy] showed up, driven by another guy from LG [Locust Grove] who lived in Tulsa at the time. The guy who drove them loaned Suspect 3 [Buddy] his shoes because he didn't even have any. At the time my friend didn't know anything about the murders, but he thought it was strange that these two were going off to California at the time and he hadn't known anything about it. Suspect 2 [Bull] was supposed to have a cousin or something that lived in Monterey.

"When my friend came back to LG, he was threatened by one of Suspect 2 [Bull]'s cousins that he better not say anything or else he would be killed. Sheriff Weaver never talked to him, but some policemen—he can't remember who, maybe OSBI—did in the early 80's, probably when Paul was sheriff. He told them the whole story but no one ever asked him about it again.

"He doesn't have any reason to make this up, and I have no idea why it wasn't investigated at the time. I know airline ticketing was really lax then, but they could have looked up the fact that they bought tickets and were on a flight the day after the murders, at least. Also, when I was looking at the docket books from 1975-77 at the courthouse, I noticed that Suspect 3 [Buddy] had a court date scheduled for sometime in June, and he missed it, and the date lined up with when he might have still been in California. The date was rescheduled, and he did show up for it."

Once again, Faith was dumbfounded. She found it difficult to pull herself together to gather up the students and take them back to school after all she had learned that day. The students commented that she was unusually quiet and spent most of the trip home staring out the window. Faith could not have known then that there was so much more to come.

That night as she walked through the door of her house, she unhooked her bra, poured herself a glass of Pinot Noir and plopped down on the couch. Her husband could tell something was amiss. Her moodiness was unusual, because after field trips she typically came home ecstatic . . . those were her class's most delightful days, when they left the confines of the school walls and found joy out in the world together, laughing and free. This time was different. Faith was stressed. She knew it was time to contact the authorities. The information that had come to her in just the span of a month or so had become much larger than herself, much more important than any student podcast or book. She knew what was happening now was the last shot at justice for Lori, Denise and Michelle.

Faith explained all these things to her husband, Mark, who felt equally stunned by the implausible series of events. They were discussing the implications and appropriate next steps when Faith's cell phone alerted her that a new text message had arrived. She picked up her phone and saw an unidentified number. She opened the message and read this:

"Hi Faith. My name is Jennifer Morrison. Paul Smith gave me your phone number. He says you are interested in the Girl Scout case. I have some information that was recently sent to me. Give me a call if you would like to visit."

Faith stared at her phone for what felt like fifteen minutes. She took a deep breath and read the message out loud to Mark. He said, "Well, what are you waiting for? Call the woman!" It was the call-to-action Faith needed to push her out of the nest.

Over the duration of that phone call with Jennifer Morrison, Faith became privy to the details of the 'death bed letter' written by David Sack. David wrote that Flea came home that morning with two acquaintances, acting suspiciously, thus confirming the accounts Faith had heard from both Paul Smith and the Locust Grove poet.

And, of course, the letter claimed that one of the suspects, Thurman, was a half-brother to Gene Leroy Hart. Jennifer had searched obituaries and found that Hart did have a brother by that name.

Faith and Jennifer knew all of these things had not happened in such a short time by accident. This was no coincidence. This was a grand design. Faith felt somewhat relieved that there actually was another woman in the world whose obsession with the case matched, and perhaps surpassed, her own . . . her new friend, Jennifer Morrison.

After they hung up, Faith immediately rang up a close family member and active law enforcement officer. All doubt and hesitation were removed from her mind. She no longer worried about whether or not people would think her crazy. She had no need for any more signs from above. It was time to call an acquaintance of hers at the OSBI. Jennifer warned Faith that the OSBI would not be interested, but Faith was confident her OSBI contact would be. She would do her duty as a citizen.

CHAPTER 13
BETTER TOGETHER

Jennifer Morrison and Faith Phillips made a date to meet each other in person. On April 20, 2021, twelve days after they had first spoken by phone, Jennifer shook hands with both Faith and her husband, Mark. Jennifer had a feeling about the stunning six-foot-tall blond, who bought the three of them an early dinner at La Mansion Mexican Restaurant in Locust Grove. Faith had a presence and confidence about her that Jennifer liked. Jennifer was so excited, she barely ate anything. After a final sip from their drinks, with Locust-Grove-native Mark as their tour guide, Jennifer drove the trio around the areas of what were once Camp Scott and Twin Bridges. They also went to the old closed-up structure that had been Sam's Corner. It was helpful to Jennifer to travel down Cavalier Road and see the layout of all the locations that had been elementary in the crime and investigation.

As the sun began to set, Jennifer said goodbye to her new friends and headed to Owasso, Oklahoma, to see an old one. Carla, Jennifer's friend since middle school, greeted her with a hug. Then, the two of them curled up on the sofa, so Jennifer could fill Carla in on all of her new adventures. Sometime just after 10 p.m., Jennifer stopped mid-sentence and gasped, "That's one of my girls!" Lori Farmer's face was filling the television screen. The Tulsa 10 o'clock news was on, and Lori's mother was pleading, as she had been for almost forty-four years, for anyone with information about the Girl Scout murders to come forward. "This case will only be solved by someone telling what they know," Sheri appealed to the audience. Early the next morning, Jennifer phoned Paul to tell him about Sheri's newscast appearance. Paul said, "Well, she sure doesn't want *my* information." His voice was woeful.

Being a mother who had buried a child and fought for help with the circumstances surrounding his death, Jennifer's heart ached for Sheri Farmer. She felt like she owed it to Sheri to do anything she could to assist her. Late one evening, she finally got Sheri on the phone and told her that she had gotten a letter in the mail and that it identified three suspects in the Girl Scout murders. Jennifer even gave Sheri the names of the three. After a pleasant conversation, Jennifer was satisfied that she had done the right thing. Now it was time to see what could be done, not only for the Farmers, but the Milner and Gusé families, as well.

Jennifer and Faith began reading the two-thousand pages of newly-accessed transcripts from Hart's preliminary hearing. They wanted to understand the evidence that had gotten Hart bound over for trial. The pair pored over every word of sworn testimony and began to take copious amounts of detailed notes. Jennifer was confused by the differing accounts of the wiped-or-not-wiped-up footprints on the floor of the murder tent. Faith's attention was drawn to the print of the jungle boot that seemed to be showing up everywhere. That was the beginning of them getting their feet wet in the complex story.

On April 29, 2021, as promised, Faith once again loaded her school kids onto a bus, and they went to interview Paul about the case: they even brought him ice cream for a belated 98th birthday treat, which he relished. Incredibly, Paul got another present: A Cold Case Unit (CCU) from Tulsa showed up to hear what Paul knew about the murders. It was a dream come true: people with badges were finally listening to him with an open mind. By the end of the day, the CCU found themselves drawn in by Paul and his story.

Two weeks later, on the morning of May 11, 2021, a meeting was held in the conference room of Paul's apartment complex in Bristow. Four individuals from the CCU came to see Paul, and Paul got Jennifer to drive down from Kansas City to be there, as well. Jennifer passed off information from her investigation a decade earlier and pointed out the sad reality that many of the primaries in Paul's original investigation were now dead: only two of Paul's suspects, Bull and Flea, remained alive. They also went over the death bed letter Jennifer had received. The CCU said they could not promise any results, but they were willing to do some follow-up investigation. They handed Jennifer and Paul their business cards as they left, with instructions to call anytime.

That same afternoon, after the CCU was gone and Paul and Jennifer had done lunch together (Ensure for Paul, vending machine snacks for Jennifer), Bo and Sheri Farmer, at Jennifer's invitation, showed up with one of Lori's now-grown sisters to discuss the case. They all crouched together in Paul's small living room to go over everything again. The new aspects that had been introduced into the case since Paul's visits to the Farmers back in the days when he was sheriff were: some inconclusive DNA tests and the letter Jennifer now held in her hands. Sheri made notes and did most of the talking for her family. Jennifer could tell she was a sharp lady. The Farmers hugged Paul as they were leaving, thanking him for all his years of caring, and Bo Farmer told Paul they loved him. Once again, Paul felt that, even though their emotions for him were real, they were still skeptical of his information. Jennifer was more hopeful: she expected the Farmers might become powerful allies.

Faith and Jennifer became a forceful team. They both began researching every detail or thought that came into their heads about the case and bouncing ideas off of each other. They even created a separate document for each item of evidence to see where all it appeared. And Jennifer began to notice a pattern in the preliminary hearing testimony. Any time the defense attorney, Garvin Isaacs, questioned a witness that could have been in the position to plant evidence (the first on any given scene, etc.) he would ask them if they knew members of Gene Leroy Hart's family. Isaacs named the siblings one by one. Answers varied, but nothing telling was squeezed out of anyone. *Gene Leroy Hart had told his lawyer that only someone within his own family circle would have had access to the evidence that had gotten him charged*, Jennifer concluded.

Jennifer, who had spent fifteen years as a computer programmer, began to develop an algorithm that would deposit each piece of evidence to its final location of discovery. She attempted to thread in Paul's theory that Sheriff Pete Weaver had planted everything that had been discovered beyond the immediate death scene.

On June 4, 2021, something astounding happened. Faith went to the Mayes County Courthouse in Pryor to look at old property records at the behest of the CCU. The CCU was hoping to be able to search for the Super Bee and wanted to pinpoint the location of the now-demolished house where Flea had lived in 1977. This would give them a starting point for their search and narrow down the area of the river where the car most likely would have been dumped. While at the Courthouse, Faith stumbled upon a bombshell. Comparing records, she determined that the squirrel hunters, Johnny Colvin and WR Thompson, who had uncannily discovered the evidence that had tied Hart to Cave Number 1, were directly related to Paul's suspect, Flea. Johnny Colvin was married to Flea's sister, Patricia. Jennifer immediately called Paul with the news. This brought a whole new dimension to the case.

Jennifer made it a habit to call Paul every single day (sometimes multiple calls in a single day) to report anything new . . . or even if *nothing* was new. On Thursday, June 10, 2021, she called him about a problem with his theory of Sheriff Weaver planting all the evidence against Hart. The show-stopper was a roll of masking tape that would not fit into her algorithm. The masking tape had appeared in three places: 1) around the lens of the flashlight found with the bodies 2) torn into small pieces lying with scraps of the green trash bag near the fence, 200 yards from the Kiowa staff tent and 3) at Cave Number 1. Jennifer pointed out that Pete could not have been in possession of the masking tape at the time it was applied to the flashlight, unless Pete had personally applied it himself, and that was too big of a stretch for Jennifer. Paul could not come up with an explanation. Jennifer contacted Mike Wheat, who had taken the original crime scene photos, and he assured her that the flashlight was already with the bodies when he had arrived. Pete could not have possibly slipped in something so obvious next to the sleeping bags with the Girl Scout staff hovering around, so Jennifer knew she had to go back to the drawing board.

On June 11, 2021, Jennifer texted Faith the first algorithm that would actually work: there were two separate crimes at the camp that night. By Monday afternoon, Jennifer felt sure enough that she was on to something that she dug out the business card of one of the CCU team members, Rick Lawrence, and used it for the very first time. She dialed the number and urged Lawrence, "Hear me out." He sat quietly and listened.

Jennifer laid out her theory:

Gene Leroy Hart may have been there and robbed the counselors, but he left and went home well before the girls were killed around 4 a.m. Paul's suspects, Bull, Buddy and Flea (who Jennifer had begun to refer to as "the three amigos") had somehow gotten access to Hart's 'dimmed' flashlight, as well as the duct tape and rope that Hart had most likely stolen from Jack Shroff's house before going to the camp. This is where Hart's half-brother came in. Michael had seen the half-brother with Flea and Buddy that night "about 2 or 3 a.m.," and Jennifer believed Hart's half-brother had taken the items from Hart after Hart had fallen asleep. The roll of masking tape was the key. It had been taken near the scene, was used to dim the flashlight, then had somehow made it to Cave Number 1. If Hart had committed the murders, why would he have left his flashlight and the rope and duct tape from his Shroff robbery there, but not the masking tape? What was so special about the masking tape? And where was it while he was committing his brutal acts? In his pocket? Jennifer had gone to Lowe's Home Improvement with her husband, Larry, and had Larry try to fit a roll of masking tape into one of his jeans pockets . . . it was too big, even with the size it would be with most of the tape rolled off. If a bloodied Hart had picked up the masking tape afterwards, from the area where he had used it to dim the flashlight, why was it in pristine condition when it arrived at the cave? No blood had been found on it: if it had, that would have sealed the deal for the jury.

When Jennifer finished speaking, she was unsure if Lawrence believed a thing she had said, but then she found out that he repeated it to Faith in a text the following day (Tuesday). That validated to Jennifer that her theory seemed plausible to experienced investigators, but, for the first time, Jennifer held something back from Paul. She had just introduced a fourth suspect into the crime, and she was unsure how to break it to him.

On Saturday, June 19, 2021, Jennifer made her usual daily call to Paul. This time she caught him at the ER, saying that he thought he had suffered a mild stroke because of a sudden onset of weakness in his left side. Also, his feeding tube had popped out of his stomach, and the doctor re-inserting it (with no anesthesia) had caused excruciating pain. They were going to keep him overnight to watch him. Jennifer began praying and also notified Faith and Mark to pray, as well.

The next day, Sunday, June 20, 2021, Paul sounded great, but they had decided to keep him for at least another night, he said. Paul lived alone, and the medical personnel wanted to make sure he was ready to go back to his apartment and take care of himself. However, things did not go well. By Thursday, June 24, 2021, he started sounding breathless and weak on the phone. Jennifer began praying harder. On Friday night, June 25, 2021, she was awakened from a dead sleep with a voice in her head saying, "Go get that briefcase." She had no idea what it meant, but it felt urgent. The following morning, Saturday, June 26, 2021, Jennifer called Paul to tell him she was coming to him: he seemed grateful. She sensed that it was taking every bit of his energy just to speak to her. She packed a bag and drove to St. John's Medical Center in Tulsa. She arrived at 4 p.m. and found an extremely sick Paul in Room 949. He seemed very relieved that she was there.

On Sunday, June 27, 2021, Paul's blood pressure dropped to 80/40. The nurses responded by pushing lots of IV fluids into Paul's veins. While it brought Paul's blood pressure back into normal range, by the middle of the night it had caused him to retain fluid to the point that he could not get his breath. Jennifer had been forced to leave at 9 p.m. when visiting hours ended. "It was scary," he told her when she arrived back the next morning. All fluids had been discontinued by doctor's order, both IV fluids and the liquid nutrition that was attached to his feeding tube.

Paul was weak and slept much of the time now. Jennifer sat quietly in the corner of his room, reading *Someone Cry for the Children*, written by OSBI Agents Mike and Dick Wilkerson.

Paul had always told Jennifer not to waste her time reading that book, because it was filled with inaccuracies (Paul had used a stronger word). Regardless, Jennifer had decided to familiarize herself with the Wilkerson brothers' account of the crime. While the book was 100% intended to convince the public that the right man had been charged when Hart was indicted (which Jennifer did not believe), she still picked up some nuggets that bolstered her theory.

WR Thompson and Johnny Colvin, the squirrel hunters, were driving a *pickup* the day they lured law enforcement to Cave Number 1. Buddy's confession had included a pickup truck being used to push the Super Bee into the river. *Could it be the same pickup? If* it was Colvin's pickup that had pushed the Super Bee into the river,

Colvin was already involved in a cover up before he led the highway patrolmen to Cave Number 1.

Another thing that sent Jennifer's mind into overdrive was a story of how the OSBI's informant had come into the knowledge of where Hart was being hidden out. Medicine Man Smith would not have been going around the ceremonial fire telling every 'Tom, Dick and Harry' standing there that Hart was okay. *Oh my goodness, Smith was trying to reassure Hart's much-younger half-brother, who he assumed might be worried about his big brother*, Jennifer reasoned. She was thoroughly convinced that the letter she had received in the mail had provided accurate information: the writer had mistaken *no one*. The half-brother of Gene Leroy Hart *was* involved, she thought.

Anytime Paul was up to it, Jennifer ran things past him that she had come across while turning pages. When hospital personnel would come in to check on things, Jennifer would tell them, "We're solving a murder case in here." It always brought a chuckle from Paul, and the nurses began to love it. They began to understand *who* they were taking care of . . . not just your typical 98-year-old patient.

On Monday, June 28, 2021, Paul was weaker than ever. He was scheduled to go to a rehabilitation center at 3 p.m. to try and rebuild his strength. Ten minutes before the transport arrived, he passed a greenish-black tarry stool that indicated he was bleeding somewhere in his upper intestinal tract. His hemoglobin was checked, and it was half of what would have been the lower end of a normal reading. Rehab was canceled, and a blood transfusion was ordered. Due to collapsed veins, it took three different nurses several different tries to get an IV into Paul's arm to deliver the blood. He became so weary of them digging around in his arms and finally his feet, he was ready to just give up and tell them to stop. But, during the night, after

Jennifer had been kicked out, they finally were successful on the eighth try.

Paul's health continued to decline, and, by Tuesday morning, June 29, 2021, he told Jennifer he wanted her to take him home. He wanted to sit in his own recliner in his own apartment. By now, he had pneumonia, was bleeding internally, his kidneys and liver were failing, and he was gasping for breath most of the time. He was, in a word, dying. Jennifer went into the bathroom and cried. Her own father had died in late June many summers before, and Paul had become like a father to her.

Paul whispered to Jennifer to get his special friend and 'business manager,' Lois, back in Bristow, on the phone. He requested that Lois meet Jennifer at his apartment at 2:30 that afternoon and get his briefcase, that he was turning the case over to her, that she would have to finish it. Despite the voice she had heard in her head the previous Friday night, Jennifer had not made any mention of the briefcase to Paul. Until now, she had been sure that Paul would live to see the case solved.

When Jennifer picked up the briefcase, she was instructed by Faith (ever the lawyer) to make copies of everything in it, because she feared the CCU would come and take it, and Jennifer might not ever get it back. This gave Jennifer a thought: while in Bristow, she would ask librarian Donna Lawrence to make the copies at the Bristow Library, where Donna had first introduced Jennifer to Paul. Donna had been rehired by the library on a temporary, fill-in assignment after having taken several years off. She was thrilled that she just happened to be back in place and available to make the copies. While she and Jennifer were meticulously pulling out every item from the briefcase, they noticed two mini-cassette tape cases tucked into an inner pocket. One of the cases was empty, but the other had a cassette in it. Jennifer stuck the tape in her purse, excited to find out what might be on it. She texted Faith, and Faith was equally curious.

When Jennifer returned back to the hospital with the briefcase, Paul was barely able to talk, but he said one of the sweetest things he would ever say to Jennifer: "You are a comfort to me." Jennifer sat on the side of Paul's bed, held his hand and spoke to him about what was about to transpire. "Paul, I know if Jesus shows up in this room, you are going to want to go with Him. And I know you will be so happy to see your mama and daddy." Paul's blue eyes twinkled like they always did when he had a surge of love come over him. Jennifer sang a song that she had written years before that was sung at her own mother's funeral. "Sail me, sail me, sail me on home . . ."

Then Jennifer said, "You tell those little girls that there are two ladies who will not stop until they have justice for them." At that, Paul seemed to gain a new determination to stay, to make sure he had done everything he could personally do to make justice happen. Jennifer felt reassured.

Remarkably, a gastroenterologist (GI doctor) came in and told Paul he wanted to put him 'out' the following morning and run a scope into his esophagus: the doctor thought that was most likely where the blood was coming from. Paul's medical team had not given up on him!

That same night, Bo and Sheri Farmer came to see Paul. He was too weak to say much to them, but he was touched by their visit. Within minutes of the Farmers leaving, Faith and Mark came up, and Mark had everyone hold hands while he prayed a simple, child-like prayer over Paul: Mark did the same again before he and Faith left. Mark had just been through a quadruple-bypass heart surgery less than a week before, and he was a walking miracle himself. He believed that Paul could beat all the enemies that had attacked him. Mark felt the Holy Spirit at the elevator and was almost overcome with joy. He told Faith that he *knew* that Paul was not going anywhere—not yet. Mark practically danced the rest of the way through the hospital and parking garage.

Paul went down for the esophageal scope before Jennifer arrived at the hospital on Wednesday morning, June 30, 2021. The first time she laid eyes on him Wednesday was when he came back to his room following the procedure around 1:30 p.m. Paul was breathing quietly, his color was good, he was fully alert, and he looked like a changed man.

"How you doing, Paul?" Jennifer asked.

"You know, I feel pretty good." Paul's tone was that of pleasant surprise. Jennifer could not help but notice the new strength in his voice.

In a little while, the GI doctor came in and said that the bleeding had "somehow resolved itself" and that Paul's pneumonia was completely and suddenly gone. His collapsed veins that had been nearly impossible to insert a needle into on Monday night were now, on Wednesday, suddenly plump and easy to find. Bloodwork was taken and sent to the lab to get a new read on kidney and liver functions. Paul was himself again. He turned the television on to watch the evening news for the first time since Jennifer had been there.

On Thursday morning, July 1, 2021, a team of kidney doctors came by and said that Paul's kidneys had somehow begun functioning again the day before (on Wednesday). By order of the GI doctor, Paul was taken down to Nuclear Medicine to do a lengthy, specialized test to observe his liver and gallbladder in action. Not long after he was returned back to his room, the GI doctor came in and said everything was great, and there was no treatment of any kind needed. Paul's liver and gallbladder were functioning perfectly. Paul was told he would be released to rehab the following day for a month of strength-building exercises. Jennifer went into the bathroom and cried again, this time happy tears.

Paul was in a good mood and talkative that evening. Paul was always full of stories, one of Jennifer's favorite things about him.

Paul told her about the one and only time in his life he believed he had seen an angel. Some of Paul's family had headed through the desert between Tuscon, Arizona, and El Paso, TX. Miles and miles from anything but sand, their Buick had sputtered and stopped: it was out of fuel. Rev. Smith laid his head on the steering wheel and began to pray. Paul's brother, Don, got out and pulled a plug out of the gas tank and drained it into a little jar provided by their mom. Don took the gasoline to the front of the car and poured it into the vacuum hose, which, in those days, worked the fuel system. Rev. Smith re-started the car, and, just as they headed back out, they went over a hill, and there sat a little shack with a gas pump in front of it. Nothing else was around . . . no cars, no horses, nothing. After filling the car up, they went in to pay. Paul never forgot the glow on the man's face as he took their money. Paul spent the remainder of his life believing the shack had only been there for them and did not exist for anyone else . . . another story Paul could never tell without crying.

Paul remembered to Jennifer some things from his days as sheriff.

A prisoner's belongings were always put in a brown paper sack when they were booked, and their name was written on the sack. The sack was then put into a safe that was similar to a bank vault. The safe was twelve to fifteen feet long and ten to twelve feet wide. The door was six inches thick, was secured with a combination lock and was directly across the hall from Paul's office door. There was no way, Paul asserted, that Gene Hart could have taken any of his belongings with him when he escaped from the jail.

Paul had to fire one of his dispatchers for giving her drug-selling son a heads up about planned raids, and he once arrested a man who had contributed to his election campaign, because he found out the guy was molesting a child (the molester's wife actually got angry at Paul). There was no screen on one of the jail windows, and a bug got in and bit one of the inmates: the guy sued Paul over it. Paul was required to provide 1600 calories per day for inactive inmates, 1800 calories for active ones. They got either milk or Tang to drink. His cook, Floyd (yes, the same Floyd who had sired Buddy), was quite the chef. Paul would give Floyd cash to go up the street to the grocery store and buy ingredients. One such day, Tulsa DA Jack Graves happened to be in town and caught Floyd at the store. Graves grabbed the cook by the arm and marched him back to the jail, where Graves, in a fit of rage, ordered Paul to remove Floyd's trusty status. There went Paul's cook, just like that. Jennifer could swear she was hearing Andy Griffith whistling again. She was bent over double, almost in tears by now. It felt so good to be laughing with Paul again . . . but the mood was about to turn somber.

Just before visiting hours were to expire that same Thursday night, Jennifer once again sat on Paul's bed next to him and related to him the algorithm she had come up with. She told him she believed he had a fourth man in the ring of murderers. She shared with him that it was also now the working theory of the CCU. Paul was quiet. Jennifer knew he was having trouble wrapping his mind around it and needed some time to process it all. When she left that evening, she left his briefcase with him, but she took the mini-cassette that she and Donna had found (with his blessing). She knew that she would not see Paul for at least a month, because the rehab center had strict COVID-19 restrictions. She would be heading back home to Kansas City early the next morning.

Jennifer went to Faith's house to spend the night. She awoke to a smiling Faith, who had begun listening to the mini-cassette. The tape was in a very fragile condition, and, afraid it might break, she had stopped it. Faith had heard just enough, though, to recognize it was Paul's voice, in addition to another male voice. Jennifer and Faith were jubilant at the thought that it might possibly be Baby Joe or Buddy from the day Paul had gone to Stringtown Prison.

On Friday, July 2, 2021, as Jennifer and Faith were making plans to send the cassette off to have it digitally restored, a much-improved Paul was being loaded onto a transport van for his move to Arbor Village in Sapulpa, Oklahoma, to rebuild his strength. He would need it. God had healed Paul for a reason.

CHAPTER 14

IF TOMORROW NEVER COMES

Jennifer gave Paul a couple of days to settle into Arbor Village, then she rang him up on Sunday, July 4, 2021, to check on him. He sounded okay, but was bored and lonely. No one was coming into his room because of the COVID-19 protocol. Due to the holiday, he had not been able to begin rehab yet, either, but he would be starting the next day, Monday, July 5, 2021.

When Jennifer called back late the next day to see how the first day of rehab had gone, Paul said they had tried to "kill" him. Paul had not walked in years, and a male therapist had gotten on Paul's last nerve when he had shouted at him to "stand up!" Jennifer could tell the former Sheriff of Mayes County was in a bad way. It went no better on the second day of rehab, nor the third.

It was then that Jennifer got word through Paul's special friend, Lois, that Paul had no desire to talk about the Girl Scout case. He said it had blown his mind up, and he could not take it anymore. Jennifer was devastated: she felt like it was her fault. Had her introduction of the half-brother into her theory of the crime upset Paul? Jennifer reached out to Faith about her heartache. Mark, who had become close to Paul, went to see him to make sure he was all right. No mention was made of the case.

Jennifer determined to continue on, even if it meant without Paul. Paul had told her, during their stay in the hospital together, that someone should get in touch with Donald Trammell's surviving family and friends. Paul suspected that Donald probably would have told someone what Janice had intended to tell Paul the day the OSBI had kidnapped them from the toll gate. After quite a lot of research, Jennifer was able to locate Donald's widow and stepson. Through his widow, she was able to find two of Donald's siblings—one brother and one sister. The brother had never been close to his siblings and thought they were all deceased, but the sister talked at length about Donald. She said he had issues and hurts in life, but would have never gone to the police about the murders if he had not fully believed he knew something helpful in solving the case. Donald was not the type to make things up. Donald's widow also connected Jennifer to a dear friend of his. The friend said Donald was an unbelievably talented wood carver and worked in his shop to keep his mind off things, which he bottled up. Donald apparently had never confided to anyone about Janice or the murders. It was a strike-out.

Faith had found a company to restore the mini-cassette. Even though it came back with a lot of friction noise, Jennifer and Faith could easily recognize the conversations were between Paul and the Trammell men. No Baby Joe or Buddy. Still, the walk back in time to the edge of a fishing hole was enchanting. It backed up Paul's story in a tangible way.

By the end of July 2021, Jennifer was hoping that Paul was missing her as badly as she was missing him. With Faith's encouragement, Jennifer called Paul just to say hello, and he immediately began talking to her about the case. It was clear he was not done with it. Paul was back! He was in a bit of a quandary, though. The Veterans Administration (VA) had only approved one month of rehab for him, and, though he was much stronger, the therapists did not believe, with all of his issues, he needed to live alone anymore. Paul had limited financial resources, so he took an offer to move over to the "nursing home" wing of Arbor Village and let them bill the government under "hospice care." Paul assured Jennifer that "they will still provide me the same care as everyone else in the nursing home," but the hospice angle would mean Paul would not be charged for anything.

Jennifer felt a bit of angst about the situation, because she knew that Paul was on the blood thinner Eliquis, due to a heart condition known as A-fib. Jennifer had gone through hospice with her own mother and had learned that they discontinue any life-prolonging medications. When Jennifer's mother had been taken off of her blood thinner after a fall, her A-fib had caused her to get blood clots, which were what had landed her in hospice in the first place. Hospice had merely let nature take its course, and the blood clots eventually took Jennifer's mother from her. But the hospice route seemed like the only option Paul felt he could afford, so Jennifer tried to stay positive. After all, there was none of his family still around who could live with him, and he did not have funds to hire a full-time nurse.

On August 24, 2021, Faith took her 'proof of vaccine' papers and a nice video camera, and, with special permission from the Arbor Village administrator, recorded a luminous Paul telling his story. He had been transformed by the difficult rehab routine (like the old saying goes, "What doesn't *kill* us makes us stronger"). Paul sat up straight, crossed his right foot over his left knee, adjusted his

WORLD WAR II VETERAN-embossed cap and, coming across like a sixty-year-old, told his story to what he hoped would be the world. NOTE: Faith was sure she was about to get a contract to produce a documentary about the Girl Scout case with the same production company who had adapted her book *Now I Lay Me Down* for the Oxygen Network. (That episode, under the name *Killer Secrets*, was later aired on Oxygen February 27, 2022).

Paul slept well that night, knowing that his decades-long agony was finally being taken onto the shoulders of two women who would never drop it. Jennifer refrained from calling Paul every day. Even though he had always vigorously thanked her for taking the time to keep him informed, she felt like maybe she had overwhelmed him. She could not bear the thought of him withdrawing from talking about the case again, so she tried to limit her calls to no more than once a week.

On September 2, 2021, Faith excitedly told Jennifer that she had found a 501c3 non-profit in Illinois that did underwater recovery for *free*, using high-tech "side image sonar ." They were called Team Watters and enjoyed a high rate of success in locating drowning victims, sunken automobiles and the like. They had worked with many police agencies across the country and were familiar with the area where the Super Bee might be. He told Faith that, after forty-four years, it was unlikely the car would come up in one piece, so divers would have to be sent down to identify it and do any looking they wanted to do before bringing it out of the water. Since the CCU had next to no budget, Faith was eager to pass along the phone number of Team Watters. This would hopefully be a boon to the CCU. Faith, Jennifer and Paul all crossed their fingers.

On Sunday night, Sept. 5, 2021, Paul, proudly wearing his WWII cap, sat in his wheelchair and threw out the final pitch for a Tulsa Drillers minor-league baseball game at ONEOK Field. It was followed by a fireworks display in his honor. Paul was tickled pink and smiling from ear to ear. It was The Drillers's way of recognizing Paul as their "Hometown Hero." It made the news, which touted Paul's twenty-five months with the Army and his fifteen years with the Tulsa Police Department. "I am just an old soldier who loves my country," Paul told them.

The old soldier was enjoying life. He had even confessed to Jennifer, "This Arbor Village place has given me a whole new perspective on nursing homes. I have great care and company, and the place doesn't smell like pee!" Jennifer giggled at that.

Then . . . two weeks later, on September 21, 2021, Jennifer received a message from Paul's niece, Jo Ann, who lived in Arizona. Jo Ann, as executor of Paul's estate, had been informed by Paul's caregivers that her uncle was not doing well physically, and he was telling everyone that he was "ready to go." Jennifer immediately called Paul's cell. Lois answered and put the phone to Paul's ear.

"Paul, it's Jennifer. How are you?"

"I may live through this day and I may not," he said. His voice was filled with a special kind of tired.

He tried to explain to Jennifer that he had no idea what was going on with his health exactly, but he was unable to finish his thought: his breath gave out. Lois took the phone back and told Jennifer she would keep her informed. Jennifer had a sinking feeling she knew *exactly* what was going on with Paul's health: a blood clot had most likely hit his lung. He was needing his Eliquis. Jennifer also knew Paul was not going to get it.

On the afternoon of Wednesday, September 22, 2021, Paul told Lois, "I would love to have some ice cream." Paul had not consumed anything by mouth in days: he had just had the usual Ensure poured through his feeding tube. But the nurses rummaged around and found Paul a fudgesicle. Paul attacked the frozen treat with a passion and said, "If I was to die right now, I'd die happy." When he was finished, he had melted chocolate all over his face. Lois mirthfully cleaned him up.

That night, Paul spent the whole night looking at the ceiling and talking. His voice was so weakened that Lois could not understand what he was saying, but she knew he was being visited by relatives and was in a transition to the 'other side.' At times he would chuckle. He was happy.

Paul left this world on Thursday, September 23, 2021, from Arbor Village in Sapulpa, Oklahoma. His funeral was scheduled for exactly one week later, September 30, 2021. As Jennifer drove from Kansas City to Bristow for his funeral, the Oklahoma sky cried again, just like it had the night before the girls were murdered. How symbolic, Jennifer thought. Thunder boomed and lightning flashed above Jennifer's car. She knew the spirit of Paul Dean Smith had gotten to where it was intended to go.

The funeral service was simple. Paul's nephew-by-marriage read the obituary, followed by several of Paul's own writings. Jennifer looked down into Paul's face and cried like the proverbial baby. She had witnessed courage and unfailing faith that was beyond human description. Paul had taught her to never give up. It was that simple. And she knew she would not. She could not. She was more determined than ever to get justice for Lori, Denise and Michelle.

There was none of the fanfare that Jennifer and Faith felt Paul deserved, but Paul had left the world on his own terms, and he was the Dragon Slayer until the very end. He requested no one follow his steel bluish-gray casket to the cemetery. And no one did. Several mentioned that Paul could not have known what a horrible rainfall would be coming down that day. Who knows if it had even been forecast? Perhaps the sky just could not help but weep when the most honest sheriff who had ever lived was put into the ground alone. But actually, Paul was not alone at all. He was now with Lori, Denise and Michelle.

"We will finish it together," Faith told Jennifer. Jennifer's love for Faith soared that day. They were bonded together by a Force that was bigger than either of them.

Unfortunately, Paul's briefcase had been given to someone else the day he had died. Jennifer was ever so grateful that Faith had advised her to make copies of everything. Not only had Jennifer and librarian Donna discovered the mini-cassette, but Paul's life was contained in that bulging black-leather attaché, the sides of which were supported by silver duct tape. It was not lost on Jennifer that, had Paul not almost died at the end of June, she would have never heard the conversation on the mini-cassette . . . that is why she had been awakened by the voice in her head saying, "Go get that briefcase." This gave her goosebumps. The good kind.

Jennifer knew beyond a shadow of a doubt that *Shattered Justice,* with a red cover and the title in big, white, cracked block letters would soon be introduced to the world (she had already been working on it). This would cause things to get *really* interesting.

CHAPTER 15

INTO THE LION'S DEN

On Monday, October 18, 2021, the mother of little Lori Farmer let Jennifer know that she was not happy about Jennifer progressing forward with a book featuring Paul's story. As a matter of fact, Sheri Farmer was downright upset. In no uncertain terms, she demanded that Jennifer tell everything she knew to Mike Reed, the current sheriff of Mayes County. Jennifer let Sheri know that Paul had given all of his information to Sheriff Reed many years earlier (in 2013) through his special deputy, Dean Majors, and Paul had not received so much as a phone call in return.

Jennifer was hesitant to go to Sheriff Reed now, because she had made every effort not to step on the toes of anything the CCU was doing. The CCU was the first law enforcement entity that had ever shown any interest in fully investigating Paul's leads, and it had meant everything to Paul. But, with Sheri agitated and concerned that Jennifer only cared about getting glory for herself and not the truth, Jennifer agreed to tell the current sheriff everything she believed about the case. Sheri promised she would have Mike Reed call Jennifer.

On the evening of Wednesday, October 20, 2021, Jennifer was on her way to cashier an auction when she answered her cell to Sheriff Reed's devil-may-care attitude. He said, "I heard you are wanting to talk to me."

"No, not really, but Sheri Farmer has asked me to, and I am willing." Jennifer did her best to be polite.

During their conversation, Jennifer sensed a defensiveness in Sheriff Reed's voice. It was the kind of tone that says, "I don't like you." Jennifer did not have time right then to go into everything she knew, but she advised the Sheriff that, if she were in his position, she would have the Ace bandage and terry cloth gag run through an M-Vac machine. The M-Vac is a brand-new technology that can extract DNA from cloth and has already been used in solving many ice-cold cases, she explained. Sheriff Reed did not sound as though he had heard of the M-Vac.

The sheriff let Jennifer in on the fact that he gets calls all the time from people claiming to know who killed the Girl Scouts, and he has to tell them they are wrong. He said a lady had angrily argued with him for an hour not long before that, and he had set her straight. He even went as far as to tell Jennifer that Garvin Isaacs had brought him a DNA expert from California to check the DNA against someone that Isaacs was *sure* was the real killer. Reed had told Isaacs that, even though he knew Isaacs was wrong, they would check it. When the DNA was not a match, Isaacs had gone away with his head hung in defeat. Reed had told Isaacs, "See, I told you."

Even though Sheriff Reed had made it explicit to Jennifer that she had no information that would be of value to him, he told her that he would clear his calendar for Friday, October 22, 2021 (two days later), and Jennifer agreed to be at his office at 10 a.m.

At 6 a.m. that Friday morning, as Jennifer left Kansas City for the four-hour trip to Pryor, she punched in a text message to Faith, asking that Faith and Mark pray for her. Jennifer felt as though she was going into the lion's den. As Jennifer closed in on Green Country, Faith agreed to meet her at Sheriff Reed's office to personally give him the news that Faith's production company would test anything Reed wanted for *free* at Othram Laboratory in Houston, TX. Othram is a world-renowned laboratory that is credited with solving cold cases by retrieving DNA from the oldest, most degraded samples in history. Othram's website displays the following: "JUSTICE THROUGH GENOMICS - Othram's scientists are experts at recovery, enrichment and analysis of human DNA from trace quantities of degraded or contaminated forensic evidence. We enable human identification even when other approaches fail."

A young-looking-for-his-fifty-two-years Sheriff Mike Reed greeted Jennifer, Faith and Mark (who had accompanied Faith) right on time and showed them into his office at the end of a long hallway. The sheriff was housed in the grandiose setting of a newly-constructed Mayes County office complex. Jennifer could not help but think of the dilapidated structure where Paul had been required to work four decades earlier.

Faith broke the ice by letting Sheriff Reed know that she admired him for something he had said when he had first been elected—that he would work on the Girl Scout murders and would try to be 100% objective. Jennifer thought Reed sounded terribly ill-mannered when he replied to Faith, "I didn't say that, and I'm not looking for any fans."

Sheriff Reed pointed out that he had only been eight years old when the murders had taken place. He said the case was on his desk when he came into office [January 2013] and will be on his desk when he leaves, whether he solves it or not. The sheriff wanted to verify that no one was taping their conversation before he made an unflattering comment about a certain OSBI agent. Reed had questioned the competence of the OSBI's investigation when he had first become sheriff, he said.

Reed let his visitors know that he had been trained to read body language and always enjoyed meeting with people in person. Jennifer saw it as a subtle intimidation tactic.

Reed moved to talking about the horrendous nature of the crime. Faith and Jennifer assured him that their only motive was to try and get justice for the little girls. "Justice is hogwash, there is no justice," Reed said. The women were stupefied that the sheriff had such a cynical view of the American legal system.

"It was overkill," the sheriff went on. Reed said he would not allow his own employees to see the photos of what was done to the girls. It was the worst thing he had ever seen, and "it doesn't bother me to wipe brains off of my boots." He said he had just held Michelle's sleeping bag in his hands on Wednesday (only two days earlier), and his countenance now betrayed that it had newly bothered him.

Sheriff Reed launched into a monologue differentiating various levels of rape. In essence, there is the drunk girl at a rock concert scantily clad, then there is the girl in a bikini in her yard (and a person might be able to understand in either of those situations) . . . but raping an eight-year-old girl? It is so beyond the pale. Other men, even men who would rape an adult woman, will not stand around and allow that to happen. "That's another kind of animal," Reed was adamant.

Jennifer pointed out that Hart had pled guilty to the rape of an *adult*, which had entailed going to an *adult* venue to find his victim: this indicated that Hart was not a pedophile, not "another kind of animal." That was only because Hart had assumed the Girl Scouts were adults until it had been too late, Sheriff Reed countered. *Wait a minute, Hart had been at the adult tent stealing glasses and purses: he knew exactly where the adult women were. He had even been just outside the fence making his weird noise and watching counselor Carla as she had pointed her flashlight right at him, had he not?* Jennifer was concerned by the county sheriff's lack of distinction between the two cases.

Faith explained that she and Jennifer had been providing their information to the CCU and had assumed that the CCU was going through the proper channels to coordinate with Sheriff Reed. Reed denied that the CCU had ever contacted him asking for permission to search for the car or to operate within Mayes County in any other capacity. "They are just private citizens, anyway," he said. "They have no jurisdiction over this case."

Faith reminded Reed that Sheriff Paul Smith had had three suspects, one of whom had confessed details to Paul that only the killer(s) would know. She also told Reed that the squirrel hunters who had found the evidence at Cave Number 1 were directly related to one of Paul's suspects, Flea. Faith had talked to a witness who had observed Bull and Buddy at the airport leaving town. Sheriff Reed seemed aware of the two suspects having flown to California, but it meant nothing to him. "All three of these guys [Paul's suspects] have been checked out and passed polygraphs," Reed assured Faith. They may all be thugs and bad guys, but they did not kill the Girl Scouts. Jennifer knew better, because Paul had gotten good information that at least one of them (Bull) had refused to take a polygraph.

Faith stated her opinion that the river needed to be searched for Bull's Super Bee, since that was a key element in Buddy's confession. Sheriff Reed said Bull had told the OSBI who he had sold the car to, the OSBI had found that individual, and the guy had said the car had sat out beside his house for two years, and then he believed he had taken it to be crushed. The OSBI had all they needed to know: they had checked off that box. Crushing yard records were not needed, apparently. Jennifer found it strange that Bull had his car Sunday night, June 12, 1977, as seen by Paul, yet was walking without shoes and a shirt at daybreak the next morning. Surely whoever bought his car during the night would have given him a ride home.

Jennifer revealed to the sheriff that she had gotten a letter implicating Thurman, a half-brother of Gene Leroy Hart. When Thurman's name was mentioned, Sheriff Reed said, "Oh, yeah, we know Thurman." Faith had been warned early on by a local that Thurman had "powerful political connections." Reed said Thurman had been ruled out, because he had been known to be with a group of friends that night, who had provided him with a firm alibi. He did not say who the group of friends were. Jennifer wondered if what Faith had heard might, indeed, be accurate. Jennifer asked Reed if the DNA of Hart's siblings had ever been tested. "Every one of them," Reed said. Jennifer suspected the statement was untrue, but did not argue. Reed never asked to see the letter, nor did he ask who had mailed it to Jennifer. NOTE: Jennifer was able to verify later, through Hart's family members, that no DNA testing had been done on all of Hart's siblings.

Jennifer once again brought up the M-Vac, and Reed said he had checked and gotten information that the M-Vac was too unreliable, often yielding false results. So much for that. All the decades-old cases that are currently being solved through M-Vac technology (and being aired on *Investigation Discovery*) are apparently just an accident to Reed.

Faith had carried in a list of loose ends she felt needed to be tied up. Reed told her to (verbally) throw things out, he would respond and they could bounce the ball back and forth: the ball was in her court. Faith said she did not wish to bounce the ball back and forth, that she would simply leave her information with him. Faith had a lot on her plate, and she had already calculated this meeting to be a waste of time. But Reed talked Faith and Mark into staying there with Jennifer and him. He wanted to hear what they 'thought' they knew.

It was at this point, just a half hour into the meeting, that Reed said he needed to go to the restroom and refill his coffee cup, so they took what turned out to be at least a fifteen-minute break. Jennifer was surprised that Reed had not already gotten all that taken care of ahead of time: Jennifer certainly had. Jennifer wondered if Sheriff Reed was needing to make a phone call to notify someone or, perhaps, get guidance. During the break, Jennifer made use of the time by checking her email. She discovered a reply from a publisher regarding a query letter she had sent out the previous afternoon about publishing Paul's story. Jennifer was ecstatic: it was the only thing going her way so far on this particular morning.

When the four finally reconvened in his office, Sheriff Reed wanted to hear everything that Jennifer and Faith believed had happened the night of the murders. For Faith, it was more about the *who*.

Faith informed Sheriff Reed of the conversation Paul had recorded of the Trammell men talking openly about Flea's involvement in the killings. Reed said there was a simple explanation as to why Janice had told that story about her brother: Flea had wagged his penis at his sister Janice, the younger Trammell's wife, and, to get even, Janice had decided that she would report to the cops that her brother had helped murder the Girl Scouts. Reed said Janice was later given a polygraph that proved she had been lying about it. Sheriff Reed made no attempt to deny that the Trammells had been kidnapped at the toll gate, though.

Once again, Jennifer found the current sheriff of Mayes County to be a bit unbelievable. Paul and his deputy, Ted LaTurner, had been there the day that Janice had emerged from behind the door of the OSBI's office in Tulsa. The OSBI had scared her out of her wits (most likely by painting pictures of what it would be like for her mother to watch her brother be executed, Jennifer figured). Janice and Donald had left town: Janice had been done with talking. Jennifer was betting now that Janice had been just as closed-mouth to any potential polygraph technician.

Jennifer explained how she had looked at the crime from a computer programmer's standpoint and had developed an algorithm. Reed did not like the word "algorithm." He immediately let Jennifer know that he might not have a degree nor any formal education, but he had plenty of common sense. Jennifer told him she would try to refrain from her use of the word "algorithm," but she went into detail how the roll of masking tape found at Cave Number 1 had dispelled the rumors that Sheriff Weaver had planted the evidence found at Cave Number 1. She walked through the three appearances of the masking tape in the transcript of the preliminary hearing: 1) on the flashlight, 2) two-hunderd yards from the staff tent and, finally, at Cave Number 1.

Sheriff Reed contested the fact that any scraps of tape and plastic were found 200 yards from the staff tent, like the OSBI had testified to in court. He said he had seen pictures, and there may have been one little piece of plastic that was torn from the center of the plastic covering the flashlight (in spite of the fact the hole in the plastic covering of the flashlight had been described by witnesses as "pinpoint" in size). The sheriff insisted Hart had altered the flashlight at the cave and left the masking tape there, and that was the reason it was not bloody.

"How do you get from the camp back to the cave?" Reed asked, then awaited a reply, which did not come. "By way of the creek," he answered his own question. The creek water had washed the roll of masking tape clean, Reed opined. That is all there was to it. Sheriff Reed had just contradicted his own story of the masking tape having never been taken from the cave.

Jennifer gave the sheriff a theoretical timeline of the crime, and when she got to the end, he cleared his throat, shifted in his chair and said, "I can see where a person could let their imagination run wild and their thoughts trick them, but the simple truth is everything from the scene has been DNA tested, and there is no one there except Hart."

"What all has been tested?" Jennifer was only aware of three DNA tests that had been run, and she thought it had been on the girls' swabs, semen on a pillowcase and maybe a mitochondrial test on a hair. The OSBI had announced no conclusive findings in any of the tests. The media had reported that the first test results had been a 'partial match' to Hart: it had come back as having belonged to "1 in 7700 Native Americans," which really was not much of a revelation, since the crime had taken place smack-dab in the middle of the Cherokee Nation. The results of the second test were announced as "inconclusive," and the findings of the third test had remained strangely quiet. Jennifer questioned Reed about this: what was the deal with the third test? Reed explained that there were not enough markers to get a complete reading, so their lab had had to rule it "inconclusive." The lab would have lost their federal certification if they had ruled any other way, in light of their findings, he claimed.

Sheriff Reed leaned back and, with his left hand, fanned through a stack of hundreds of sheets of white paper on his side table, indicating that was how many items had been tested. Faith disclosed to Reed that her production company would run any further, more sophisticated tests that he needed, and it would be at no charge. He declined the generous offer. "I can only use certain labs," he told her. Othram was obviously not deemed good enough to be among them.

Jennifer voiced her surprise that they had been able to test so many items, because she had heard, due to too little funding, Sheriff Reed had had to personally raise $30,000 from private individuals to do the most recent DNA testing. His response was that they had gotten a new OSBI director since then and now had a huge budget. And guess what? Every one of those items that had been tested had pointed to Hart and Hart alone. There was no "unidentified" DNA from the scene, Reed announced more than once. He said he had personally tried to get just one more tiny bit of DNA out of the test tubes Janice Davis had collected from the autopsies, scraping the bottoms of them with the tip of a cotton swab, but, alas, there was nothing left to test.

"People's word means nothing to me," Reed said: he has to go on cold, hard evidence. Sheriff Reed and his special deputy, Dean Majors, along with the OSBI, had taken all their evidence to the National Center for Missing and Exploited Children, who had agreed with them: Gene Leroy Hart had done all of it by himself. *I am sure they would with Janice Davis's deformed sperm reports,* Jennifer facetiously imagined. *And I will bet NCMEC never heard Sheriff Paul Smith got a detailed confession out of one suspect and a tape of the family of a second suspect discussing where a getaway car was put into the river. And the chances that NCMEC was told a half-brother of Hart was in the picture were probably nil.* Jennifer's thoughts were interrupted by Sheriff Reed explaining how he had even been able to act out how one man could have done it. He re-enacted it again right there in his office. He stood up, and with a hammer-swinging hand motion, he said, "Boom [Lori], boom [Michelle]", then, reaching out like he was motioning to Denise to come to him, he interpreted that now he was telling Denise exactly what he wanted her to do, and he judged that she would have done anything he wanted because of fear, having seen what he had just done to the other two girls.

Jennifer noticed that Sheriff Reed had no explanation as to why Hart would have carried all three girls, two of them dead already, so far (398 feet, to be exact) to the back gate. Why would Hart have needed to take them close to the back gate? He had no car to load them into. And, if he was kidnapping Denise after killing the other two, why not just take Denise and leave the others in the tent? *Seems like a lot of extra work, especially for a guy who was night blind,* Jennifer thought.

Realizing that Sheriff Reed was acting as a spokesman for the OSBI, Jennifer asked about the first thing from Hart's preliminary hearing that had sent her into mental gymnastics: what about that smeared-or-not-smeared blood on the tent floor? Reed offered that the blood was smeared on the tent floor by the dragging of the girls in their sleeping bags across it. Jennifer silently searched her gray matter and was sure that she had seen in either the preliminary transcript or the Wilkerson book that the bodies were not dragged, that they had to have been carried. The 'official' opinion had been that the floor had been wiped using the missing mattress covers in more of a circular motion, which would not leave straight drag marks.

Buddy's confession that the girls had only been raped by instrument was disputed by Sheriff Reed. Reed could personally tell by looking at the autopsy pictures that the girls had been "raped with a penis." The Wilkerson book says the OSBI had doubts it was a penis at first because of the lacerations. *If penises caused lacerations, I doubt much sex would occur in the world,* Jennifer mused to herself. But who could argue with the indomitable sheriff of Mayes County?

The OSBI messed up stuff: lots of things might could have been done better, Reed admitted. For instance, the print of the jungle boot, which Faith had zeroed in on, was not really described correctly in court: there were no clear footprints. The "caves" were merely crevices in the rocks with overhangs, not a place someone could live: the OSBI had used misleading terminology to describe them. Jennifer wanted to discuss the testimony about the puzzling actions of the "wonder dogs," but Reed had no interest. He dismissed the dogs as "useless."

Sheriff Reed asked his guests if they had ever heard of "touch DNA."

"Yeah, we have actually heard a little about that." Jennifer was not sure that Reed picked up the sarcasm in her voice.

Reed made quite a big show of twice swiping his finger across his desk and stating, "Now I am *there*."

Jennifer, having gotten pretty steeped in statistics when getting her BA in Mathematics, found Reed's claims to carry impossible odds. The crime had occurred in 1977. The first DNA test had not been run until twelve years later, in 1989. How would all the DNA from the scene have been identified? Jennifer had been to church camp in her teens and remembered the thrill of getting to purchase new items to take along. *How would the OSBI have gone back and identified every stocker, cashier and sacker that had touched the items the girls had brought to camp?* Jennifer remained silent, but was inwardly shaking her head. She decided to introduce a new topic.

"I think your killer is probably your snitch," Jennifer told Sheriff Reed.

"*What* snitch?" Reed bolted forward in his chair. *Now there is some body language,* Jennifer calculated silently. She told him the Wilkerson brothers' book had talked extensively about their informant. Why would Reed not know about this person's existence?

Jennifer and Faith both got the feeling that Sheriff Reed was merely an OSBI stooge that had been given the 'company line' to regurgitate and was not up on the details for himself. He obviously fully believed what he was saying, though.

Sheriff Reed eventually got around to personal criticism of Paul.

"Let's say hypothetically there was a sheriff who got some bad information," Reed began. And then Reed went on about how Paul had spread his 'bad information.'

Sheriff Reed, while he was on hypotheticals, said he might could see another one of Hart's half-brothers, Millard, being there that night. "Would I be surprised if he was there that night? No, I wouldn't. He was a 'snapper head [annoying jerk].' But I can't put him there, because his DNA is not there." Reed said he had interviewed Millard, who had shown up with his attorney: Millard hated cops, hated authorities. To Faith, that was the one and only time Reed acknowledged that 'we still do not know or have the truth.'

The meeting ended with Faith being told by Sheriff Reed that she was welcome to search the river for the Super Bee. "It has been searched before: Lowrance [Machine & Fishing Electronics] came down here a few years ago and used their high-tech equipment and were unable to find anything. Actually, I think the river has been searched at least three times, but you are welcome to search again. Heck, you might find all kinds of Super Bees down there. It won't matter, because the DNA is all Hart's." Reed seemed satisfied that, if the Super Bee was in the river, Lowrance would have found it. But what he did not realize, is that Jennifer and her husband, Larry, had recently sat in a class at Bass Pro, sponsored by Lowrance, who was introducing new sonar fish-finding equipment that would make an angler's head spin. A fisherman could actually watch, in real-time, a fish nibble at his bait underneath his boat. The demonstration had been mind-blowing.

"What if I find the Super Bee that has the VIN number that matches Bull's Super Bee?" Faith asked.

Reed: "It will tell me that Bull has been lying to me about where his Super Bee ended up."

Faith: "Wouldn't that be a red flag to you if a suspect lied about something like that?"

Reed: "Nah, Bull lies to me all the time."

Reed's voice was playful. Jennifer was intrigued by the statement. *How much time does he spend with Bull? Does he arrest Bull* that often, or does he merely hang out with him? And what would the sheriff do if the murder weapons and mattress covers were discovered, still inside Bull's car? Would Reed even care? After all, nothing else mattered except that all the DNA from the scene matched Hart.

It was abundantly clear that Sheriff Reed just wanted his questioners to go away. He had done everything he could do to discourage them.

Faith, in her capacity as an attorney, told Jennifer as soon as they got outside, "We need to create a shared document and dictate every word he told us to the best of our memory between the three of us."

Faith was conspicuously followed home after the contentious meeting with Sheriff Reed, by a marked Mayes County sheriff's car. Had Reed put Dean Majors on standby with a phone call during their fifteen-minute break? Jennifer was suspicious. If this was the way people were being treated who came forward with information, Sheri Farmer was on the television stations asking for help in vain.

Jennifer texted Faith as she pointed her car back to Kansas City: "This is all so troubling to me. Why don't I feel peace? Something in my gut just can't settle all of what I've heard today. Why do I still want to search for that car so bad?" Faith comforted Jennifer with a vow that they *would* search for the Super Bee.

If the CCU was nothing more than a group of "private citizens," then Jennifer figured she was just as qualified, so she put the job of investigating the murders of three innocent Girl Scouts back on herself. The more she dug, the more she learned: and the more she learned, the more frustrated she became at the incompetence and arrogance demonstrated by law enforcement throughout the course of the case.

The OSBI and Sheriff Weaver could have demonstrated due diligence in the quest for truth during the summer of 1977. Justice could have been delivered for three innocent Girl Scouts and their families. Instead, they opted to scapegoat a man who had embarrassed the local white man's social order, who was doing his best to lay low and eke out an existence in the backwoods of the Cherokee Nation. Fortunately, for Hart, the jury saw through the ruse, the OSBI's subterfuge, and the sham prosecution. Unfortunately for the three little girls, the expectation of justice was shattered, and the current sheriff of Mayes County was still grinding the pieces.

The CCU was denied access to Mayes County by Sheriff Reed the following Tuesday, October 26, 2021: they were not welcome in his jurisdiction. But one of the CCU team, Rick Lawrence, had already interviewed the witness who had seen Bull and Buddy on the plane to Monterey . . . and Lawrence had already learned the name of Bull's cousin who had threatened the witness's life if he told what he had seen. Reed had not cared about that, of course. And he had spent a good deal of time arguing with the CCU that all suspects that had been named, including Thurman Buckskin, had all been cleared.

Jennifer knew *Shattered Justice* was going to now go well beyond Paul's original mis-treatment by the law enforcement community of Mayes County and the State of Oklahoma. She had an even bigger story to expose.

CHAPTER 16
READY OR NOT, HERE I COME!

Jennifer set about getting herself an interview with 'Squirrel Hunter Extraordinaire' WR Thompson. She figured *if* it had been WR's hunting buddy Johnny Colvin's pickup that had been used to push the Super Bee into the river, WR might be keeping some juicy secrets. Thompson was easy to find: he was in prison serving a life sentence for having his wife murdered. Thompson's wife was the sister of Johnny Colvin, who had been with Thompson the day the two of them had stumbled upon the Hart-incriminating evidence at Cave Number 1. Jennifer reached out to Thompson's case manager at the prison.

With COVID-19 protocols in place, in-person visitation had been tightened at the medium-security penitentiary. The first hurdle Jennifer had to clear was getting Thompson to put her on his personal visitors' list. The second hurdle would be passing a background check, so she could be wedged into the limited number of slots on the prison's visiting schedule. Jennifer began with the first hurdle: she wrote a letter to Thompson.

On Tuesday, November 30, 2021, Jennifer's phone rang. It was an incoming call from Oklahoma's Lexington Correctional Center.

To be specific, it was inmate WR Thompson on the line. Jennifer explained to Thompson that she was reaching out as an author who wanted to question him about his testimony in the Gene Leroy Hart trial. Thompson was cordial, almost friendly. He told Jennifer he knew stuff, but could not prove it. Jennifer told Thompson she knew stuff, too, and, if they both knew the same stuff, they would find a way to prove it.

Jennifer asked Thompson whose pickup he and Colvin were driving the day they went squirrel hunting and found the sack of flour at the cave. Thompson said it was his. Now Jennifer knew for certain who had owned the pickup. This left her wanting to know if it was *the* pickup that had pushed the Super Bee into the river.

Thompson said he would be happy for Jennifer to interview him in person, that he could tell her "everything that went down that night." She went into action to start clearing the second hurdle: she filled out the required paperwork for a background check and sent it off to the appropriate agency. Now she had to wait for her application to slowly drift through the sludge of governmental bureaucracy.

In the meantime, God was answering prayers. The doors were opening for Faith to go into film production. Faith let Jennifer know a "sizzle reel" for her Girl Scout documentary was finished and would now be shopped to HBO, Netflix, Fox Nation and other major streaming services. Jennifer met Faith at Old Chicago in Joplin, MO, December 9, 2021, to watch the sizzle reel. Jennifer was amazed by how professionally it was done. It was, however, bittersweet to see Paul's face in his final interview that he had granted to Faith at Arbor Village a month prior to his death.

Over lunch, Jennifer and Faith went back over everything they had learned since that fateful day back in April when Paul had suggested that the two of them get together.

Faith shared something with Jennifer that made Jennifer's skin crawl. Since the two of them had last seen each other, Faith had been contacted by Mayes County Special Deputy Dean Majors. Majors had invited Faith to meet him in an old, empty warehouse in Locust Grove. Majors had tried to convince Faith that she had no idea what she was talking about and had no business producing a 'Girl Scout Murders' documentary. Majors was equally as adamant as Sheriff Mike Reed had been that Thurman Buckskin could not possibly have helped kill the little girls. Majors had put the 'maybe Millard' story forth just like Sheriff Reed had. When Faith had disagreed with him about Thurman, Majors had taunted, "Well, Thurman will get a good laugh out of it when he hears he is being accused of murder." Talk about overt intimidation.

Faith had told him, "I am not accusing anyone of anything. I am just gathering facts."

Jennifer was floored. *Why would a sheriff's deputy go and clue in a suspect that he was being named by someone in a death-bed letter?* Something really strange was going on here. Once again, the warning that Faith had gotten about Thurman being "politically connected" came rushing back. Jennifer determined right then and there that she would look into Thurman's connection to Sheriff Reed and Deputy Majors. It seemed like those two were trying way too hard to protect him.

On the way home from meeting with Jennifer, Faith drove through the small town of Seneca, Missouri, and noticed a street sign that said "Thurman." She turned around and got a picture of the sign to send to Jennifer. As Faith was making a U-turn, she noticed she was on Cherokee Street. What a coincidence . . . a 'Jennifer moment' for sure. Jennifer was always hyper-aware of little "signs" that would indicate she was on the right path with something—"God winks," she called them. Faith was starting to get in on the fun, as well. Jennifer confidently told Faith it was not Millard they were interested in: it was *Thurman*!

Jennifer continued to work diligently on *Shattered Justice*. One day in late December 2021, she was writing about Cave Number 3 and became strangely curious about who had written "THE KILLER WAS HERE" on the wall of the cave. Paul had told her the person would have had to have been left-handed, because of the small size of the cave and the weird position they would have had to have been in when they wrote the message. As Jennifer reviewed the pre-trial transcript, she came to believe that there were only two people who were possibilities. Either Sheriff Pete Weaver had written it, or the juvenile delinquent Darren Creekmore, who had taken Weaver to the cave, had written it. She needed to find out if either of them was left-handed.

Jennifer texted Faith to ask if any old video footage Faith had collected for the sizzle reel might make it obvious as to whether Sheriff Weaver was left-handed or right-handed. Faith said she had not paid attention, but she would try to keep her eyes open for anything that might lend a clue.

However, Jennifer could *not* get it off her mind. Finally, she did a Google search for Sheriff Weaver to see if there might be some helpful video out on the Web. She failed to find any old footage that would give up the answer, but something else popped up: it was Sheriff Weaver's obituary. Jennifer took note that Weaver had been survived by a son, Herb, and it listed the city of Herb's residence at the time of the sheriff's death. Jennifer did a new search, and a place of business came up bearing Herb's name, along with a phone number. She asked the lady who answered the phone if that was the Herb Weaver who was former Mayes County Sheriff Pete Weaver's son. The lady was unsure, but promised she would have Herb call Jennifer back. Sure enough, that very afternoon, Herb called.

Herb seemed more than thrilled to talk to Jennifer about his dad and the case. In a deep, velvety, made-for-radio voice, he said, "You want stories? Girl, I can give you stories." Jennifer immediately liked Herb. She told him she wanted to hear his stories and accepted an invitation to his home. They set a date. Before they ended their call, Jennifer learned that Sheriff Weaver was right-handed, and Herb had let it out that he had a full transcript of the Gene Leroy Hart trial packed away in an old ice chest left behind by his father. And the best part? Jennifer was welcome to borrow it.

Jennifer's hands were practically trembling when she texted Faith. Jennifer and Faith had been having to rely on the transcript of Hart's preliminary hearing, so this was a big deal to be offered a transcript of the actual trial. The Mayes County court clerk had told Faith they wanted $10,000 for a copy: now Jennifer and Faith would be able to see the transcript for *free!* NOTE: Jennifer later determined that no complete trial transcript had ever been placed on record by the court reporter.

The next excitement came on December 31, 2021. Jennifer spent the last morning of the year in Oklahoma at the Lexington Correctional Center. WR Thompson greeted her with a smile and a friendly hand-shake. The aging Cherokee attempted to hug her, but was scolded because of COVID-19 rules. There was to be no more touching: six feet apart, that was the rule. The two sat down across from each other at a six-foot wide table as Jennifer scanned the room to see inmates visiting with their wives and children. A couple of toddlers were noisily unaware of their surroundings.

A cheerful Thompson went first. "Where do you want to start?"

Jennifer said, "Well, you said you don't believe Hart did it, so tell me what you *do* believe."

Thompson had made statements on the phone that the investigation had gone the wrong way from the beginning, but he said nothing like that now. He explained that he had only told the press he no longer believed in Hart's guilt, because he was trying to help the Farmers get the case "reopened." This made no sense. Thompson had also told Eric, his case manager, that he did not believe Hart "did it" after they had both spoken to Jennifer about Thompson testifying in the case. Eric had told Jennifer as much.

Jennifer quickly noticed that Thompson was not the same as he had been on the phone. Something was off. Had a recorded jailhouse phone call been heard by the wrong individual(s)? Had someone gotten to Thompson? Jennifer was baffled. But Thompson seemed to want to give Jennifer something to keep her there.

Thompson blurted out that three guys did it (including Hart). They supposedly had flirted with the counselors at the Dairy Boy, and they went out there that night to find them and "get with them." Thompson explained that the killers had come in from the McClain cemetery, which sits on the east side of SH-82 and due east of the camp (Thompson explained that people could party at the cemetery without being bothered by cops). Jennifer found the account unlikely, because there is a lot of real estate between SH-82 and the boundary of the camp that would have been closest to the cemetery.

Then she realized that was it, that was all he had to offer. She had come all this way to hear *that*? What a waste of time and gasoline.

Thompson would not go on record with who had been with Hart. Thompson said he knew Hart had done it, though, because Johnny Colvin's wife had seen Hart in the area of the camp the evening before. *How could Hart have been at the Dairy Boy flirting with counselors if he was hiding out down in the area where Colvin's wife had spotted him?* Jennifer kept her thoughts to herself and quietly waited for Thompson to continue.

The first thing Jennifer told Thompson she knew about anything he had said was, "Johnny Colvin has a brother-in-law named Flea, right?" Thompson squirmed and said yes, but his demeanor changed between two beats of his heart. He was no longer warm and friendly to Jennifer: he was now just politely cordial.

Jennifer sat up, as if starting a new subject, and inquired as to whether anyone had asked to borrow Thompson's pickup "that morning" (referencing the morning the bodies were discovered). His reply was a terse, "no, I didn't have anything to do with it." Jennifer had made no mention whatsoever as to why she had brought up his pickup. *Why did he immediately associate a pickup to the crime? And especially his pickup? Why had he not merely said "no?"*

Jennifer confessed to Thompson that she found it suspicious that two men directly related to Flea had 'found' the evidence that pointed the cops to Hart (and therefore conveniently away from Flea). Thompson was quick on the draw. He vehemently denied that he and Johnny Colvin had intentionally sic'd the cops on Hart. He kept insisting that he and Colvin just happened to be hunting and found the stuff at Cave Number 1 by "freak accident." He shored up his defense by saying the first question Sheriff Weaver had asked him on the day he and Colvin had notified the cops about the cave, was if he knew Hart. "They were already looking for Gene Hart," he contested.

Jennifer told him she suspected a half-brother of Hart's may have provided the incriminating evidence that had been placed there and then notified the OSBI. What Jennifer kept to herself was that she had asked Herb Weaver who it was that had given Herb's dad "reliable information" that Hart was living in Cave Number 1, which had caused his dad to send up an airplane looking for it. Herb had revealed that it was Cary Thurman, the first OSBI agent on the scene. Cary Thurman was not from Locust Grove, so he would not have figured out on his own that he needed to look for a cave: someone would have had to have told him that. It had been public knowledge that the airplane scout was unsuccessful, so Jennifer told Thompson she had reasoned that Flea might have told his brother-in-law to take a witness and go hunting: someone needed to find that stuff quick, before it got ruined.

"Johnny and Pat (Flea's sister) would have told on Flea if they had known he did it," Thompson insisted. When Jennifer asked if Pat would have stuck with her family to protect Flea's mother from watching Flea die, Thompson conceded that might be different. But that still did not make Thompson believe Johnny *personally* knew anything about it.

Jennifer suggested that the items being strewn out all over the ground was kind of weird. "It seems like Hart would have wanted to keep the photographs he had supposedly carried around for almost a decade safe from the elements."

Thompson went 180 degrees from his trial testimony and said that everything besides the sack of flour, with the salt and pepper in it, was inside the cellar, not strewn out. He obviously did not know that Jennifer was familiar with how he had testified in court that everything was out in the open, and had even estimated that the photographs were ten yards away from the cellar entrance. But what about the salt and pepper? *How did Thompson know there was salt and pepper in the flour?* In all the reading and research that Jennifer had done, she had *never* seen any mention of the flour having salt and pepper in it. Hmmm. She kept quiet, but she added that to her mental list of things to check out.

Thompson was very protective of himself and Johnny Colvin and kept repeating that "Johnny was not close to Flea, Johnny wouldn't have helped Flea cover up anything" and that "it wasn't Johnny's idea to go hunting that day, anyway." Thompson was pretty sure it had been his own idea to go bag some squirrels in that sauna-like heat.

Thompson acted ignorant that a flashlight was found with the girls, but he said Hart was known to dim his flashlight like that, with tape and plastic. Jennifer told him Hart could not have carried the masking tape back to the cave. Thompson argued with that. *Why would he bicker about the masking tape? Was it because he knew it had been planted?* Jennifer wondered.

Jennifer asked Thompson if he knew Bull or Buddy. He said he had not grown up in Locust Grove and had no idea who they were.

When Jennifer mentioned that Buddy had said Flea had used a pickup to push the Super Bee into the river and that another brother-in-law of Flea's, Donald Trammell, had also spoken of the car being in the river, Thompson got really quiet and was nervously sliding his flattened-out hands back-and-forth across the table like windshield wipers. Then, Jennifer sprung it on Thompson that they were going to be looking for the Super Bee, and, she believed that if they found it, people would start talking and someone would tell *everything*. Thompson shut down and became downright cool to Jennifer. He wanted to change the subject.

He shared with Jennifer his intentions to file a "McGirt challenge" to his conviction, so Jennifer asked if that would put him in the custody of the Cherokee Nation. He said the Cherokees could either consider his time served and release him, or they could re-try him. He had no problem with them re-trying him, because an individual who could have kept him from being convicted of killing his wife in the first place had since become available to testify on his behalf. He had had "proof" that he was innocent, but his witness had been in Afghanistan at the time of his conviction. NOTE: In July 2020, the Supreme Court of the United States ruled in *McGirt v Oklahoma* that Native American tribal citizens who commit crimes on tribal lands are not under the jurisdiction of the State of Oklahoma, due to a treaty that was signed with the tribes at the time Oklahoma became part of the United States in 1907.

Thompson seemed to be on edge and more than ready for Jennifer to leave when the time came. He had not enjoyed his time with her. She had pushed hard. She left with the feeling he would never want to speak to her again. No goodbye, nice to have met you, be careful going home, or happy new year came from him: he just kept eye contact with the guard as he walked out of the visitation room back in the direction of his cell. That was that.

Jennifer drove to Herb Weaver's home for the in-person interview they had scheduled the day they had visited by phone. Herb did not disappoint . . . he had stories, alright. Fascinating stories. The Girl Scout murders had affected the Weaver family in ways that no one had ever realized. Herb's mom had been convinced that his dad, Sheriff Weaver, was having an affair with OSBI Chemist Janice Davis. She went so far as to have Herb bug the family home to try and catch them. Nothing was captured, but his mom was resentful that Sheriff Weaver spent all his waking hours with Davis.

After sitting and listening to some gruesome stories that Herb told from his dad's days as sheriff, Jennifer made sure she had all the information she had come for. She was able to check most of the boxes, other than taking possession of Sheriff Weaver's ice chest.

The ice chest was at Herb's sister's house, and he had not had a chance to retrieve it yet. Jennifer put Herb on the phone with Faith. Since Jennifer lived four hours away in Kansas City and Faith lived in Locust Grove (much nearer to Tulsa), Herb agreed to let Faith pick it up for Jennifer at a later date.

On March 17, 2022, the world was celebrating St. Patrick's Day, while Faith was sitting with Herb Weaver asking a few questions as she picked up the ice chest from his place of business. As she loaded it into her vehicle, she took the opportunity to open the lid . . . and she almost convulsed.

Faith realized it was *not* what Herb had assumed. The ice chest contained no copy of Hart's trial transcript: the only transcript it contained was a copy of his preliminary hearing, which Faith and Jennifer had already read. That, in itself, would have been a huge letdown, but . . . what *was* in the ice chest was more than they could have dreamed, *much* more! This was an are-you-sitting-down moment! It was a treasure trove of hand written investigative notes made by Sheriff Weaver in addition to several OSBI documents . . . everything from the Girl Scout murders/Gene Hart files that Sheriff Paul had assumed had been burned! Sheriff Pete Weaver had apparently put them in an ice chest and taken them home to prevent Paul from benefitting from them. Now Pete's wife was also deceased, and his son, Herb, was in possession of the ice chest. Herb had freely turned it over to Faith, just as he had promised Jennifer.

Faith could scarcely believe her eyes! She immediately sent the documents to have them scanned into a digital format. She texted Jennifer that Jennifer was going to "flip her wig" when she saw what was in the ice chest—Jennifer would "be in heaven."

On Tuesday, May 10, 2022, Jennifer traveled to Locust Grove to be interviewed for Faith's documentary about the Girl Scout murders. Faith got footage of herself and Jennifer looking through the files that should have been turned over to Paul the day he took office as Sheriff of Mayes County. More encouraging was when Faith told her the Attorney General of the Cherokee Nation was reaching out and asking for their evidence.

After shooting her part for the documentary, Jennifer went to Siloam Springs, Arkansas, and checked into the hotel room that the production company had booked for her. She settled in, and over dinner in her room, she began to review the ice chest files.

One of the first things Jennifer noticed was nearly all the OSBI reports in Sheriff Weaver's files were initialed by Janice Davis. It appeared as if Davis had taken care to give Sheriff Weaver copies of anything she had worked on as an OSBI employee.

Jennifer observed that Davis had submitted "#EEE2 Undershorts from Gene L. Hart" on April 18, 1978. Then, forty-four days later, on June 1, 1978, Davis had submitted:

PPP1 Vaginal slide from Lori Farmer
PPP2 Anal slide from Lori Farmer
PPP3 Oral slide from Lori Farmer

PPP4 Vaginal slide from Michelle Gusé
PPP5 Anal slide from Michelle Gusé
PPP6 Oral slide from Michelle Gusé
PPP7 Vaginal slide from Denise Milner
PPP8 Anal slide from Denise Milner
PPP9 Oral slide from Denise Milner

So . . . Janice Davis did not submit the slides from the little girls (which, according to her, contained "deformed sperm") until *after* having access to Hart's underwear and semen (which, in her eyes, also contained "deformed sperm"). *Hmmmm. Perhaps Davis was going above and beyond the call of duty to help her intimately close friend, Pete, get his man.* Jennifer was perplexed.

The *Pryor Daily Times* reported on Sunday, June 11 1989, that, at Ted LaTurner's urging, "Gov. Henry Bellmon requested the slides [still in the possession of the Medical Examiner] be reviewed. Consequently, they were reviewed in August 1988. A written response from Dr. Fred B. Jordan, M.D., states that smears taken from the three victims contain no sperm although 'It is ... our understanding that spermatozoa were identified by the Oklahoma State Bureau of Investigation laboratory.' Hart had undergone a vasectomy prior to the Scout murders and was thought to be incapable of producing sperm. However, Dr. Jordan states in his letter to LaTurner that a review of 'slides of the testis (of Hart) contain sperm.' Pathologist Dr. Neil Hoffman performed autopsies on the three victims. 'I spoke with Hoffman on Thursday and he told me the vaginal traumas and lacerations were caused by a blunt instrument, not necessarily a male member,' said LaTurner. He said the question in his mind is where the sperm samples on the OSBI slides came from."

Jennifer was caught up in disturbing thoughts, before digging further.

In Sheriff Weaver's files were pictures of some of the evidence: the message written on the wall of Cave Number 3 . . . the plaster casts made of the jungle boot and tire track . . . the muddy print of the jungle boot on the entry rug at Jack Shroff's house . . . the piece of rope from Denise's wrists that had hairs caught in the knot, etc. Jennifer noticed how *clear* the pictures of the jungle boot print were (despite Sheriff Reed's description). A picture of the entrance of Cave Number 3 illustrated what Paul had said to Jennifer about how tight it was, and how whoever had written the message there would have had to have been left-handed.

The most interesting thing (to Jennifer) that had been resurrected with the ice chest was a sheet of notebook paper bearing Sheriff Weaver's handwriting about things which involved Thurman—some of them incriminating. Why had Weaver never investigated Thurman? *Why had Thurman seemingly been protected by the Mayes County Sheriff's office from the very beginning?* A picture was beginning to come into focus in Jennifer's mind . . . and it was not a good look for the members of Mayes County law enforcement or the OBSI.

Jennifer made a pledge to herself that she would do whatever it took, as long as it took, to shine a light into every nook and cranny of the Girl Scout murder case. And she could feel Paul's spirit propelling her forward.

CHAPTER 17
NOOKS AND CRANNIES

Jennifer put out feelers to some of Michael Nott's family to try and find out whether any of them had ever personally heard Nott recount the information that was put into the 'death bed letter' Jennifer had received in the mail. She eventually got a response from Nott's nephew, Jeremiah Bear. Jennifer told Bear that she had received information passed on by his Uncle Michael before his death, and the information had to do with the Girl Scout murders. She asked Bear if Nott had ever talked to him about the murders. Bear immediately said yes, that Nott had told him several times that Buddy and Thurman had come running out of the woods one day at Spring Creek, near Twin Bridges, and excitedly told Nott and some other guys that they had found a place on the creek where they could crawl up the bank and see where the Girl Scouts showered. Nott had not known if it was true or not, but he had been troubled by the fact that they were so aroused by the thought of seeing little girls naked.

Bear did not recall his uncle mentioning Flea or Bull, but he said Nott had always been *thoroughly* convinced that Buddy was one of the killers. So, what about the guy Nott had seen running from the creek with Buddy? What about Thurman? Bear said Nott had never told him that he thought Thurman was one of the killers. Jennifer found it odd that Nott had never named Thurman until Nott knew he was dying and wanted to make sure his own uncle (David Sack) knew what he knew. Then Sack had refused to repeat the information while he was still alive, fearing repercussions, but insisted a letter, complete with names, be mailed to Jennifer as soon as he was dead. Jennifer took note that Buddy also, in his detailed confession to Paul, had not named Thurman. Was everyone that afraid of Thurman? NOTE: Buddy *did* name Thurman to some of his closest friends, according to Locust Grove natives.

Jennifer dug back through the ice chest files and pulled out a page where Sheriff Weaver had scrawled down some notes the day he had talked to a local man we'll call Wayne. Wayne told Weaver that he was close to Hart and his brothers, that he would pick up Hart at Ella Mae's house to give him rides, and that he had once worked on Hart's flashlight. Wayne described how he commonly added folded up newspaper behind the battery of a flashlight to tighten the battery contact. Wayne said he had worked on Hart's light in what could have been the spring of 1977. Based on the date of the newspaper, April 17, 1977, found in the crime scene flashlight, Jennifer could verify that the timing fit.

Wayne had also told Sheriff Weaver that Thurman was known to wear an Ace bandage for a headband, and he had most recently seen Thurman with such a headband in the summer of 1977 down on the creek. Jennifer looked at another hand-written note made by Sheriff Weaver: "[G]ag was in place on victim at [the] time of abrasion below lip. Saliva stains on gag."

Jennifer was captivated by Thurman's choice of headbands, since little Denise had been found with an Ace bandage wrapped around her neck. Now Jennifer knew the Ace bandage had also apparently served as a gag. Jennifer located ME Hoffman, who had personally removed all the items from Denise's body at her autopsy. Dr. Hoffman referred to old photographs still in his possession and explained the configuration of the gag: "It looks like the Ace was at least partially covering the terry. Both probably were pulled out of her mouth when the rope was tightened."

Having once been a Licensed Practical Nurse, Jennifer knew that an Ace bandage would not absorb sweat. *Could it be that Thurman had fashioned a piece of terry cloth to place between the Ace bandage and his forehead to keep his brow dry?* He was known to be 'artistic,' according to his family, so perhaps he would have known how to stitch the terry cloth into a roll, which is how it had been found. The Ace bandage and terry cloth *really* needed to be put through an M-Vac machine: Jennifer was more convinced than ever. Why would Sheriff Mike Reed be opposed to at least *trying* that?

While speaking with Dr. Hoffman, Jennifer brought up the topic of the deformed sperm found by Janice Davis. Dr. Hoffman was still dismayed about that topic. "I took the slides to the best medical examiner around at that time, an Austrian doctor who spoke German, and he agreed that there was no sperm."

Lastly, from Sheriff Weaver's notes, Wayne had told Weaver that he had loaned a hand axe to Thurman and had never gotten it back. Jennifer checked the ice chest files and found where Agent Linville had submitted #WWW1 Crowbar and #WWW2 Hatchet on June 14, 1978. Jennifer called Agent Linville to ask why the items had never been presented as murder weapons at trial? Linville, after asking for identifying information about Jennifer and typing loudly on his computer, eventually told Jennifer that if they were not determined to be the murder weapons, it was because they had been microscopically examined and no biological material had been present. Five minutes after they hung up, Linville rang Jennifer back and asked her what The Cherry Tree Club is. (The Cherry Tree Club was an organization that Jennifer had founded years earlier to help young adults struggling with mental illness). *More overt intimidation*, Jennifer thought, as she let out a sigh. *Why had he felt it necessary to be so rude?*

Jennifer went to visit Attorney Garvin Isaacs in Oklahoma City. Isaacs re-iterated to her what Isaacs had always firmly believed: Gene Leroy Hart was innocent of killing the Girl Scouts. Isaacs gave Jennifer a tour through his offices, which contained thousands of pages related to the case, as well as framed pictures and documents from those days. Jennifer's favorite was the "Hotel Hart" sign.

Jennifer gained a strong desire to learn everything she could about Gene Hart. Had Hart gotten off unrighteously? Was he the kind of guy that could mercilessly beat innocent little girls to death?

Jennifer dug again through Sheriff Weaver's files and found the interview the OSBI did with Patricia, Hart's ex-wife. The OSBI asked Patricia explicit questions regarding Gene's sexual habits with her, the kind of questions that would make a sailor blush. The one question Jennifer found conspicuously missing from the interview, though, was whether Hart ever made a weird noise when he was sexually excited or at any time at all, for that matter.

Jennifer moved on to an in-depth psychiatric evaluation of Hart, performed by the highly-qualified Dr. James White, Jr., of Joplin, MO, who had sent a copy to Paul. The protocols administered to Hart by Dr. White were as follows:

Minnesota Multi-phasic Personality Inventory (MMPI), Rorchach, Bender-Gestalt, Rotter Incomplete Sentence, Word Association (Jungian), Kinetic Family Drawing (KFD), Draw-A-Person, Lifestyle Analysis (Adlerian), Dream Analysis and Early Recall and Personality Priorities Interview.

Dr. White had then followed up in a report: "Based upon the results of the above-mentioned protocols, it was my clinical judgment that Mr. Hart's characterological make-up was not of the type that would be necessary for the commission of the kinds of crimes for which he stood accused. Mr. Hart manifested no deep-seated sociopathy or psychopathy – of either a discreet or overt nature. In fact, Hart manifested precisely the opposite: a propensity for kindness, relative nonviolence and sensitivity. Given the condition of his surroundings, Hart's answers were spontaneous and unguarded, which reinforces the judgment that certainly no one capable of committing crimes of such monstrousness could hide the kind of pathology necessary for their commission. The protocols aside, the actor who could hide the telltale nuances associated with such behavior is extremely rare – if he exists at all.

"The composite picture reveals that Hart was a careful man, and a man of above average intelligence. The crimes of which he stood accused had a character all their own about them. Since the bodies were moved quite a distance from the murder scene, whoever did commit them took a considerable chance of being caught by moving them. Further, fear of sexual inadequacy is a common trait among child molesters. During the nearly three and one-half years that Hart was at large from McAlister as an escapee before the crimes were committed, he did not appear to have been suffering from sexual deprivation. It is interesting to note, regarding the consideration of poor impulse control as a factor in the crimes, that just a short distance down the road from the general vicinity where Hart had been living is the Christian Children's home with an overabundance of potential victims but none was ever bothered.

"And yet, had not Hart earlier been arrested, charged [and pled guilty] of kidnapping and rape? Yes. However, the circumstances surrounding this matter were entirely different. The individuals who were involved were not children. They were mature adults and experienced."

Jennifer next went back to the crime Dr. White had brought up—the 1966 rape case.

Paul had told Jennifer that he had always found the story told by the victims in Hart's 1966 rape case to be "suspect." Paul had heard on the street that it had been a consensual threesome, and the girls were embarrassed by it afterwards. After reading the transcript of the preliminary hearing in the case, Jennifer did a lot of digging and snooping to locate the two young ladies who had been the victims. She first located Kathy, who had been nineteen at the time the incident took place. Kathy told Jennifer she did not like to talk about the rape, which was understandable. Jennifer assured Kathy that she had read her testimony in Hart's preliminary hearing and did not need to hear the sexual details. NOTE: Since Hart had taken a plea deal, there was never a trial, and therefore, no trial transcript.

Jennifer was only interested in the two aspects of the rape case that the OSBI had used to tie Hart to the Girl Scout murders: a weird noise and his having tried on the rape victims' glasses. Kathy did not recall hearing Hart make any weird noise, and she did not wear glasses. She felt that Margie, the other victim (who did wear glasses), would have been able to better answer Jennifer's questions, but

Margie had passed away in 2017. Kathy said Margie had a twin sister, though, Marylyn, who was still around and probably more than willing to talk about all the things Margie had confided to her. Kathy had run into Marylyn a couple of years earlier, and Marylyn had broken down crying. Since that time, Marylyn had tried to reach out to Kathy a few times, and Kathy assumed it was because Marylyn wanted to talk about the rape case. Kathy seemed averse to the idea of talking to Marylyn about it, and Kathy did not provide contact information for Marylyn so that Jennifer could talk to her.

Kathy was locked in on Hart being guilty of killing the Girl Scouts and thought it was a travesty that he had gotten away with it. In retrospect, Kathy now felt that he would have come back and killed her and Margie if they had not gotten themselves loose and found help, she said. Kathy described to Jennifer how terrified she had felt when she had been in Hart's trunk out behind Foreman's Mountain View BBQ. She had recognized that Hart was backing the car, and, because she could hear fish jumping, she had sensed that they were near water. She was scared that he was going to back her into the water and entomb her in the trunk, drowning her. Jennifer asked Kathy about why Margie had not testified in Hart's preliminary hearing. Kathy sounded a bit aggravated about that. "Margie was off with her doctor, or something, so it was all left on me."

A little more digging led Jennifer to Marylyn, and sure enough, Marylyn was very willing to talk about everything that had happened to her twin sister, Margie. Marylyn told Jennifer that her eighteen-year-old (at the time) sister had stayed at their parents' home for two days after that dreadful night. Marylyn was still living there, as well, and her twin had confided everything to her. Margie had said that

Hart had only wanted *Margie* to go with him from the Fondalite Club, but Margie had talked him into letting Kathy go, too. When it was over, at daylight, Hart had told them he had to go home to make an appearance, because he was married with a kid, but he would come back.

Marylyn said Margie had not testified in court, because the *prosecutor* had refused to let her. Marylyn seemed unsure as to why. Jennifer found this to be suspicious. *What was the prosecutor afraid that Margie was going to say in front of the judge or Hart's defense attorney?*

Margie's parents had been angry at her over the entire situation. Her mother was in complete denial that she had been raped. Margie's abusive husband had pretty much raped Margie again when she went back to her marital home. Sadly, Margie later got into heavy drinking and drug abuse and had died from Hepatitis C. Whatever had happened, it seemingly had eaten on her mentally and emotionally for the remainder of her life. NOTE: Hart told his attorneys that he and another man had 'picked up' Margie and Kathy that night at the Fondalite Club, and the four had spent a steamy night having consensual sex. Then, at daylight, when the men both had to go home to their wives, things went south. Margie and Kathy were mad that the men were leaving them there and tried to prevent the men from going, despite the fact that Hart had promised to return for them. The men had to get away from them, so they loosely tied them up. Hart would never name the other man and had pled guilty so he would not have to. Kathy and Margie had never mentioned a second man, obviously.

Marylyn had gone with Margie the day the OSBI had Margie come to Pryor to be interviewed on camera. Some of the footage was included in the documentary *Someone Cry For the Children*. Marylyn invited Jennifer to watch the documentary with her from an old VCR tape, and when it came to the segment featuring Margie, Marylyn said she was surprised at Margie talking about Hart's 'noise'. Marylyn had no memory of Margie ever mentioning Hart making a weird noise, either before or after the taping session. Jennifer wondered how hard the OSBI had worked to nonchalantly slip in suggestive questions to Margie. They had seemingly tried to tie the 1966 rape case to the 1977 murders so they could introduce Hart's prior crime into his trial for the murders.

Jennifer had taped the *Someone Cry For the Children* documentary on her voice recorder while she and Marylyn had watched it, so she went back and listened to it again to get Margie's exact description of Hart's sound.

Margie: "He wasn't speaking, he was just making strange noises, real strange noise. It's not, it wasn't a real, you know, like somebody in pain, or somebody just ouch or a, a growl or, it was, I don't, it was, I guess, um, and so we went to [unintelligible] his own little sound that he has, or he made."

Margie had seemed to struggle for words to describe the sound Hart had made (apparently during sex). Her friend, Kathy, had testified in court and stated, in essence, that there was no remarkable sound.

County Attorney Longmire: "How do you know that he reached a climax?"

Kathy: "You could tell from the way he acted."

Jennifer compared the court testimony given by Kathy with the descriptions given in court by counselor Carla Wilhite.

Carla: "I decided it was an animal" . . . "kind of like in between a fog horn, a frog or a snore."

After comparing the two descriptions, Jennifer was unconvinced that they were the same sound. She contacted Carla Wilhite and asked Carla to listen to a lineup of unidentified sounds to see if any of them were close to the sound she had heard near the back gate that night. Unbeknownst to Carla, Jennifer included:

1) the grunt of a whitetail buck deer, 2) a hunter using a deer calling device ("deer call") to imitate a deer grunt, 3) a bullfrog croaking, 4) a human trying to make the sound of a bullfrog, 5) a human trying to make the sound of a foghorn, 6) a human trying a second time to make the sound of a foghorn, and 7) a human trying a second time to make the sound of a bullfrog.

Carla chose sounds 1 and 6 as being the closest, but pointed out that the sound was "deeper, more uhhhh than muhhhh, and drawn out." (The human in sound 6 had inadvertently added the muhhhh).

Jennifer sent Carla an 8th sound: the same hunter that created sound 2 used a deer call to make a second sound imitating a deer grunt. Carla said it should be a "slower temp and slightly deeper."

Sound 9 was a different hunter with a deer call. The main thing wrong with his grunt imitation was that it needed to be a bit slower (he also drew it out a little too long and failed to "trail off" enough at the end).

Jennifer lastly sent the YouTube video entitled "Doe Grunting Like Crazy" for Carla to consider. Carla made no suggestions for change.

Jennifer researched what is going on with deer in June. Fawns are born in late May or early June. Their mothers grunt to call them when they are moving around. Jennifer felt it was possible that, once the rain had stopped and the camp had become quiet, a deer was moving her fawn(s), and the giggles from tent #5 had interrupted the process. Carla's light shining directly at the doe would have caused the animal to momentarily freeze in indecision (sometimes referred to as "a deer in headlights"), explaining the silence while her flashlight was pointed in that direction.

Jennifer had created an algorithm that had put Hart at the camp at 1:30 a.m., based on the OSBI having said that the noise Carla had heard was the same as a sound Hart had made when he had raped the women in 1966. Jennifer now had to re-program the night, using different input. She still believed the fact that stolen glasses indicated that Hart was the one who had been at the camp stealing things. But there was one thought that bugged her. *Why were both pairs of Carla Wilhite's glasses not taken? If both pairs of her glasses had been there in her tent, why would he have taken only her spare, less expensive pair?* Jennifer was not at all sure that both pairs of Carla's glasses were in her tent when Hart was there.

Jennifer once again returned to the pre-trial transcript to review Carla's testimony. *Everyone* in the camp had left their units to go down to the Great Hall for supper by 6 p.m. Carla had estimated that it was 6:30 p.m. when the rain had begun. *Could it be that Hart spent that 30 minutes stealing Kathy Elder's purse from the Quapaw unit, and then, as he was in the Kiowa unit stealing Susan Emery's purse and Carla's glasses and capo, the rain had caused him to scurry off over the back gate? Was this the possible reason he had dropped the glasses and capo in the grass and had taken no time to stop and gather them (if he had even realized he had dropped them)?*

NOTE: The fact that the guitar capo was stolen might be attributed to the fact that Hart had two half-brothers, Jimmy Ray and Millard, who played guitar. Perhaps Hart had intended to give the capo to one of his musical half-brothers? Who knows.

Jennifer next reached out to more of Hart's family and friends, who told her some great stories. Her favorite was how Ella Mae had made a compartment in the bottom of her couch, where she would hide "Sonny" any time someone would come around that might cause trouble for Hart.

Thurman would laugh and brag about how he had convinced the OSBI that Ella Mae, using "Indian medicine," had made Hart invisible at times. The OSBI could be in Ella Mae's house standing right next to Hart and not be able to see him, Thurman would say. That was because Hart was in the couch. One OSBI agent was even convinced that Hart could "shapeshift." That agent described how Hart had once turned himself into a cat and pounced him one night. And the agent just knew that Hart had changed himself into a bird and flown away one day when the dogs were searching for him: that was why the dogs had lost the scent in Cavalier's field. *No, that's most likely where the Super Bee was last parked, the point from which the culprits got in and drove away,* was Jennifer's thinking. Though she couldn't prove it, Jennifer suspected that Thurman Buckskin was the one who had gone to Agent Cary Thurman and told him they needed to find Cave Number 1, which had caused Agent Thurman to instruct Sheriff Weaver to send an airplane up.

Another thing that Thurman liked to brag about was that he had had the OSBI running circles through the woods looking for Hart in a cave, when Thurman knew all the time that Hart was at Ella Mae's house. Thurman got his jollies by manipulating people, Jennifer was told. NOTE: Whenever Thurman would say anything about Hart living in a cave, their brother, Millard, would call him out on it. "You know Gene never lived in a cave. He always lived with [Ella Mae]."

Thurman would say of that night, "Sonny came in with some stuff" . . . then, the story would hit a fork in the road. One time Thurman would finish the story by saying that Hart had blood on his shoe when he came in (Thurman would say he thought probably from rabbit hunting). The next time Thurman would tell the story, there was no blood on Hart's shoe when he came in. *Had Hart gone home to Ella Mae's house, and Thurman was there when "he came in?" Was this when Johnny Colvin's wife had seen Hart in the area of the camp?* It would make sense, Jennifer supposed.

This reminded Jennifer of the last interview Hart had given to *The Cherokee Advocate* on June 1, 1979, only three days before his untimely death. Attorney Garvin Isaacs had referred to law enforcement planting evidence.

Hart: "Well, let me tell you, now, talk about a gross miscarriage of justice...or, better yet, abuse of power on the part of the officials who took the pictures from here and placed them here (gesturing with his hands)...whoever done it."

Isaacs: "I think it was the guy who got the $8,000 for turning you in, is who I think it was. Now, who would stand to benefit more? If I'm not mistaken, if Gene had been convicted, that guy would have gotten $42,000."

Hart: "*Another* $42,000."

Advocate: "Do you know who that was?"

Hart: "Yeah."

Isaacs: "Do you?"

(Laughter)

Hart: "I do. I know who it was, but I'm not going to say so-and-so done this or so-and-so done that unless I can prove it. I'm not going to lay the blame on anybody unless I can prove it. And, if I can't prove it, I'm not going to say a word."

Isaacs: "Yeah, we've got a hunch, you know."

Hart: "We know almost for certain who did it, but we can't prove it. It's best at this time just not to say anything until maybe we can come up with a witness that can verify what we feel to be the truth. Then and only then will we say who we think it was."

Pitchlynn: "Chances are there is going to be more than one person up the creek."

Hart: "You bet. There will be a bunch."

Jennifer re-read Hart's last statement on the topic: "There will be a bunch." *Had Hart seen who Thurman had been hanging out with that night when Hart came in with his stuff? Had the four killers been together at Ella Mae's house when Hart had gone to bed? Had Hart also known that the evidence at Cave Number 1 was discovered by close relatives of one of the guys Thurman had been with?* Jennifer's mind was racing.

If Jennifer was right, after Hart had gone to bed, Thurman and the three amigos had taken Hart's dimmed flashlight and some of the stuff that Hart had possibly brought in from Shroff's house (duct tape and rope) to do the killings. Thurman would also have had access to the sunglasses (from counselor Susan's purse), the roll of masking tape, the photographs that Hart had kept from his time at the Granite Reformatory and the newspaper that Wayne may have left behind when he worked on Hart's flashlight: what a perfect set of items to plant at Cave Number 1 the following day. Wayne had told Sheriff Weaver he had fixed a switch in Hart's flashlight at Ella

Mae's house the day he had put the newspaper in it. NOTE: Wayne was shown the actual red and white box flashlight that was found next to the girls, and he said the switch in that flashlight had been fixed in the same manner that he fixed Hart's flashlight (which looked identical). At the time Wayne was shown the flashlight from the scene, it did not have the newspaper inside it: Wayne brought that up on his own.

Jennifer thought back to the items that were found at Cave Number 1. There had been little made of the pair of green cotton gloves that Agent Linville had collected. Had Thurman planted Hart's gloves there, as well? Their presence would give Law Enforcement a way to explain the lack of any of Hart's fingerprints being found at the scene. *But they were noticeably absent of blood stains. Had Thurman failed to think this through?* Jennifer wondered. *The gloves needed to go for a soak in the M-Vac machine, as well.*

Then there were the jungle boot prints: found first in the murder tent, then outside Jack Shroff's farmhouse, then between the Kiowa and Arapaho units, then at Sam's Corner and, finally, at Cave Number 2.

Jennifer wondered if Thurman had gone intentionally and left his boot print on the rug at Mr. Shroff's house while Thurman was out messing with the minds of the OSBI later the same morning that the bodies had been discovered. After all, *if* Jennifer's new algorithm was right, Thurman would have *known* that items taken from Shroff's place by Hart were used in the killings: he would want to make sure the same print that had been found in the murder tent was also found at Shroff's house. But, there was no need to go inside and muddy up the floors. That would explain why there were no footprints inside the house. Shroff had testified that the prints would have had to have been made after the Sunday-night rainfall: Monday morning would work. Thurman may have even heard from the press by then that the boot print had been discovered in the murder tent. Jennifer felt relatively certain that the individual who had robbed the inside of the house, leaving no footprints, was not the same person who had left the outside footprints that matched the print in the murder tent.

The fact that Sheriff Weaver had gotten down on his knees and found the jungle boot print on the trail between the Kiowa and Arapaho units, heading toward the Kiowa unit, made Jennifer believe the killers had perhaps initially made their entry into the camp through the front gate. Buddy had confessed they had been at the camp earlier in the evening, but too many people had been up and around.

Perhaps they had regrouped, and the second/final time they went to the camp they drove onto a remote service road on Cavalier's property, near the Cavalier family cemetery. WR Thompson had said, after all, that a cemetery was a normal place for area 'partiers' to hang out in those days. This would explain Cavalier's neighbor hearing traffic on a remote road between 2:30 and 3:00 AM. Michael Nott had seen three of them come in at Flea's house in that same timeframe and knew, by the way they were acting, they were up to something. The final plan (that was executed) may have included leaving the Super Bee next to the cemetery and walking over to the camp. Maybe this was why Buddy had been sent to get the car and move it as close as he could to the back gate—without getting stuck in the mud. The killers knew by then they had cargo that needed to be loaded. Buddy had lied to Paul. He had not been moving the car when the killing happened. He may not have personally killed anyone, but he was there when it happened.

The dog that had been released from behind Tent #7 tracked through the Arapaho unit, up Cookie Trail, out to the section line, then west to the corner at Cavalier Road. It had been unsure whether to go north to Ella Mae's house or south to Mr. Shroff's farm. Maybe it should have gone north.

And it seems it would fit Thurman's egomaniacal nature to want to sit on the ridge overlooking his mother's house to watch the goings on there. He probably wanted to watch and see how quickly the law would show up there looking for Hart. *If* it was Thurman, that would explain why the huge manhunt had not netted Hart.

With the jungle boot print being found at Sam's Corner, that meant, if Buddy's confession was accurate that the three amigos had gone and stolen beer there, Thurman was most likely with them at the time. All the puzzle pieces were beginning to fit, as far as Jennifer was concerned.

Jennifer settled again on an algorithm that accounted for every single piece of evidence available to her. But who could she tell? Sheriff Reed was not interested, and he had gotten the Tulsa Cold Case Unit dismissed from looking into any new information.

On Wednesday, May 4, 2022, the OSBI announced through the press that the Girl Scout murder case was about to be closed by the OSBI, with Gene Leroy Hart as the confirmed killer. KOCO News 5-ABC in Oklahoma City aired Andrea Fielding, Director of Criminalistics for the OSBI. "I started looking into the case and realized that we had done some DNA evidence in 1989 and nothing since then." So, with new technologies they looked at all the autopsy samples that were submitted from the three victims, as well as some of the clothing items and a sleeping bag. But DNA was too hard to detect. "Unfortunately, because the items were collected in 1977 and preservation techniques have changed, collection techniques have changed and testing techniques have changed, some of the items were not preserved the way they should have been, and so a lot of the items were too degraded to actually get any DNA results." But they were able to get partial DNA profiles from fingerprints on the flashlight and semen on a pillow. "They were not able to exclude Gene Leroy Hart as being a contributor to that DNA profile." The other partials connected to the victims. "There were none that were not linked to somebody known in this case. As far as the OSBI goes and the evidence that we have, our belief is that Gene Lerory Hart committed the murders, and the evidence we have doesn't exclude him, and it doesn't point to anyone else, and so we will close the case that way."

Jennifer figured (and worried) this was so the OSBI could dispose of evidence. Faith went into action, working the proper channels to protect their work.

What interesting timing. Why, after forty-five years, was the OSBI closing the case *now*, so soon after Thurman Buckskin had been brought forward as a possible suspect? It felt like, to Jennifer, that Thurman was *still* being protected for some reason.

Sheriff Mike Reed then appeared on a couple of local Tulsa news programs, as well as a Hulu documentary, stating that he needed to put all the "conspiracy theories" to rest. Gene Leroy Hart was the one and only killer of Lori, Denise and Michelle, and he could prove anyone wrong who said anything any different. As Jennifer had learned on October 22, 2021, the way Reed 'proved' anyone wrong was by hanging his hat on the DNA testing, which, to Jennifer, was as full of holes as Swiss cheese. Having evidence that the killer was

Native American would by itself meet the measure that Fielding had used: it would not rule Gene Leroy Hart out, and it would not point to any other individual. But it meant absolutely *nothing*!

Just after the Hulu documentary aired, Jennifer received a phone call from the daughter of one of Gene Leroy Hart's jurors. She was upset by the news reports. The daughter told Jennifer that her parents were harassed and threatened by Sheriff Weaver to stop answering questions or making any statements to the press. It had worked. Jennifer inquired as to whether her parents were afraid of Sheriff Weaver. The daughter said that, having been raised in Pryor, her family saw Sheriff Weaver as a crook, and that was partly the reason the jury had so easily believed that he was capable of planting evidence against Gene Hart.

It brought to Jennifer's mind a situation Paul had once told her about. While Sheriff Weaver was still in office, he had apprehended a suspect that was wanted in a huge jewelry heist in Texas. The suspect was in possession of some of the jewelry that had been stolen. It was Sheriff Weaver's job to preserve the jewelry until it was needed for the trial of the suspect. Paul observed Weaver and his deputies wearing the jewelry—notably big diamond rings. When Paul had taken office there was no sign of the jewelry, even though it had never been needed in Texas: the suspect had taken a plea deal. A lot of the jewelry ended up in a pawn shop just south of Pryor. Paul never saw any record of proceeds going into the sheriff department's bank account.

Sheriff Weaver had believed that if they could have only presented Gene's prior record of the 1966 rapes to the jury hearing the Girl Scout case, they would have gotten a conviction—something the U.S. Constitution prevents for a reason. You cannot be found guilty solely due to a bad reputation. Obviously, the judge had seen no legitimate tie between the two cases and, therefore, had not let any evidence or testimony from the 1966 case taint the 1979 trial.

Jennifer asked around and was told by the locals that Sheriff Mike Reed and Deputy Dean Majors had been close buddies since high school (some even said they were like brothers), and Majors and Thurman lived within walking distance of each other and were friendly.

Deputy Dean Majors privately scolded a woman who had been posting on a Facebook page dedicated to the cold case. He did not mention his status of being a deputy. He accused the woman of spreading lies and, in early July 2022, told her that Sheriff Mike Reed had DNA that matched Hart 100%, that the information had just not been released to the public yet. He also invited her to meet him in person. It all sounded too familiar. That was exactly what Deputy Majors had told Faith the day she had met him in the empty warehouse seven months earlier.

The Wednesday before Memorial Day, 2022, Faith presented all the evidence to the Cherokee marshals. Because of *McGirt v Oklahoma*, the marshals possessed the right to act—all three living suspects were tribal citizens and Lori, Denise and Michelle had died on tribal land. The case was now in the hands of Almighty God and the Cherokee Nation.

On September 30, 2022, the *Tahlequah Daily Press* informed the public that Marshal Service Director Shannon Buhl had informed the Cherokee Nation Rules Committee a day earlier that he had recently assigned a Missing and Murdered Indigenous People investigator to look into the 1977 Girl Scout Murders, due to one of the victims being Native American. What the *Tahlequah Daily Press* did not report was that sonar was showing the frame of a car seventy yards downstream from where WR Thompson had told Jennifer Morrison the Super Bee had most likely gone into the Neosho River. It turns out, WR Thompson *had* wanted to speak to Jennifer again.

CHAPTER 18

DNA = DO NOT ASK

One evening in late September 2022, Jennifer was watching the OWN channel on television when she came upon the case of a man who was wrongly convicted of murdering a young woman after a confession was forced out of him by police. In the television presentation of the case, a woman named Cece Moore, working for a company named Parabon, used genetic genealogy to correctly identify the killer and free the wrongly convicted man, who had languished for nineteen years in prison.

It made Jennifer curious as to whether genetic genealogy could be used to identify the killer of Lori, Denise and Michelle. Jennifer did some poking around and found out Cece Moore had shown interest in the case, but was unable to move forward after conferring with the OSBI lab. It was Jennifer's understanding that there was not enough DNA to build a genetic profile, but she wanted to find out more.

There were a lot of questions about the specifics of DNA testing that *had* been performed in the Girl Scout case. All the results that had been made public were vague, at best—terms like "partial match," "inconclusive," "incomplete profile," or "degraded DNA" were thrown around.

The reporting of the first test set the tone. On October 25, 1989, *The Oklahoman* proclaimed, "DNA Tests Link Gene Leroy Hart to Girl Scout Deaths." It sounded like a bombshell until the details below the headline were scrutinized. In testing conducted by the FBI, Hart's body fluids matched only three probes of DNA out of five, according to "two separate sources, both with knowledge of the confidential tests." The sources asked not to be identified. "One person in 7,700 American Indians would match the crime scene sample as Hart did . . . If all five probes had matched it would have been one in 3 billion . . . With three of five matching it is one in 7,700. That means if you got tests from 7,700 American Indians one of them should match, which is the reason why the test is not conclusive."

And then, on June 25, 2008, *The Oklahoman* ran an article stating "recent DNA tests failed to identify the killer or killers who raped and murdered three Oklahoma girls June 13, 1977, at Camp Scott in Locust Grove. However, the tests revealed a partial female DNA profile, Mayes County District Attorney Gene Haynes announced Tuesday in a news release. Testing from a semen-stained pillowcase found at the crime scene failed to exclude all three of the victims or the possibility of a female attacker, adding to the stockpile of questions that already surround this enduring mystery." The article went on to explain "in April, the [OSBI] received permission from Haynes to conduct specific DNA tests on semen stains from pillowcases and a swab taken from one of the victims. Haynes signed off on the test even though they would exhaust the evidence from the swab. The DNA test conducted is capable of separating female and male DNA. But results from tests conducted by Houston-based Identigene returned inconclusive. Two months later, OSBI sent the remaining evidence from the pillowcases to Sorenson Forensics in Salt Lake City for further testing. This time a DNA profile that genetically types as female was obtained from one of the pillowcase stains." Buddy Fallis, who prosecuted Hart, was quoted: "It would be nice if we had pristine DNA samples from all parties involved, but we don't. Now the case becomes murkier, and that's real sad."

Jennifer phoned Gene Haynes, who had been in the Mayes County District Attorney's office from 1986 to 2010. Haynes explained the 1989 test fell short of the four-marker match required to be legally useful. Then, as had been clear from the newspaper report, the tests in 2008 had not yielded any conclusions. Haynes had left Mayes County before any further testing was done. NOTE: Garvin Isaacs was told by a lab technician that the samples tested in 2008 contained *no* DNA belonging to Hart, and Isaacs was furious about the reporting done by the media.

When Haynes had first been hired by Jack Graves, he had been instructed by Graves to familiarize himself with the Girl Scout case, because people would be calling from time to time with questions. Haynes had read every document he could get his hands on, including the OSBI investigative reports that had never been provided to Hart's attorneys. Jennifer asked Haynes if he ever recalled seeing any report having to do with Flea. Haynes did not remember Flea's name: he even asked Jennifer to spell it. Haynes pointed out that it had been thirty-four years since he had looked at the reports, and he could not 100% guarantee the accuracy of his memory. Buddy's name did ring a bell, however. Jennifer named off some of Buddy's subsequent convictions, and Haynes concluded that Buddy having been a regular at the DA's office could explain why his name sounded so familiar.

Jennifer then asked Haynes the million-dollar question. Had Haynes seen in any of the reports that any of Gene Hart's half-brothers had been cleared as suspects? The answer was negative. He didn't think the half-brothers had ever been looked at.

This was important to Jennifer, since Sheriff Reed had recently begun telling people in various circles that he had snatched a cigarette butt smoked by half-brother Thurman from an ashtray, had it compared to the killer's DNA and ruled Thurman out. Jennifer had become wary of Reed's whack-a-mole style of sheriffing. She checked with extremely close family members of Thurman's, and they were surprised to hear Thurman was still smoking. They were adamant that he had stopped five years earlier, due to health issues. But, even if Thurman had fallen off the clean-lung wagon, there were other problems Jennifer had with Reed's account. Her understanding was the OSBI crime lab would not legally be able to process Thurman's DNA that had not been obtained through 1) a warrant or 2) if he had discarded it in a public place with no intention to retrieve it (one example would be putting it out on the curb in his garbage). Reed's account included neither, which meant Thurman's Fourth Amendment rights may have been violated.

Sheriff Reed had publicly stated that he uses CODIS (Combined DNA Index System). But, according to the American Bar Association's *Standards for Criminal Justice, Third Edition*, "DNA Evidence," published in 2007, "a profile developed from DNA evidence collected by consent as provided in Standard 24 should not be entered into a database or compared with profiles in a database (for example, by keyboard search) without the written consent of the person who is the source of the profile." Furthermore, "a profile developed from a DNA sample collected from a location other than a crime scene solely for the purpose of obtaining the profile of a person should not be entered into a database."

Another thing that bugged Jennifer was how Reed had made no mention of having used a cigarette butt to rule Thurman out on October 22, 2021, when she, Faith and Mark had met with Reed in his office. As hard as he had tried to veer his visitors away from Thurman being a valid suspect, the strongest argument he had come up with was to say he believed Thurman had been ruled out through an alibi provided by some of Thurman's friends. Jennifer called Rick Lawrence to ask if Reed had mentioned the cigarette butt when the CCU had met with Reed October 26, 2021, and he had tried to convince them of the same. "Nope," came the answer.

Jennifer became a student of DNA science. She spent hours reading and researching everything she could find about it. She called up crime labs and spoke to experts. Her nursing background aided her understanding. She learned that every human being has their own recipe, a ridiculously long string of instructions, all running together, end to end. The recipes of all humans are 99.9% identical, with a .1% difference that makes every individual unique. Everything from gender and race to the size and shape of a person's ears is written in their recipe.

In simple terms, each trait (each instruction in the long string of instructions making up the recipe) is known as a marker. Scientists are learning the exact location within a human recipe that the instruction for a particular trait (marker), can be found. As an example, they know how far down the string to look for the instruction that says what eye color to give the human that is being created.

In the original test that had been performed in 1989, three out of five markers found in the assumed killer's DNA allegedly matched Gene Leroy Hart. This was how it was determined that the killer was a Native American. One of the markers Hart had matched, obviously, was race (Native American). Jennifer (safely?) assumed that another marker indicated gender (male). She wondered what the third marker was that Hart matched, and, more than that, she wondered what the two markers were that were inconclusive.

Five markers were all that could be compared in 1989. That changed in 1997, when thirteen markers were located in the human recipe (genome) for use by law enforcement to identify criminals. As of January 2017, it became twenty. Twenty markers now make up what is known as a "complete profile." Anything less is a "partial profile." The National DNA Index System (NDIS) currently requires that twenty autosomal STR markers be tested, and the profile must contain information for at least ten. State and local databases are less stringent—states require seven or more and local databases require at least four. CODIS (Combined DNA Index System) which operates local, state and national databases, is what Sheriff Reed uses, so . . . that means Sheriff Reed has matched Hart to less than ten and possibly as few as four. Yet, he claims his DNA evidence is strong enough to trump any other evidence brought to him. NOTE: Jennifer suspects he has matched Hart to less than four, which means he has nothing definitive.

People Magazine, on January 31, 2018, reported that "with $30,000 raised locally last year by Mayes County Sheriff Mike Reed, surviving evidence from the crime scene is undergoing DNA testing that Reed thinks may reveal a forensic profile of the killer that was unavailable four decades ago."

Jennifer was told by a strong source that a 'whistleblower' from inside the OSBI had contacted Garvin Isaacs to say the most recent DNA testing performed in 2018 would be announced as "inconclusive" (if anything was announced at all), but that the results actually excluded Gene Hart as a suspect. These were the results that Jennifer had tried to pin down Sheriff Reed about at their October meeting, when he had said they were inconclusive. Jennifer took the whistleblower's report with a huge grain of salt, since the whistleblower had not given their name, but it did make her curious to see the exact details of the 2018 results. It seemed unusual that the results of the 1989 and 2008 tests had been presented to the public through the press, but there had only been silence regarding the 2018 test until 2022. Reed said it was due to the parents wanting the results held until the Hulu documentary was filmed.

"Inconclusive" results can mean any one of three things: 1) too many contributors 2) too little DNA to test (not enough lines from the recipe) or 3) the DNA is too degraded (the instruction on any given line of the recipe is partially destroyed, for example).

Jennifer asked Sheri Farmer if she was in possession of a copy of the lab reports or a list of comparisons. Sheri told Jennifer that the parents had never been provided with that information.

Jennifer and her youngest son, Quentin, began digging deeper into how meaningful the closely-guarded, secret DNA results could possibly be. While looking, they found some spell-binding information about the genetics of Native Americans.

According to the article *Native American Populations Share Gene Signature* published by *New Scientist* February 14, 2007, "a new study shows a distinctive, repeating sequence of DNA [that is] found in people living at the eastern edge of Russia is also widespread among Native Americans.

"The finding lends support to the idea that Native Americans descended from a common founding population that lived near the Bering land bridge for some time.

"Kari Schroeder at the University of California in Davis, US, and colleagues sampled the genes from various populations around the globe, including two at the eastern edge of Siberia, fifty-three elsewhere in Asia and eighteen Native American populations. The study examined samples from roughly 1500 people in total, including 445 Native Americans.

"The team looked for a series of nine repeating chunks of DNA, known as 9RA, which falls in a non-coding region of chromosome 9.

"They found the 9RA sequence in at least one member of all the Native American populations tested, such as the Cherokee and Apache people. The two populations in eastern Siberia, where the Bering land bridge once connected Asia to North America, also tested positive for the 9RA sequence.

"The 9RA sequence did not appear in any of the other Asian populations examined in the study, including those from other parts of Siberia, from Mongolia or Japan. According to Schroeder, the high prevalence of this gene marker among native populations of North and South America – and its absence in most of Asia – lends strong support to the idea that Native Americans can trace their ancestry to a common founding population. NOTE: Journal reference: *Biology Letters* (DOI: 10.1098/rsbl.2006.0609)"

The University of Kansas went further in the article *DNA Sequences Suggest 250 People Made Up Original Native American Founding Population,* published May 1, 2018. Michael Crawford, KU professor of anthropology and head of KU's Laboratory of Biological Anthropology helped publish a study in the journal *Genetics and Molecular Biology* that estimated the parameter for the original founding population of Native Americans to be about 250 people.

The Abstract of a lengthy study published online by The Oxford University Press February 12, 2009, in the article *Haplotypic Background of a Private Allele at High Frequency in the Americas,* states:

"Recently, the observation of a high-frequency private allele, the 9-repeat allele at microsatellite D9S1120, in all sampled Native American and Western Beringian populations has been interpreted as evidence that all modern Native Americans descend primarily from a single founding population."

The results of the study, indeed, "supported the hypothesis that all modern Native Americans and Western Beringians trace a large portion of their ancestry to a single founding population that may have been isolated from other Asian populations prior to expanding into the Americas."

All of this newly discovered data troubled Jennifer. The fact that the hair found at the murder scene was "Mongoloid or Indian" was used to point the finger at Gene Hart, was flat-out wrong. If his blood type being O is one of the traits that Sheriff Mike Reed and the OSBI were/are still using to say the DNA 'points' to Hart, that is wrong, as well.

Jennifer called Patrick Abitbol, who was the Assistant DA of Mayes County under Jack Graves (now deceased) when the first test was run in 1989. Abitbol was not at all sure that *any* markers had ever been conclusively matched to Gene Leroy Hart or anyone else. It was his understanding that the DNA had been too degraded to ever yield anything meaningful. He referred Jennifer to the OSBI.

And round and round the bureaucratic shuffle goes. This is the same not-so-merry-go-round that Sheriff Paul Smith was put on. The same nothing-to-see-here-move-along that so disturbed the one honest cop on the case. Surely someone in a position of authority would realize that the Girl Scout killer(s) is still a free man and roaming at will within the community of Locust Grove. Why, after all these years, are the current sheriff of Mayes County and the current officials at the OSBI still neglecting to pursue the killer(s)?

Jennifer Morrison is using this book to publicly request here and now that Sheriff Mike Reed and the OSBI disclose how many DNA markers have *ever* been *conclusively* matched to Gene Leroy Hart. And, if Thurman Buckskin's DNA has, indeed, been compared to the killer's DNA, how many markers does he match?

CHAPTER 19

OVER AND OUT

COVID-19 changed the course of the world in the year 2020. It also changed the Buckskin family, when Millard died and left Thurman as the only living sibling of Gene Leroy Hart. What the world was unaware of was Thurman's attempt to sell the 'Hart family' story for a nice payday. He had called Millard a couple of years before his death and had also reached out to Don Eddie Dawson (Gene's son with Patricia). Millard was not so sure about the idea. Thurman talked Don Eddie into taking his Hart last name back. Thurman felt if they could sell an exclusive 'after forty-five years of silence, Gene Leroy Hart's family speaks' to a publisher or producer, it would be worth a pretty penny. Thurman was always seemingly disappointed when someone came around looking for his story . . . after he teased them a bit and they offered no monetary reward, he would go silent. But not before he would convince anyone who was listening that Gene was a monster and that Gene had master-minded the murders.

Paul Smith desired no such gain to tell his story. On October 10, 2022, with Faith Phillips as the executive producer, Fox Nation dropped *The Girl Scout Murders* onto the world. A ninety-eight-year-old Paul posthumously told his story to anyone and everyone who was willing to hear it. The world finally knew what had been done to him. And more importantly, to Lori, Denise and Michelle.

Paul Dean Smith (1923-2021)

AUTHOR'S NOTES

According to the ice chest files, at the time Sheriff Pete Weaver left office in 1981 and took the Mayes County Girl Scout murder investigative files with him, the following specimens and evidence had been taken from the listed individuals. Sheriff Mike Reed has stated publicly that every suspect he has ever heard of in this case has been ruled out by DNA. It is left to the reader to decide if the specimens have ever been compared to the alleged killer's DNA.

#CCC4	Head hairs from D.J. Cooper
#CCC5	Pubic hairs from D.J. Cooper
#CCC6	Saliva sample from D.J. Cooper
#DDD1	Head hair from Alva Joe Zarnes
#DDD2	Pubic hair from Alva Joe Zarnes
#DDD3	Saliva sample from Alva Joe Zarnes
#EEE1	Head hair from Tommy Joe Sanders
#EEE2	Pubic hair from Tommy Joe Sanders
#EEE3	Saliva sample from Tommy Joe Sanders
#FFF1	Head hair from Darren Creekmore
#FFF2	Pubic hair from Darren Creekmore
#FFF3	Saliva sample from Darren Creekmore

#GGG1	Head hairs from "Wayne"
#GGG2	Head hairs from "Wayne"
#GGG3	Head hairs from "Wayne"
#GGG4	Head hairs from "Wayne"
#GGG5	Head hairs from "Wayne"
#GGG6	Head hairs from "Wayne"
#GGG7	Pubic hairs from "Wayne"
#GGG8	Saliva sample from "Wayne"
NOTE:	"Wayne's" family requested that his real name not be used in this book.

The following items were taken from Dewayne Peters at Kansas State Industrial Reformatory in Hutchinson, Kansas by Chemist M. Janice Davis and Agent Larry Bowles, OSBI.

#JJJJ1	Blood sample on sterile gauze by pricking a finger.
#JJJJ2	Saliva sample.
#JJJJ3	Pulled head hairs.
#JJJJ4	Pulled pubic hairs.
#JJJJ5a	Seminal fluid contained in a sterile container.
#JJJJ5b	One (1) unfixed and unstained seminal smear slide made at 1:30 pm on January 9, 1979 by Janice M. Davis, OSBI.
#JJJJ5c	One (1) unfixed and unstained seminal smear slide made at 1:30 pm on January 9, 1979 by Janice M. Davis, OSBI.
#JJJJ5d	One (1) unfixed and unstained seminal smear slide made at 7:00 pm on January 9, 1979 by Janice M. Davis, OSBI.

The following items were taken from William Alton Stevens at Kansas State Industrial Reformatory in Hutchinson, Kansas by Chemist M. Janice Davis and Agent Larry Bowles, OSBI.

#KKKK1   Blood sample on sterile gauze by pricking a finger.
#KKKK2   Saliva sample.
#KKKK3   Pulled head hairs.
#KKKK4   Pulled pubic hairs.
#KKKK5a Seminal fluid contained in a sterile container.
#KKKK5b One (1) unfixed and unstained seminal smear slide made at 2:12 pm on January 9, 1979 by Janice M. Davis, OSBI.
#KKKK5c One (1) unfixed and unstained seminal smear slide made at 2:12 pm on January 9, 1979 by Janice M. Davis, OSBI.
#KKKK5d One (1) unfixed and unstained seminal smear slide made at 7:00 pm on January 9, 1979 by Janice M. Davis, OSBI.

PRAYER FOR SALVATION

If Paul Smith were still alive, he would tell each reader of this book that the most important thing they will ever do is to ensure that their soul is saved. Jesus Christ once told His disciples, "Where I go you know and the way you know . . . I am the way, the truth and the life." According to the Holy Bible there is no other name under heaven whereby men must be saved, and every one of us must be born again to see heaven.

Being saved is as simple as ABC:

- Acknowledge you are a sinner
- Believe in your heart that Jesus Christ is the Son of God and trust Him to take the punishment you deserve
- Confess to others that you are a follower of Jesus Chris

Here is a simple prayer to help you get started:

Heavenly Father,
   I declare that you are God – the only God – who created heaven and earth. I have sinned before you, going my own way instead of following the light that You have sent to me. I come before You, not to plead my case, but to plead guilty and throw myself upon Your mercy. Please forgive me of my sins: cleanse me from all wickedness.

I accept your Son, Jesus Christ, as my Savior. I dedicate my life to learning and following His ways through the study of the Bible, Your Holy Word. Thank You for receiving me and sending Your Spirit to live in me.

Amen.

Author Contact Information:

JDMorrison1960@gmail.com
(816) 674-8350

Made in the USA
Columbia, SC
04 March 2025